Complaints Against Police

Complaints Against Police

The Politics of Reform

Colleen Lewis
BCom (Hons), PhD

Hawkins Press
1999

Published in Sydney by

Hawkins Press
A division of The Federation Press
71 John St, Leichhardt, NSW, 2040
PO Box 45, Annandale, NSW, 2038
Ph: (02) 9552 2200 Fax: (02) 9552 1681
E-mail: info@fedpress.aust.com
Website: http://www.fedpress.aust.com

National Library of Australia Cataloguing-in-Publication data:
Lewis, Colleen
Complaints against police: the politics of reform

Bibliography.
Includes index.
ISBN 1 876067 11 X

1. Police – Supervision of – Australia. 2. Administrative remedies – Australia. 3. Police – Complaints against – Australia. I. Title

363.20994

Typeset by The Federation Press, Leichhardt, NSW.
Printed by Ligare Pty Ltd, Riverwood , NSW.

CONTENTS

For John as a small token
of my appreciation

ACKNOWLEDGMENTS

During the first stage of this project numerous people gave generously of their valuable time by either granting me interviews or reading and commenting on draft chapters. Because their numbers are many I will not name them individually, but that does not detract from the sincerity of my appreciation to them all. There are, however, a few people who must be singled out for mention. At various times. Keith Bryett and Ciaran O'Faircheallaigh painstakingly read through draft chapters. I thank them for their comments and support. My special thanks to Patrick Weller. His wise counsel, encouragement and support over many years made a difference.

I have been particularly fortunate in having the support of several colleagues during the second stage of the project. My thanks to Brian Costar and Dennis Woodward for reading and commenting on draft chapters hurriedly placed on their desks and quickly returned with enlightening comments. Very special thanks are due to Scott Beattie who read the entire penultimate draft and made many wise suggestions. Eleni Goimil did more than use her exceptional talents to type and format the book, she also cared. Thank you Eleni. My thanks also to Andrew Goldsmith for kindly suggesting several titles for the book. The one I finally settled on reflects one of Andrew's ideas.

The Faculty of Arts, Monash University, assisted in bringing the second stage of this project to completion with a grant from their Project Completion Scheme (using SMURF II funds). I am grateful for their assistance.

It has been a pleasure to work with Chris Holt, Vanessa Playford and Kathy Fitzhenry from Hawkins Press. I thank them for their encouragement and support.

The writing of a book requires more than professional and collegial assistance. Personal support is imperative. Throughout the long and arduous doctoral journey, which laid the foundations for this book, and during the writing of the book I have had the unconditional support, encouragement and love of my husband John. I thank him for always being there. Without his patience and understanding neither the doctoral thesis nor the book would have been possible.

Colleen Lewis
July 1999

INTRODUCTION

Nearly two millennia ago Decimus Junivus Juvenalis posed the vexed question "*Quis custodiet ipsos custodes?*", commonly translated as "who should guard the guardians?". It is a problem which has occupied the thoughts of those who govern and are governed ever since. For countries such as the United States, Britain,[1] Canada and Australia, which operate according to liberal democratic principles, the dilemma about how to address Juvenalis's question is compounded by the need to ensure that citizens who have been granted the authority to legitimately deprive other citizens of their freedom, the police, are held accountable to society for the way in which they exercise their powers.

Police have been given particular powers and also in many instances the discretion to decide if and how to use them. They are the coercive arm of liberal democratic governments but, by virtue of their oath of office, are said to have an independence from government direction when enforcing the law. In terms of the doctrine of the separation of powers, this independence would seem to align police more closely to the judiciary than the executive. However, a reading of the statute law governing police departments and agencies would show that the police chief, commissioner of police or chief constable is accountable managerially and administratively to the executive for the superintendence of the force while retaining some operational independence. This somewhat paradoxical situation adds to the police accountability quandary in liberal democratic societies and, in part, accounts for the profusion of methods already used to hold police accountable for their actions.

At the formal level, these methods include accountability to the courts and to parliament, primarily through the doctrine of ministerial responsibility or by means of accountability to parliamentary committees. Depending upon the country and jurisdiction, police are also accountable to governments at the federal, central, state, provincial or local level, and to police boards, commissions, committees and authorities.

Internal police accountability procedures include rules, regulations and internal investigation units. Ad hoc, external processes such as

1 The word Britain is used to denote England and Wales. This book has not undertaken any analysis of the Scottish situation.

government-initiated commissions of inquiry, royal commissions or reports are further examples of formal accountability methods. On an informal basis pressure groups and the media are said to contribute to the process by bringing police misconduct to the public's attention.

Some of these accountability methods have been used since the establishment of Peel's new police in 1829. The first joint commissioners of the "modern" police, Charles Rowan and Richard Mayne were conscious of the coercive nature of police powers. They tried to maintain discipline by imposing strict sanctions on police misconduct and encouraged all "respectable" people to bring complaints about police behaviour to them. This entrenched the notion of an internal system for handling complaints against police, a system which by the 1950s was badly in need of reform.

This book is about reforming the complaints against police process. Because it is about change in a politically sensitive area of the public sector it is also about political relationships.

At the centre of political relations is the notion of power. While this is not a book on the exercise of power, it is interested in who, within a particular system, has the capacity to exercise power, either directly or indirectly. In other words, who can have issues placed on the political agenda for debate? who can influence the outcome of that debate? And who can use their power to keep things off the agenda so that a matter does not require a decision?

Broadly speaking, the book examines relations between police and government, police and civilian oversight body and oversight body and government, and analyses how the nature of these relations can affect the success or otherwise of police accountability policies. More specifically, it focuses on a relatively new method for dealing with complaints against police: civilian oversight bodies. This method of police accountability is increasingly being used in liberal democratic societies and, while each jurisdiction has introduced its own variation, a common feature is the emphasis placed on a reactive approach to complaints handling. The reactive approach is not effective as many oversight bodies are not granted the powers they need to achieve their accountability objectives, and even when they are, reactive bodies can only treat symptoms.

If the civilian oversight policy is to change behaviour, civilian bodies need to address the cause of police misconduct. To be able to do this, governments must broaden their activities to include proactive, preventative functions which focus on changing police conduct in the long term. They must also adequately resource them. The evidence suggests that, because of the nature of relations which often develop between key players (police, government and oversight body) at various steps of the policy process, this rarely happens.

Police are powerful players at all stages of the complaints process. They use the special position they occupy in liberal democratic societies to influence the shape of the civilian oversight policy. However, despite their special, even unique position, in the final analysis police power is limited through legal and administrative structures. They rely on governments for their powers and resources, indeed for their very existence. Police power is also limited by party political imperatives. Thus, when it is considered electorally prudent, governments will respond favourably to opposing pressure group demands for a more open and accountable police service by establishing external, independent, civilian oversight bodies, rather than listening to police demands that they be allowed to maintain control of the complaints process.

But the civilian oversight policy invariably has a sting. Such bodies are established to solve a set of problems relating to police behaviour, yet governments often find that the policy has produced another set of problems. Independent civilian oversight bodies can create competing demands of control which tend to muddle clear notions of accountability. They also expose politically damaging findings in relation to the behaviour of public servants. As this book argues, of vital importance to the success of any oversight body is the way in which governments respond to the sting.

Definitions

Before proceeding to outline the structure of the book, there are some definitional issues which need to be clarified.

Independent, external civilian bodies have been referred to by a variety of titles: for example, Police Review Board, Police Complaints Authority (PCA), Criminal Justice Commission (CJC), Police Complaints Tribunal (PCT), Office of the Police Complaints Commissioner (OPCC) and Office of the Ombudsman, to name but a few. While these institutions invariably have different legislative frameworks and hence different functional powers, they share common elements which allow them to be jointly classified as external, independent, civilian oversight bodies.

Several writers, including West (1988), Goldsmith (1991a), and Walker and Wright (1995) have highlighted the growing problem of interpreting the terminology used in the complaints against police literature and the difficulty which can arise in decoding the different terminologies used without lengthy definitional explanations. Having said that, this writer is probably about to add to the problem by explaining how particular words will be defined in this book. How other researchers define key words will not be canvassed. This at least avoids a lengthy but rather pointless discussion on why one person favours a particular interpretation over another.[2]

- *Oversight* is used as a generic term to imply some form of external, (usually) independent, civilian superintendence of the complaints against police process.
- *External* implies that to varying degrees the complaints process is undertaken externally, in a physical and organisational sense, to the police department being oversighted.
- *Independent* is used to imply that the oversight agency is accountable to a body or person other than the police or government. In the Australian context it implies that accountability is to a parliamentary committee or to the parliament, not to the government.
- *Civilian* denotes non-police people, including those who are not sworn members of a police department.
- *Monitor* refers to investigations undertaken by the police which are watched over (often in a physical sense) by the oversight agency.
- *Supervise* is used to suggest that the oversight agency is directing the police investigation, in other words that the police are acting under instructions from the oversight agency.
- *Review* implies that the oversight agency retrospectively scrutinises the police investigation. This is usually by way of a paper review.

Some other words which attract different labels in the four countries referred to in this book are the titles given to the chief executive officer of a police force or service. In the United States and Canada this person is referred to as the police chief or chief of police, in Britain as the chief constable or commissioner of police and in Australia as the commissioner

2 The exercise is pointless in the sense that each person's interpretation is valid for the context in which they are writing. Nevertheless, some attempt needs to be made to standardise the key concepts used in the civilian oversight literature. Perhaps an organisation such as the International Association for Civilian Oversight of Law Enforcement could address this issue.

of police or chief commissioner of police. It should also be noted that the term "police commissioner" often has a different meaning in the United States and Canada than it does in Britain or Australia. In North America and Canada it can refer to the chief executive officer of a police commission. Police commissions can be appeal bodies for disciplinary and personnel matters or bodies which have statutory control over the entire operations of a police department (Wilson and McLaren 1972, 21-22). To try to minimise any confusion when the term "police commissioner" is used, it will be used to mean the head of the police service in the British and Australian context. Any exception will be specifically noted at the time of use.

Outline of the book

This book has twin hypotheses:

(1) that an integrated, reactive-proactive approach is fundamental to the long term success of the civilian oversight process; and

(2) that external relations need to be factored in when evaluating the success or failure of this relatively new form of police accountability.

The book's structure is loosely divided into two sections. The first (Chapters One to Five) deals with general issues in the debate about civilian oversight bodies and emphasises the need to extend the traditional models beyond the reactive "big stick" approach. The second (Chapters Six to Nine) presents two case studies on the civilian oversight process from the Australian State of Queensland. These case studies are used to support the hypotheses of the book, but particularly the second, which focuses on external relations.

To be more specific, Chapter One places the role of police in the appropriate political context. It then addresses the issue of police discretion and police independence before discussing the inevitable intertwining of police and politics and the "police are different" thesis.

Chapter Two addresses the problems which led to the rejection of internal police-controlled methods for handling complaints against police in two cities in the United States, Philadelphia and New York; in Britain; Toronto, Canada and Australia. Different historical, social and cultural factors have influenced which level of government should have responsibility for police. The result has been a diverse set of policing structures within and between these countries and differences in the way police and governments view their relationship. Despite these differences, Chapter Two shows that there are shared difficulties which cross city, county, state, provincial and national boundaries. These problems include unacceptable and illegal police behaviour, the police culture and the failure of internal police accountability processes to hold police accountable for their actions.

Citizens' reactions to the problems raised in Chapter Two and the government's response to those reactions are discussed in Chapter Three. The impetus to change from the discredited, secretive police-controlled method for handling complaints against police to a system which was more open, independent and involved non-police grew out of the 1950s, 1960s civil rights movement. As citizens' demands for greater police accountability increased, expressed primarily through pressure group politics, governments were forced to act. They often did so by establishing commissions of inquiry, royal commissions or commissioning reports. While, in many instances, the recommendations from these reports were not acted upon, this ad hoc form of accountability did have an incremental effect on the introduction of civilian oversight bodies.

Chapter Four examines how other writers explain this method of police accountability. It analyses the more common models used to monitor, supervise, investigate and/or review complaints against police and highlights the limiting and confining nature of them. Given the trend toward the use of external, independent, civilian oversight bodies, this chapter argues that there is a need to pay greater attention to the proactive aspect of the complaints process.

Chapter Five discusses methods used by governments to limit the capacity of civilian oversight bodies and the impact their actions can have on effective police accountability. It concludes by arguing that there is a need to broaden the way in which oversight bodies are evaluated. The chapter proposes the adoption of a new model which incorporates three levels of analysis: the reactive, the proactive and external relationships.

The first of the two case studies begins in Chapter Six, which analyses why Queensland's first attempt at civilian oversight, the Police Complaints Tribunal, was such an abject failure.

Chapter Seven commences the second case study. It looks at Queensland's second attempt at civilian oversight, the Criminal Justice Commission. This brief chapter discusses the conditions which led to the creation of what is a unique and powerful external, independent, civilian oversight body.

The current structure, functions and jurisdiction of the Criminal Justice Commission, and how this powerful organisation is held accountable is the subject of Chapter Eight.

Chapter Nine focuses on government-oversight body relations. It shows how they can impact on government intent and the way in which that intent can be directed toward destroying the credibility of the organisation which is charged, among other things, with oversighting complaints against police and devising policies to help prevent them from occurring and recurring.

1

POLICING IN LIBERAL DEMOCRACIES

Introduction

Countries referred to this book – the United States, Britain, Canada and Australia – are classified as liberal democratic societies (Emy and Hughes 1988, 188). Theoretically, they share certain fundamental beliefs about what constitutes a just society; of paramount importance is freedom and the rights of the individual. These countries' political systems are said to embody the following principles: freedom of speech, association and religion; free media; freedom from arbitrary arrest and imprisonment; equality of opportunity and a view of justice which is based on equity (Phillips and Rielly 1982; Emy and Hughes 1988; Jaensch 1991).

With the primary emphasis on the rights of the individual, state power is supposedly limited in a number of ways, such as constitutions which define and constrain governmental power. In Britain, Canada and Australia, citizens elect their parliamentary representatives and in the United States the members of congress and the president and vice-president. In all four countries this is done through free, open and regular elections. In Britain, Canada and Australia, which adhere to the principles of a Westminster system of responsible government, the party that wins the majority of seats in the lower house of parliament forms the government.[1] Theoretically, a politically neutral public sector, accountable to the government, performs the administrative functions of the state and the judiciary is independent of executive power. In the United States, which has a presidential style of government, the executive (president) and the congress function independently, as does the judiciary. With the exception

1 When no one party wins a majority of seats in its own right, a coalition between parties may be formed. The coalition then forms the government.

of certain levels of the Senior Executive Service, the United States' public sector is also expected to be politically neutral. Importantly, in relation to this book, in both the Westminster and presidential systems, governments govern with the consent of the people and sovereign power remains with the people.

In reply to liberal philosophy, citizens voluntarily consent to the state having the necessary power to maintain social control and protect their civil, political and economic freedoms through the enforcement of laws (Lessnoff 1986; Alderson 1993). However, as they are also suspicious of concentrated forms of power, power is checked and controlled through accountability processes. Regardless of how circuitous the route, accountability ultimately leads back to the people.

Adherence to the rule of law is an important fundamental tenet of liberal democratic societies. It institutionalises the notion that all citizens have formal equality before the law and equal protection from it.

> This concept and the principles of natural justice combine to establish a series of basic legal safeguards . . . the right to trial in open court, by jury; the right to call witnesses in your defence; right to bail, legal representation . . . and to appeal; the generalised protection of habeas corpus and certain restraints on the powers of police to arrest and interrogate subjects (Emy and Hughes 1988, 214).

No citizen or organisation is considered to be above the law.

Although, according to liberal theory, protecting freedom and the rights of the individual are central tasks of liberal democratic governments, it is simultaneously accepted that individuals derive benefits from being part of an organised community. This means that citizens must accept some restrictions on their freedoms (Chisholm and Nettheim 1988, 113). As explained by Clifford (1981, 4), "the need for regular trading between controls to maintain freedoms and freedoms jeopardised by controls, is the heart of democracy".

The dilemma for liberal democratic governments is in striking an acceptable balance. The expected formal minimum standard of behaviour is laid down in the criminal law,[2] which is concerned with "the protection of individual liberties *within* a system of social order" (Skolnick 1966, 7). To protect society as a whole, the state can prosecute individuals who break the law and transgressions are dealt with through the criminal justice system which embodies the coercive powers of the state. Criminal

2 Other institutions such as the family and religion also contribute to setting minimum standards of behaviour but they do so at an informal level.

justice systems comprise an investigative/enforcement component (the police and other enforcement agencies), an adjudicative component (the courts), and a corrections component (prisons and other correctional agencies). The specific structure of these components reflects the society they serve.

The police[3]

The police are the "gatekeepers" of the criminal justice system. If they do not act in the first instance, other parts of the system lie dormant. The police have been entrusted with considerable coercive powers and a significant degree of discretion. These two factors help contribute to the thesis that "police are different" from other public servants.

Police powers

Broadly speaking, police are able to stop, question, detain and arrest people. They can search and seize their property, fingerprint and photograph them, conduct intimate body searches and use force, even violence, to control a situation. Police have the power to deprive people of their freedom, autonomy and dignity and, under extreme circumstances, their lives. These potentially oppressive powers have been granted to police so they can regulate and protect society in general and people's individual rights in particular. However, they are formally required to do so according to the law and to abide by the procedural rules and policies laid down by society.

Even though policing is accepted as a licit form of social control, community acceptance of police authority is contingent on their "good behaviour", their compliance with the rule of law, and on there being processes which can deliver effective police accountability (Uglow 1988, 15). Accordingly, police in liberal democratic societies are held to account through a variety of formal and informal processes.

Despite the plethora of accountability processes, the evidence presented in Chapter Two shows that for decades many police abused their discretion and misused their power, but it was not until the 1960s and 1970s that the gravity of the situation became known to the general public.

3 When police or policing is referred to in this book it is in the context of what Bayley (1992a, 509-45) calls "general purpose policing" and not the more specialised functions provided, for example, by the Federal Bureau of Investigation in the United States.

Even then, most governments did not move decisively or swiftly to remedy the situation. Their reluctance to act may be related to problems which need to be addressed when tackling issues of police accountability. As Robert Reiner (1993, 1), a highly respected writer on policing issues, argues, "Police accountability is one of the thorniest conundrums of statecraft. . . [It] poses peculiarly problematic issues both of principle and practice, particularly in a democratic society". Some of these "peculiarly problematic issues" relate to police discretion and police independence.

Police discretion

Police discretion is necessary in a liberal democratic society where full and rigid enforcement of the law is undesirable (Clifford 1981, 23). Its importance to the policing function has been recognised in common law. For example, in *Enever v The King* (1906) 3 CLR 969 the court held that a constable's authority "is original and is not delegated, and is exercised at his own discretion by virtue of his office, and on no responsibility but his own". The constable's right to exercise discretion was also recognised in an Australian case, *Wright v McQualter* (1970) 17 FLR 305, when Kerr J noted that the inspector in charge of a peaceful demonstration "very properly and wisely exercised his discretion". In this instance police discretion was used to prevent an escalation of disorder. Discretion was also an issue in the much cited *R v Commissioner of Police of the Metropolis; ex parte Blackburn* [1968] 2 QB 118, in which Lord Denning held "that the police have a wide discretion in enforcing the law". While the common and statute law have accepted that police need to have discretion, it is also overwhelmingly accepted that it is only permissible and desirable when it is exercised fairly in the interest of justice, and when it conforms to guidelines set by community standards. What is not permissible or acceptable is the abuse of police discretion.

But as Bowden (1978, 14) points out, police discretion is most frequently applied in "the court of first instance – the street". Consequently, the decision to arrest or not often takes place on a one-to-one basis or, more accurately perhaps, with a member of the public and the police. As a result, the police officer's discretionary decision, particularly the decision not to arrest, is placed beyond the formal procedures implemented to make other public servants accountable for their actions. This means that despite the variety of accountability processes, many police decisions cannot be scrutinised. This creates a dilemma for governments: how to keep police in line on the one hand but allow them to exercise their "low visibility" discretion on the other. The dilemma is further compounded by the doctrine of constabulary independence which, in terms of operational policing, further shields police actions from scrutiny.

Police independence

Police accountability is complicated by the controversial theory of constabulary independence. Because of the independence accorded police by common law, which has been preserved and recognised by statute, they are said to exercise original powers which cut across traditional notions of accountability. These powers, which are embodied in police discretion, evolved through the belief of judicial authorities that, like the courts, the police occupy a special position in society and, as such, should not be subject to the arbitrary interference of the executive (Milte and Weber 1977; Stenning 1981a; Oliver 1987).

The degree to which police are, or should be, independent from political direction in operational issues is a matter of great debate (Marshall 1965, 1978; Goldstein 1977; Stenning 1981a; Clifford 1982; Jefferson and Grimshaw 1984, Hann et al 1985; Pike 1985; Lustgarten 1986; Oliver 1987; Reiner 1993; Finnane 1994) much of which has centred around the *obiter dicta* in several celebrated court cases in England and Australia (some of which were referred to in the section on police discretion) and, to a lesser extent, Canada and the United States of America.[4] Many of the cases were concerned with whether those who employed the police (the government) were liable, at common law, for the torts of their employees when they were exercising their public duty as peace officers. In other words whether there was, in law, a master-servant relationship. Even though these cases did not deal directly with the constitutional status of the police, they have served to reinforce the notion that the police occupy a special position in society in that they exercise an original not a delegated power when enforcing the law.

While the doctrine of constabulary independence does not render police unaccountable for their behaviour, in relation to operational policing they do possess an independence which is somewhat unique.

Hann et al (1985, 44) argue this uniqueness means that "There are some areas of police decision-making . . . in which the police are not subject to the same degree of external control by and/or accountability to

---

4 A summary of these cases and their contribution to the debate on police independence can be found in the study paper by Philip Stenning (1981a) prepared for the Law Reform Commission of Canada and in Marshall's (1965, 1978) seminal work.

governing authorities, ministers or others charged with responsibility for police governance, as is the case in other areas of decision-making".

Police are said to possess "substantial autonomy" (Uglow 1988, 139). Ritchie (1992, 209) claims that this is a problem for police accountability. She says that "operational activities of the police cannot in fact be adequately controlled by politicians". Sanders (1993, 106) goes so far as to suggest that constabulary independence ought to be abolished. He sees it as an "historical anachronism" which "simply serves as a barrier to effective supervision and control".

Not surprisingly, the police do not share Sanders's sentiment. David Hunt (1993, 2), former commissioner of police for South Australia, echoes the thoughts of other police commissioners and police chiefs when he says that:

> The police need some independence from the government of the day. This is not to say that the police should not be loyal to the government. We should. We must be accountable for our performance and use of resources as any other employees of the government. Without operational independence though there is potential for us to become merely the tools of the executive and with that goes abuse of individual rights.

The notion of police as mere puppets of government is an anathema to liberal democratic societies which have adopted the "kin" rather than the "*gendarmerie*" style of policing. The difference in these styles was addressed by Reith (1975, 20) who claims there are fundamentally two police systems in the world "the kin police or Anglo-Saxon police system, and the ruler-appointed, *gendarmerie*, or despotic totalitarian police system. The first represents, basically, force exercised indirectly, by the people, from below, upwards. The other represents force exercised, by authority, from above, downwards" (Reith 1952, 20).

The *gendarmerie* system has an explicit top down political dimension whereas the kin system embraces the Peelian notion that "the police are the public and the public are the police" (Robinson, Scaglion and Olivero 1994, 11). While this latter notion has been discussed by many authors, including Morgan (1989, 219), who claims that "The legal doctrine of 'officers as servants of no one save the law itself' is widely said to be built on sand", it has nevertheless "been a pervasive and essential prop to concepts of modern policing" (Robinson, Scaglion and Olivero 1994, 8). The foundations of modern policing, laid down by Sir Robert Peel in 1829, were designed to ensure that British police were not seen as the tool of government but rather as the people's police. It survives in various forms today.

Adherence to the concept of police being accountable to "the law and law alone" is strongest in Britain. British police, and to some extent governments and police authorities, still embrace the theory of constabulary independence, which supports the notion that police derive their power and legitimacy not from governments but from the Crown. It is not surprising, therefore, that chief constables in Britain are powerful players in the police policy arena and have always enjoyed considerable autonomy, particularly in relation to operational policing matters (see Reiner 1991b). While Canadian courts have questioned whether this aspect of English jurisprudence is applicable in Canada, qualified support for the idea that police should be independent from arbitrary, party political interference by government remains (Stenning 1981a, 161-208).

American courts, particularly in the developmental stages of modern policing, lent support to the concept of police independence (Stenning 1981a) but overt political interference by local governments undermined police legitimacy and with it any notion of independence. In the 19th and early 20th centuries, police in America were seen as "The legitimate spoils of victory at the polls" (Fosdick 1920, 119). As Reith explains (1952, 83), "the police were allowed to become corruptly the instruments and servants not of law, but of policy and of local and corrupt controllers of policy". That situation did not really change until the 1930s when police in the United States (particularly August Vollmer) moved to depoliticise the policing function.[5] They did so by arguing that police were professionals, there to serve the American community, not to satisfy the party political whims of government.

In Australia adherence to the concept of constabulary independence is closer to the British than the American practice. This is despite Australian police commissioners being directly accountable to police ministers, a fact which was confirmed by two royal commissions in the State of South Australia in the 1970s, when police commissioners tried to

5 One of the most prominent leaders in the move to professionalise American police was August Vollmer. He was the chief of police in Berkeley, California, from 1905 to 1932 and is often considered the "father of police professionalism" (Walker 1992, 13). He is credited with developing the concepts of modern police administration and of promoting higher education for police officers. Vollmer was also the author of the report on police administration contained in the 1931 *National Commission on Law Observance and Enforcement* (the Wickersham Commission). Findings from this Commission assisted police reformers who, like Vollmer, were dedicated to trying to eliminate political influence from the policing function (Walker 1992, 13, 17).

argue they were accountable "to the law and law alone".[6] Even though commissioners are subject to the direction of police ministers, most ministers try to distance themselves from any suggestion that they are interfering in police operational matters. As Finnane (1994, 39) explains, "In spite of the legislative subjection of the police to government direction, there has long been an ambiguity in understanding the proper domain of ministerial authority and that of the commissioner".

Australian police, including the commissioner, may not enjoy constitutional independence in terms of their operational, law and order role, but they usually do so in practice (Finnane 1994, 39).

While it is necessary to raise the related issues of police discretion and police independence in any discussion about the particular set of problems surrounding police accountability, in terms of this book it is also important not to get caught up in the fascinating, much discussed, ongoing but still largely unresolved constabulary independence debate. To avoid being sidetracked into an even lengthier discussion on the subject, the writer will assert that the nature of police discretion and the theory of constabulary independence sets police apart from other public servants. Their discretion is not subjected to the same degree of scrutiny and their operational independence places part of their functions beyond the direct control of governments.

But the conundrum goes on. Even though governments are not supposed to direct police to enforce or not enforce the law, there is no suggestion that governments are not ultimately responsible to the people for the conduct of the police. The onus is therefore on governments to delicately balance the perception that, while they keep police accountable for their actions, they do not interfere with police operational independence. Some governments have managed to do this better than others.

The complexity surrounding police accountability does not end there. Despite their so called independence, the police are also an arm of government and embody the peace-time coercive powers of the state. Indeed, they are "to government as the edge is to the knife" (Bayley 1985b, 189), an edge which has often been honed through the politicisation of the policing function. Even though a politicised police force is contrary to all of the principles underpinning policing in a liberal democratic society, the stark reality is that law and order issues matter.

---

6 *Royal Commission on the September Moratorium Demonstration* 1970, Report, Government Printer, Adelaide. *Royal Commission on the Dismissal of Harold Hubert Salisbury* 1978, Report, Government Printer, Adelaide.

In extreme circumstances they can affect the stability of the state; under less extreme conditions they can cost government office. The party political advantages to governments through a compliant police force are considerable.

What results is a somewhat fractured relationship between police and governments which, in terms of pressure group politics, tends to enhance the power of the police. Police power is further enhanced by the reciprocal relationship which exists between police and governments: a topic which, as David Bayley (1985b, 190) says "is too important . . . to ignore".

Intertwining of police and politics

Bayley (1985b, 190-97) identifies six general ways in which the police and political life are intertwined. First, the criminal law which the police enforce can be used as a tool by politicians to "harass and frustrate" each other to gain political advantage. Secondly, police can influence the political process. In their peace-keeping role they scrutinise conduct at political rallies and demonstrations. The organisers of such events are usually obliged to notify police of their intent and the police often have the power to issue the required permits. There have been instances where police permission appeared to be denied for party political reasons rather than for peace-keeping concerns.[7] Police can and have been used by governments to rally electoral support. They represent a "large, ready-made, and pervasive network" which, as Bayley notes, incumbent governments often find difficult to resist.

Thirdly, police are a government's first line of defence against any attempt to overthrow them. While this has not been an issue in the liberal democratic countries being discussed in this book, it is a latent police power about which governments are aware. Fourthly, the police, often through a special branch or unit, gather secret intelligence data. This data may include information on political activities and personal information on politicians. Fifthly, the police can directly affect government policy in a formal and informal sense. More and more the police executive and police unions are entering the political arena as committed spokespersons championing a particular issue. As they represent a large block of votes both government and the opposition try to woo them. In tightly fought

7 This occurred in Queensland during the 1970s and 1980s in relation to the granting of permits to conduct street marches (Hawker 1981).

elections they can help a party win or lose government. The *quid pro quo* is usually a strong law and order policy and increased police numbers and powers. Sixthly, police have the potential power to undermine government policies that rely on law enforcement to be implemented. This can be done by using their discretion to turn a blind eye or caution an offender rather than charge them with an offence or issue a traffic fine; or, in the reverse, to rigidly enforce the law. Both extremes can seriously affect the intent of a government policy and can affect the way citizens view their governments: as either the defender or oppressor of civil liberties (Bayley 1985b, 197-200).

The increased militancy of police unions has further demonstrated the inevitable political nature of policing.[8] Since the 1960s, in particular, police unions have publicly involved themselves in political debates about wider criminal justice issues and social policy (Reiner 1985; Walker 1992; Finnane 1994). Reiner (1985) likens their tactics to those of the 1960s liberal pressure groups which campaigned successfully to change laws on abortion, capital punishment and homosexuality. Reiner was specifically referring to the British Police Federations but his analysis is just as applicable to unions in the United States, Canada and Australia.

Historically, police in many countries have performed a variety of non-police administrative duties (Finnane 1994; Bingham 1994) and in several of the more isolated areas still do. The diversity of their functions serves to enhance their importance to governments and to the community (Finnane 1994).

Conclusion

Police discretion, police independence, the diversity of the policing function, the growing militancy of police unions and the reciprocal nature of police-government relations combine to strengthen the special, even unique, position of police. It underpins their power as a pressure group and as a government bureaucracy, and affords them a privileged position with government, a position they have often used to their advantage in debates about appropriate police accountability policies.

As will be shown in this book, police have chosen to exert pressure in two ways: overtly and covertly. According to Dahl, an overt use of power occurs when "A has power over B to the extent that he can get B to

8 A variety of names exists for those organisations which concern themselves with police industrial and workplace welfare issues. In this book the more generally accepted term of "union" will be used.

do something that B would not otherwise do" (1957, 203). Bachrach and Baratz (1962, 1963), however, see the exercise of power occurring in a more covert and subtle fashion and under circumstances where its distribution is not as equal or obvious as Dahl and other pluralists maintain (Ham and Hill 1984, 68). Both tactics, Dahl's one-dimensional view of power and Bachrach and Baratz's two-dimensional view, have been used successfully by police to avoid or limit external scrutiny of their behaviour.

Police behaviour did not really emerge as a political issue until the late 1950s and early 1960s. Until then most public complaints about police misconduct were made by politically weak minority groups and the so-called criminal class (Hain 1979). Consequently, they were not of real concern to politicians or the largely law-abiding middle class. But as the following chapter shows, when pressure group politics forced governments to publicly examine the internal, police-controlled methods for dealing with complaints against police, disturbing facts emerged. It became evident that when police were isolated from outside scrutiny, they often performed their duties with little regard for the rule of law. This had grave consequences for the rights of many citizens, particularly as the internal system rarely held police accountable for their deviant behaviour.

2

THE PROBLEM – UNACCEPTABLE POLICE BEHAVIOUR

Introduction

Unacceptable and illegal behaviour by police appears to be pandemic. The record of evidence suggests that over the past 50 years there has been a growing awareness of the problem and a corresponding concern about the inability of police-controlled systems to deal with citizens' complaints. This chapter demonstrates the depth of the problem. By necessity it adopts an historical approach and identifies the issues which fuelled the public's lack of confidence in police, more particularly in the methods used to address complaints against police and the penalties imposed if disciplinary charges were laid. In essence, there was a growing public perception that while police enforced the law, they did not believe that it should apply to them. The following evidence supports that perception.[1]

---

1 This chapter makes several references to various inquiries into policing. The main ones cited are:

Report of the Board of Inquiry into Allegations of Corruption in the Police Force in Connection with Illegal Abortion Practices in the State of Victoria (The Kaye Report) 1971, Government Printer, Melbourne.

Report of a Commission to Investigate Allegations of Police Corruption and the City's Anti-Corruption Procedures (The Knapp Report) 1972, The City of New York, New York.

Report of the Committee of Inquiry into the Enforcement of Criminal Law in Queensland (The Lucas Report) 1977, Government Printer, Brisbane.

Report of the Board of Inquiry into Allegations Against Members of the Victorian Police Force (The Beach Report) 1978, Government Printer, Melbourne.

Report of a Commission of Inquiry Pursuant to Orders in Council (The Fitzgerald Report) 1989, Government Printer, Brisbane.

Report of the Commission to Investigate Allegations of Police Corruption and the Anti-Corruption Procedure of the Police Department (The Mollen Report) 1994, The City of New York, New York.

Reports of the Royal Commission into the New South Wales Police Service (The Wood Reports) 1996 and 1997, New South Wales Government, Sydney.

Police malfeasance

While allegations of corruption were not new, during the 1950s and 1960s there was mounting evidence of police misconduct in many American cities (Brown L 1975; Brown D 1985a). Complaints about police malfeasance included allegations of police brutality covering physical violence and harassment and various forms of corruption ranging from accepting bribes for non-enforcement of traffic fines to taking illicit payments in relation to drugs and gambling (Brown 1975; Petterson 1991; Skolnick 1993).

In England confidence in the institution of policing was also declining as more and more scandals involving police became public. Throughout the 1950s and 1960s there were accusations of police corruption and well-publicised cases involving allegations of racial violence, attempted cover-ups, unlawful violence, pressure on suspects to plead guilty and the planting of evidence. Concern about police behaviour was further fuelled in the 1970s by more allegations of bribe-taking, theft, conspiracy to pervert the course of justice and corruption scandals involving detectives from London's Metropolitan Criminal Investigation Division (Wegg-Prosser 1979; Reiner 1985; Maguire 1991). Accusations of wrongful arrest for serious crimes, including murder, and confessions "extracted" through psychological pressure were also made against the police (Humphry 1979).

In Toronto police were accused of abusing their authority and exceeding their powers (Goldsmith and Farson 1987; Lewis 1991). In 1974 one Toronto newspaper ran a series of front page stories which documented 16 cases of police brutality. Throughout the 1970s there were further allegations of police lying under oath to royal commissions to protect other officers and of police abuse of minority groups (La Marsh 1983).

In 1981 a non-government organisation funded by private donations, the Citizens' Independent Review of Police Activities (CIRPA), was established in Toronto to give advice and counselling to citizens making complaints about police behaviour. A summary of typical complaints received by CIRPA, which dealt with abuse by police, was compiled by the La Marsh Research Program on Violence. Allegations of police misconduct included instances of people being beaten while handcuffed and of a homosexual man being stripped and having a gun pointed at his genitals. Other complaints involved police roughing up citizens who challenged their authority in relation to traffic offences. In one such incident, it was alleged that a woman in her sixties had a vertebrae fractured and in another, a person's head was allegedly pounded on a car window. An indigent complained that he was called "a '[F]---ing pervert, faggot' and threatened with arrest *after* an officer discovered he had been checking out the wrong man" (La Marsh 1983, 31).

A Study of the Reform Process and Police Institution in Toronto by McMahon and Ericson (1984) details two specific incidents, a police shooting and raids on bathhouses, as the fulcrum "around which various community, minority and other groups began to systematically, continuously and consistently articulate their opinions about the issue of complaints against the police in Toronto" (1984, 15). The shooting of Albert Johnson in August 1979 and the February 1981 raids on four gay bathhouses were seen by many in the community as indications of growing police racism, homophobia and "systematic harassment" of minority groups (McMahon and Ericson 1984, 23).

Over the past 40 years, commissions of inquiry and royal commissions in Australia have found, inter alia, that police have given false evidence to boards and inquiries, have been party to illegal assaults, have failed to properly investigate complaints against police, have obstructed the course of justice, committed perjury, conspired with other police to suppress evidence, unlawfully detained, assaulted and arrested people, corruptly received money and fabricated evidence (see, for example, Beach Inquiry, Lucas Inquiry, Fitzgerald Inquiry and Wood Inquiry).

The Beach Inquiry in Victoria in 1978, which sat for some 15 months, heard evidence of "incidents or allegations ranging in gravity from mere loutishness, through to intimidation and violence, and culminating in what might properly be described as sophisticated misconduct concerning corruption, conspiracy, the concoction of false evidence and like matters" (1978, 59).

Queensland's Fitzgerald Inquiry, which ran from 1987 to 1989, found that for many years the police had been contemptuous of the criminal justice system, disdainful of the law and rejected the notion that it applied to them. Their "disregard for the truth" meant that for 25 years verbal confession became a feature of criminal trials in Queensland (Fitzgerald 1989, 200). The Inquiry not only exposed a network of corrupt police activities, it also revealed a less than arms-length relationship between the National Party Government and the police, which contributed significantly to the lack of effective police accountability in that State.

The report of the Wood Royal Commission into the New South Wales Police Service (1997) gives a brief history of police corruption and abuse of police powers in that State. It dates back to the first official inquiry into policing in 1867 which noted incidences of misconduct and inefficiency by some members of the Force. In 1918 a royal commission investigated allegations of serious corruption and in 1936 another commission of inquiry investigated allegations of police framing people for offences, giving false evidence, wrongly inducing accused persons to plead guilty and wrongly entering private premises. These allegations were found "to be substantially justified" (Royal Commission into the New South Wales Police Service, 54).

From 1960 to 1970 the perception inside and outside the New South Wales Police Force was that "corruption was rife". In 1979 a commission of inquiry was established to investigate the administration of the Force. It uncovered grossly inadequate administrative processes and management practices; a lack of planning; inadequate supervision and control; and confusion about the lines of responsibility within the Force. This inquiry also acknowledged the existence of corruption and noted that it had been explained and addressed within the New South Wales Police Department by the "rotten apple" theory. Consequently, no attempt was made to look at complaints against police as symptoms of a wider, institutional problem. Post 1970 allegations of corruption and misconduct continued.

The 1997 Royal Commission into the New South Wales Police Service highlights more recent examples of corruption and misconduct including perjury; planting of evidence; verbals; abuse of due process; "scrumdowns";[2] extortion; alcohol and drug abuse; fraudulent practices by police; cover-ups of police driving vehicles while heavily intoxicated; serious abuse of police power; police interference with prosecutions in return for bribes; shakedowns; protection of the drug trade, clubs, vice operators, gaming and betting interests; and direct police involvement in the supply of cocaine, heroin and cannabis (Royal Commission into the New South Wales Police Service 1997).

Corruption in Australia's police forces has not been confined to the cop on the beat or the senior sergeant in charge of the local station. It has extended to the highest office. For example, in New South Wales in 1982

2 Scrumdowns were defined by the royal commission as "A police term for the practice of getting together to ensure police statements and/or evidence are consistent. The practice can be used innocently or corruptly; the latter to ensure that the evidence and statements consistently support a corrupt purpose" (Royal Commission into New South Wales Police Service (1997, xxv).

the Police Tribunal found that Deputy Commissioner Bill Allen had disgraced the force (Nelson 1986, 232). He was permitted to resign at the reduced rank of Sergeant First Class. In August 1991 Queensland's former Police Commissioner Terence Lewis was convicted of 15 counts of official corruption. He was sentenced to 14-years jail.

These widespread examples of unacceptable and illegal police behaviour in the United States, Britain, Canada and Australia were not exposed through standing police-controlled accountability processes. Rather, the catalyst by which they were made known to the public was pressure group politics which often led to the setting up of ad hoc commissions of inquiry, royal commissions or the commissioning of government reports. Standing accountability processes failed for a variety of reasons to hold police accountable for their actions, but one of the most common contributing factors to their failure was the police culture and the "blue curtain of silence" that it breeds.

Police culture

Much has been written about the police culture, which is understandably influenced by the confrontational and often dangerous nature of police work, and the conflicting public expectations that go with the job. These factors help to create a culture based on strong group solidarity (Goldstein 1977; Alpert and Dunham 1988, 81-85; Landa 1993, 5; Royal Commission into the New South Wales Police Service 1997; Chan 1997). This strong group loyalty is one of the culture's many beneficial features in dangerous operational situations. However, it has proven to be its "Achilles heel" in relation to complaints about police behaviour. A substantial body of evidence supports the view that many officers will lie to protect fellow officers who are under investigation. The exceptionally strong unwritten code, that police must stick together at all times, encourages police to cover up the misconduct, even the criminal activities, of other officers (Gleeson 1993; Skolnick and Fyfe 1993). This kind of thinking often starts at the academy where veteran police instructors explain to recruits the importance of not "dobbing in" another officer. Recruits quickly learn that if they do they will be exiled and branded for the rest of their policing career. In America police who try to expose corruption, brutality and misconduct within police departments are called "rats". In Australia the term is "dogs". These labels precede the whistleblower wherever they go within the force (Daley 1978).

Several leading authorities on policing, including Goldstein (1977), Reiner (1992) and Skolnick and Fyfe (1993), refer to the "blue curtain of silence" or the "notorious conspiracy" of silence which is common to policing across the Western world. Skolnick and Fyfe (1993, 111-12), while making the important point that a code of silence is "not unique" to police, go on to explain that:

> In the closed society of police departments . . . the pressure to remain loyal is enormous . . . having subsumed their individual identities into the whole, cops know that betraying the group betrays themselves and destroys their identities. [Police] live in a world of desperately conflicting imperatives, where norms of loyalty wash up against standards of law and order. So mostly . . . they see, hear, and speak no evil . . . [but] special efforts can and must be made to overcome these powerful prescriptions of silence and loyalty in the culture of policing.

The Mollen Inquiry (1993) demonstrated that the strength of the code of silence had not changed in the New York City Police Department since Detective Frank Serpico told the Knapp Commission in 1971, "we must create an atmosphere in which the dishonest officer fears the honest one, and not the other way around" (cited in Mollen 1994, 51). Several police of various ranks testified to the Mollen Inquiry about the pervasive nature of the code which they admitted still permeated the department. Although many police were not corrupt or abusive, they chose to turn a blind eye to those who stole property, sold drugs and/or abused citizens' civil liberties. By abrogating their professional obligations, honest police were, and still are, instrumental in facilitating and perpetuating corruption and abuse.

The Mollen Report's (1994, 53) findings on the code of silence typify those of many other inquiries into alleged police misconduct, namely that:

> Group loyalty often flourished at the expense of an officer's sworn duty. It makes allegiance to fellow officers – even corrupt ones – more important than allegiance to the Department and the community. When this happens loyalty itself becomes corrupt and erects the strongest barriers to corruption control: the code of silence and the "Us vs Them" mentality (Mollen 1994, 53).

The "them against us" mentality was noted by Beach QC in his report into allegations of misconduct against members of Australia's Victoria Police Force some 16 years earlier. Beach (1978) noted:

> [T]hat it was with regret that one observed what had been described in other reports of a like nature as the "brotherhood syndrome", or the "ghetto mentality" of a number of members of the Force called to give

> evidence before this Board. In other words, the attitude adopted by Police was that of "it's them against us" and "the team must stick together".

Marenin (1985, 107), also addressing this issue, explains how "the police think of themselves as a distinct, sometimes beleaguered, frequently mistrusted, and always unappreciated minority which must stick together, protect its own, and reject external criticism".

This mentality extends to commissions of inquiries and boards established to investigate allegations of police misconduct (La Marsh 1983; Mollen 1994; Perez 1994; Royal Commission into the New South Wales Police 1997). Like the code of silence it often begins to develop at the academy and is reinforced by fellow officers and superiors once recruits are sworn-in and begin to work the streets.

Taken to its extreme, this "them against us" mentality can result in police perceiving the community as the enemy. In areas with high crime rates, in particular, many police stereotype all citizens as criminals. A police officer at the Mollen Commission testified that on one particular occasion he and a group of officers decided they would attack an apartment building which was a known drug location and physically brutalise everyone in sight. They decided to do this to help "pass the night away". No one who happened to be at the apartment building on that particular occasion was spared the police brutality.

> The victims were all perceived as one: they were the "them" in a world often defined as "Us vs Them"; a world that far too often pits the police against the people they are sworn to serve. It is this attitude that allows cops to detach themselves from the public, and from the norms and customs that govern the "real world" from which they come. And it is this attitude that makes both brutality and corruption easier to commit and to tolerate (Mollen 1994, 48).

The police code of silence protects the kind of behaviour that the "them against us" mentality can create. This remains a problem for any system which handles citizens' grievances about police conduct but, as is demonstrated below, when police control the process the problem is compounded. The following brief look at the inadequacy of police controlled, internal accountability policies helps to explain why the handling of complaints against police emerged as a political issue in the 1950s and 1960s and why it has intermittently remained on the political agenda ever since.

Failure of internal accountability

A common and significant factor for the break-down in police accountability centred around the closed and secretive police controlled, internal system of handling citizens' complaints and the lack of effective redress it provides for complainants (Hudson 1971; Goldstein 1977; Brown 1985a; Petterson 1991).

To bring the inadequacy of existing methods of handling citizens' grievances about police conduct to public attention, the American Civil Liberties Union highlighted instances of police abuse which they considered had not received the appropriate scrutiny and action (Hudson 1971). Case studies, which clearly documented abuse of police authority, showed that the internal systems were "ineffective" (Goldstein 1977). Brown (1985a) refers to the lack of any procedural safeguards for complainants and to the failure of the internal complaints system to satisfy citizens who complained. The police controlled system lacked independence and actively discouraged complainants from lodging complaints. Brown's analysis is supported by Loveday (1987) and Petterson (1991) who also maintain that allegations of cover-ups and the exoneration of police by other police "discredited" the internal system and fuelled calls for a more open and accountable process.

In many major American cities, it was perceived that complaints about police misconduct handled exclusively by other police created a process that was unfair to the complainant and biased toward the police (Petterson 1991). Goode (1973, 62), citing an American reference, discussed how police investigations "tend to be defensive of the police and slanted against complainants... Only the most blatant offence, supported by incontrovertible evidence could induce investigators and superiors to abandon the fellow officer".

The same criticisms were echoed by those writing about the situation in England and Wales. Maguire (1991) points out that the need for a more effective system to handle complaints against police had, to a greater or lesser extent, been on the political agenda in Britain since the 1950s. Highly publicised accounts of police violence, malpractice, widespread corruption and insensitive policing caused the public to lose faith in their police force and, more particularly, in the internal processes used to hold them accountable. According to Maguire (1991, 180), the 1962 Royal Commission "largely ducked the issue of controlling individual police misconduct". It rejected calls for the inclusion of an independent element in the complaints system, preferring instead to recommend modifications to existing internal processes.

In the early 1970s a series of events increased public disquiet about police behaviour. A publication by the Parliamentary Select Committee on Race Relations and Immigration found that the handling of complaints against police was a primary cause of "friction" between black minority groups and the police (Robilliard and McEwan 1986). Robilliard and McEwan refer to the unfairness of a system that allowed police to investigate themselves with no method for reviewing their decisions. Humphry (1979) also addressed the problem of the internal system not holding police accountable for their actions.

Similar concerns were expressed in Toronto. Citizens complained that the police-controlled complaints system failed to provide them with adequate documentation and appropriate information about the nature of the system. It was also considered to be a closed and furtive process (Lewis, Linden and Keene 1986; Lewis 1991). People were reluctant to complain to members of the Metropolitan Toronto Police Force about the conduct of other officers. Some complainants were warned by police that if police found the complaint to be unfounded they (the citizens complaining) ran the risk of being charged. This was clearly intimidation. Others who had formally put in a complaint expressed dissatisfaction with the process as they were never informed of the outcome of the complaints they lodged (Watt 1991).

The Abortion Graft Inquiry[3] in Victoria, Australia, in 1970 demonstrated how police had failed to adequately investigate allegations of police corruption in that State, despite the strong suspicions of some police that other police were involved in corrupt practices. The Inquiry also highlighted the uselessness of believing that police can adequately investigate themselves when corruption is "cohesive and well planned" (Milte and Weber 1977, 3).

The Beach Report (1978) referred to earlier documented cases which showed "the futility of a civilian making a complaint to police, about the behaviour of other police" (40). One particular incident involved "a thoroughly decent and respectable married couple" (48) who had been "subjected to a harrowing experience ... without any cause whatsoever. . ." (49). They had been "foully abused, assaulted, harassed

3 *Report of the Board of Inquiry into Allegations of Corruption in the Police Force in Connection with Illegal Abortion Practices in the State of Victoria* (The Kaye Report) 1971, Government Printer, Melbourne.

and intimidated" (105) by three police officers. Beach described the police conduct as "unbridled sadism" (49). The abused citizens lodged a formal complaint about the matter which was investigated by a chief inspector. The report describes the chief inspector's investigation as a "white wash", a disgrace. Under questioning at the Inquiry, the inspector concerned made the startling comment that "no one was under suspicion" for the sadistic behaviour of the police. He went on to say that "if we are going to talk about suspicion, they [the abused citizens] more properly are under suspicion for making a false report" (106).

Beach (1978, 106-7) summed up his findings on the internal police controlled process by saying that:

> In my opinion, the Board's inquiry established beyond any doubt that prior to the 1st August, 1975, there was no satisfactory avenue through which a citizen could lodge a complaint against Police misbehaviour in the expectation it would be thoroughly and impartially pursued. Regrettably, this is apparently due in no small measure to an attitude of the Police mind, which is affronted by the impertinence of the civilian in making a complaint at all and which then in a defensive reflex, classifies him as a trouble maker, or as being anti-Police, or motivated by malice or ill-will.

In New South Wales, before any external oversight, the process for lodging complaints against police was regarded by citizens as "involving an unequal battle between them and the brotherhood of the service" (Kirby 1976, 14), especially given that anonymous complaints were rejected outright. This practice meant that citizens, unwilling to identify themselves for fear of police retaliation, had nowhere to go with their grievance.

Fitzgerald (1989, 81), commenting on the police internal investigation process in Queensland, found that:

> Some of the procedures adopted have been amazing; for example, disclosing the material available to suspected police officers prior to interrogation and seeking and acting on reports from sections which are the subject of complaint or allegation. Regularly, no more has been required as a basis for a finding in favour of a police officer than his denial of the case against him, which was seen to put one word against another and therefore make the allegation unsustainable, a proposition so absurd as to be risible.

Even when disciplinary charges were laid, the penalties imposed were often farcical. Fitzgerald cites the example of a "ludicrous" fine of $2.00 for false statements (1989, 81).

Another factor which contributes to the failure of internal methods of accountability is addressed by Goldstein (1977, 212) who makes the important point that "It is absolutely unrealistic to expect officers on special assignment, however honest and dedicated, to investigate zealously the activities of fellow officers who may one day be their partners or superiors".

This problem is compounded by what Ruchelman (1974, 3) identifies as the "closed" nature of police organisations. Regardless of an individual's previous work experience, many police departments have a policy that (except at the very highest level) anyone entering (and in many jurisdictions re-entering) the police service must do so at the lowest rank of constable and work their way up through the organisation.

This "closed" system not only supports Goldstein's argument that it is foolish to expect police to investigate future partners or superiors but lends credence to the argument that it is also unrealistic to expect them to investigate former partners, superiors or colleagues who, as members of the same closed system, have shared departmental, district and station problems and are inculcated with the same strong culture. To use the police family analogy, asking police to investigate their colleagues through internal only processes is akin to asking brothers and sisters to investigate each other or their parents.

This view has been, and in many cases still is, strongly rejected by the police who often claim that only police can truly understand the policing function and therefore only police should be allowed to judge the misconduct of other police (Kerstetter 1985, 149-82; Pomeroy 1985, 183-86). This police-centred view, however, ignores an important point in the police accountability debate which was addressed in Chapter One, namely that police in liberal democratic societies are expected to abide by community standards in terms of their behaviour, not by the standards acceptable to a police culture or subculture.

The mounting evidence that police protected their own and rarely, if ever, witnessed any wrong doing by other officers frustrated and angered the public. They became convinced that the police were not capable of investigating and prosecuting malefactors from within their own ranks or that when they did it was not done with the resolve it warranted.

Conclusion

A situation of almost complete mistrust of the police-controlled complaints process (Goldstein 1977) has meant that, regardless of the thoroughness of any internal investigations, findings that exonerate police are now treated as suspect by the community (Maguire and Corbett 1991). As Skolnick (1993, 9) explains, "Cops are not trusted to investigate and reach decisions about the alleged misconduct of other cops, even when they are perfectly capable of doing so, and even when they make the right decision". This lack of trust, Maguire (1991) argues, is perhaps permanent as findings of innocence on the part of the police, if the police alone control the process, are no longer believed by citizens.

When it comes to receiving and processing citizens' complaints about the conduct of other police and imposing disciplinary sanctions, police in the United States, Britain, Canada and Australia have been seen as part of the problem, not part of the solution. In theory, there were accountability processes but in practice they did not work. The following chapter shows that it was the practice which led to a situation where citizens, largely through pressure group politics, demanded that the system be changed to include independent, civilian involvement in the handling of complaints against police. Not surprisingly, police fought hard to retain their virtual monopoly over the process[4]: the degree to which they were successful varied, as did the way in which they chose to demonstrate and exercise their political power.

---

4 In relation to complaints involving criminal charges the courts and not the police are in control.

3

REACTION TO THE PROBLEM – GOVERNMENTS AND POLICE

Introduction

This chapter continues the historical account of the emergence of external, independent civilian bodies to oversight complaints against police. It takes the issue beyond identifying the cause of public dissatisfaction with the internal system to explaining how pressure group politics was the catalyst which placed this new form of police accountability on the political agenda.

But the chapter is more than simply an historical narrative. When explaining governments' response to pressure group politics, it also highlights the dilemma civilian oversight causes for governments. This dilemma is brought about by the symbiotic nature of police-government relations being counterpoised against the growing influence of several pressure groups opposed to the secretive, unsatisfactory nature of existing policies for handling complaints against police.

Predictably, police did not relinquish their monopolistic control of the complaints process without a fight. The tactics they used can be described as a classic example of Dahl's (1957, 203) one-dimensional view of power which is said to exist when individuals or groups are able to influence key decisions by enforcing their preferences over those of other individuals or groups.

The degree to which police were able to affect the direction or outcome of government policy varied. Evidence will be presented to show that an overt display of power was evident in New York City and, in a less volatile fashion, in Philadelphia. In other jurisdictions – Britain, Toronto and Australia – police used their power as a bartering tool to weaken the legislative powers of the oversight body and to win concessions for themselves, rather than to try to force the closure of the watchdog agency.[1] The important point is that in almost every case the police were able to influence the outcome of government policy. Before civilian oversight became a political issue, this was made possible by the nature of the policy community which set the police accountability agenda.

Closed policy community[2]

Historically, there have been few formal policies for handling complaints against the police. In jurisdictions where they existed they were formulated in a closed policy community, with the police hierarchy, police unions and governmental actors deciding the nature of the processes. This arrangement, which supports Bachrach and Baratz's (1962, 1963) non-decision-making process, advantaged the police. With the agenda being controlled by a close-knit dominant group, the policy options were restricted to "safe" issues which favoured the police retaining their virtual control of the complaints process.

The limited membership of the policy community, in particular the absence of people to represent the largest consumers of the service, the community, is not unusual in law and order matters. When examining power and policy in liberal democratic societies, Ritchie (1992, 195-217) found that "The law and order policy community is dominated by governmental actors and by the corporate professionals, the police. In general, the consumers of the policy – the citizens – are not organised and do not influence policy outcomes except in a general way through the ballot box" (Ritchie 1992, 203).

In the late 1950s and early 1960s, however, this arrangement slowly began to change in terms of police accountability. Despite being treated as "outsiders" for many years, civil rights groups, supported by the media, eventually forced the issue onto the political agenda. The civil rights movement's campaign was the catalyst, the first step in a long process,

---

1 An exception is in the State of Victoria (Australia) where power exerted by the police hierarchy eventually led to the closure of the Police Complaints Authority (see Freckelton and Selby 1989).

2 Fenna (1998, 85) defines the term "policy community" as a "closed [policy] network where a self-serving consensus exists between participating interests and the branch of the government responsible for implementing policy in that sector". He goes on to say that others have defined them as "advocacy coalitions" and that in extreme situations that can be likened to "private interest government, where the interests themselves are entrusted with authority to make or implement policy in their area, or 'capture' government agencies to work in their favour".

which eventually undermined the previously established "mobilisation of bias" (Bachrach and Baratz 1963, 642) and led to a split in the policy community. This split, which altered the nature of police-government relations, led to the introduction of civilian boards, commissions or authorities to monitor, review and/or investigate complaints against police.

Influence of civil rights movement

Demand for civilian input into the police complaints process in America is said to have developed out of an upsurge in civil rights activities (Gellhorn 1966; Goldstein 1977; Brown 1985a; Walker and Bumphus 1992). The most notable of these groups, the American Civil Liberties Union, campaigned intensely for civilian review between 1957 and 1963 (Goldstein 1977). The civil rights movement and the subsequent "heightened awareness" about individual rights across North America contributed to the civil unrest in many Canadian cities, especially in Toronto in the 1970s (Watt 1991). This unrest included protests about the way police treated citizens, particularly those from minority groups (McMahon and Ericson 1984) and resulted in the media paying closer attention to allegations of police abusing their powers.

The civil rights movement does not take the same degree of prominence in the literature which covers the emergence of civilian oversight in Britain and Australia. That is not to imply that pressure group politics did not play a part in helping to establish more effective systems of police accountability; it did. For example, complaints about police brutality, verballing and harassment by civil liberties and minority groups during the 1960s and 1970s served to highlight citizens' growing dissatisfaction with police behaviour and the lack of redress afforded them through the police-controlled complaints system (Humphry 1979; Wegg-Prosser 1979; Hawker 1981). With the support of the media, these grievances were brought to the public's attention and, as the number of complaints increased, governments in Britain and Australia were forced to act. They did so by establishing royal commissions, commissions of inquiry or by commissioning reports to investigate the allegations.

Civil rights groups have also been influential in strengthening the powers of civilian oversight bodies. For example, in Britain in the 1980s issues concerning the police and the rights of minority groups were instrumental in establishing the Police Complaints Authority, a more powerful oversighting body than its predecessor, the Police Complaints Board (Scarman 1981).

Calls for increased accountability generally

While citing the civil rights movement as a factor in the oversighting of police conduct, Hudson (1971) does not focus specifically on problems relating to police. Rather, he maintains that the movement had a much broader agenda which was to improve accountability across the public sector generally. He sees the debate about civilian involvement in the police complaints process as part of a questioning and re-examination of traditional relations between clients (citizens) and agencies (service delivery bureaucracies), not simply between citizens and the police.

By the late 1950s, early 1960s, government-delivered services had begun to play a pivotal role in the lives of many citizens and the manner and form in which those services were delivered became a "critical" issue (Hudson 1971). As the procedures and practices of service delivery institutions were scrutinised, many were found wanting. Allegations of "incompetence and mistreatment" were made against departments dealing with housing, health, education and welfare issues. Police, Hudson maintains, were only one of the institutions subjected to calls for increased civilian involvement in the accountability process. There were, for example, calls for greater community (civilian) input into the running of schools (Hudson 1971, 515). According to Hudson's argument, civilian oversight of complaints against police can be viewed as part of the push by citizens for more "open government".

Influence of television

Even though the civil rights movement focused widespread public attention on police conduct (Bayley 1991), it was television that allowed police actions to be beamed into people's living rooms and many citizens were not happy with what they saw. Police were increasingly viewed as the "oppressors of civil rights", the willing tool of governments in the suppression of people's civil liberties (Petterson 1991).

Goode (1991, 120-25) believes that police made the fundamental mistake of allowing themselves to be ideologically aligned to governments which by and large resisted citizens' rights to protest. The community may have better understood the difficult position police found themselves in if the police had operated strictly from a neutral, law enforcement perspective. But police went beyond that point by stereotyping civil rights demonstrators as "deviants" and on many occasions their behaviour reflected those beliefs.

The civil rights and peace marches also had the effect of broadening the class of people who became the focus of police attention. They often put police in direct conflict with middle-class citizens who saw protesting as their natural democratic right (Goode 1991, 120-21). Previous explanations that complaints about police lawlessness came from the "under-class" had been largely accepted by the majority who rarely came into contact with police. Police behaviour had not really been an issue for the law-abiding middle classes (Hain 1979). However, protest marches coupled with the televised police response changed all that. The middle classes were now experiencing first-hand, or in the majority of cases viewing on television, police-citizen contact. Many began to complain about police behaviour. This fuelled a growing legitimacy problem for police (Hain 1979). As citizens started to lose faith in the police, policing became an increasingly controversial issue. Governments were faced with a new set of problems which could no longer be dealt with to the mutual satisfaction of the key players in the policy community.

Governments, sensing the mood of the electorate, felt compelled to respond positively to citizens' demands. The police response to this new situation varied. The following examples from New York, Philadelphia, Toronto, Britain, South Australia and Western Australia demonstrate the range of government and police responses and the effect they were to have on police-government relations.

Philadelphia

In 1957 the American Civil Liberties Union's Philadelphia branch successfully campaigned for the establishment of a civilian review board. The Philadelphia Police Advisory Board (PAB), established in 1958 by newly elected, reforming mayor, Richard Dillworth, was "beset by litigation" (Gellhorn 1966; Brown 1985a). Opposition by the Fraternal Order of Police (FOP) was intense and relentless. It included two law suits, the first of which was filed some 12 months after the Board was established but was withdrawn after the Board agreed to institute some "modest reforms" (Hudson 1971, 526). The second suit, filed in 1965, resulted in an injunction suspending the Board's hearings and led to its eventual demise (Hudson 1971, 526; Terrill 1991). The FOP's campaign was further assisted in 1965 by a change of mayor who also opposed the PAB (Terrill 1991). The city administration suspended any appeal against the court's decision until after the 1967 mayoral elections. When Mayor Tate was re-elected, he gave no indication that he would appeal the "unfavourable court decision" (Hudson 1971, 527). Lack of action by the mayor meant that the Police Advisory Board continued to be inactive. Members of the PAB, frustrated by the situation, attempted to appeal the decision themselves but the court ruled they did not have standing. Nevertheless, their action had the desired result in that the administration proceeded with the appeal.

Even though the Supreme Court of Pennsylvania ruled in the PAB's favour, Mayor Tate claimed "there was 'no reason for haste in re-activating the Police Advisory Board'" (Hudson 1971, 527). He further claimed that he would be discussing the situation with his administration and the police commissioner (used in the North American sense of the word) whose strong opposition to the Board was publicly known. The mayor finally revealed his intention not to reactivate the board in a speech to one hundred members of the police hierarchy. He explained his decision by saying, "This is a type of a Christmas present to you gentlemen" (*Philadelphia Inquirer*, 13 Dec 1969, 1; quoted in Hudson 1971, 527). It is interesting to note that the police commissioner who was consulted about reactivating the Board went on to successfully run for mayor himself. In Philadelphia the eventual outcome was that the police, with the help of the politicians, eventually won the battle against the reformers. This meant that for the time being, at least, the policy community could return to its previous non-threatening arrangement.

New York

In the 1950s allegations of police malfeasance within the New York City Police Department reached such proportions that the Justice Department warned that unless police behaviour improved it would conduct its own investigation into the matter (West 1991, 379). It was against this background that in the early 1960s the civil rights movement became increasingly vocal about the lack of police accountability. By the mid-1960s the issue of civilian involvement in the police complaints system had become a hotly contested political issue (Walker 1983, 237) and was firmly on the agenda in the 1965 New York mayoral campaign. Republican candidate John Lindsay made his position very clear. If elected, he would introduce a civilian element even if it meant having to appoint a new police chief.

When Lindsay was elected, he set about establishing the Civilian Complaint Review Board (CCRB) and, true to his word, appointed a police chief who was disposed toward the idea. This was important as the

CCRB's authority was derived from a police department order (Brown 1985b, 151). It appears that on this occasion the politicians and reformers had won the battle for increased accountability. However, their victory was to be short-lived. The Patrolmen's Benevolent Association (PBA) acted immediately and mobilised opposition to the board. They were determined to make the issue the subject of a referendum and were successful in attracting the support needed for one to be held. Many conservative groups supported the Independent Citizens' Committee Against Police Review Board. In the pluralist tradition of American politics in the 1960s an opposing pressure group, the Federated Association for Impartial Review (FAIR) was quickly formed.

A fierce battle ensued. Skolnick (1993, 221) describes the nature of the campaign waged by the PBA to demonstrate the degree to which they were prepared to go to avoid external independent civilian scrutiny. Posters featured throughout the city graphically depicted dangerous scenarios including riots brought about because of police fear to act. The PBA campaign even went so far as to suggest that people's lives would be in danger if the CCRB was allowed to continue.

The campaign by those opposing civilian review was delivered with an initial budget of $500,000 with a PBA promise that, if necessary, it would spend all its funds, some $1.5 million (1966 dollars), to fight the board. Pressure groups opposing the establishment of the board were successful. Citizens voted overwhelmingly in favour of abolishing the civilian-dominated police review committee. This time the police had won the battle against the reformers and politicians. New York's first attempt at partial civilian oversight survived a mere four months from July to November 1966.

Hudson (1971, 528) explains the police success in opposing civilian review in America in terms of police "single-mindedness". Supporters of civilian review, he argues, are not as single-minded in their defence of the concept as police are in opposing it. Police accountability is only one of the many issues that capture the public's attention. Groups advocating the benefits of civilian review are a collection of disparate people in society. The police on the other hand were, in these scenarios, an homogenous and very powerful pressure group.

In both these American examples the inter-meshing of police and politics is a product of the historical relationship between police and governments. In the United States nearly 80 percent of general-purpose policing takes place at the local government level (Walker 1992, 37) where police are accountable to the mayor or city manager. This arrangement reflects the nation's ideological commitment to the dispersal of political power, also evidenced by its federalist structure, separation of powers and bill of rights. Theoretically, the devolution of police power to the local government level was done to make police more accountable and responsive to the community. In practice, it served to make police the "tool" of local politicians who unashamedly used them to further their personal and party political ambitions.

As mentioned previously, in the 19th and early 20th centuries American police were regarded by politicians as part of the prize of winning office (Fosdick 1920, 119). Some attempts were made to deal with this problem. Police boards were introduced to act, among other things, as a buffer between politicians and police. However, as politicians appointed the board members, and in many instances the mayor was a member of the board, they were not particularly effective in achieving their goal (Kelling and Moore 1988). Police and politics became so intertwined in many American forces that debates about who would be police chief became an important issue in local mayoral elections (McDougall 1988, 49).

In the 1930s police began to react against this situation. The law, particularly the criminal law, and police professionalism, were the basis on which police demanded their right to be free from party political exploitation (Kelling and Moore 1988, 5). Police, particularly in the larger American cities, have been successful in their campaign to be dealt with as professionals and many have used their newfound professional status to argue that their autonomy should extend to accountability policies involving police misconduct. However, in some cases their conduct in opposing external civilian oversight calls into question their claim to professional status (Chevigney 1995).

Display of police power

In New York in 1966 the announcement that civilian oversighting was to be introduced brought forth a display of raw, naked power by the police, particularly by the PBA. The power struggle between the government and the police was largely played out in public. It led to a complete breakdown in relations between the executive and the police and the disintegration of any notion of a policy community. It also led to the speedy demise of the civilian oversight body. In Philadelphia the police used the courts to try to stop the introduction of civilian oversight. Even though police tactics were not as blatantly aggressive as in New York, the result was the same; the civilian oversight body was closed down. The interesting distinction between the two was the role played by the mayor. Even more interesting, perhaps, is the fact that with or without political support the police won.

Influence of commissions of inquiry

In the United Kingdom, Toronto and Australia governments reacted to citizens' demands for improved police accountability in a different manner than in Philadelphia and New York. They established inquiries or commissioned reports to examine allegations of police misconduct and mismanagement.

Several theories have been advanced about why governments establish commissions of inquiry or commission reports. Among the principal reasons identified by Smith and Weller (1978) and Prasser (1994, 6-10) is the need for governments: to respond to a crisis situation where immediate and independent actions are needed; to help resolve public controversy and promote greater public participation and consensus over key issues; to help governments manage the policy agenda through the illusion of actions or to deflect criticism and co-opt critics; and to investigate allegations of impropriety concerning public servants or public organisations. In terms of police accountability, establishing an inquiry may also serve to distance the executive from policies which have the potential to harm police-government relations.

Many inquiries about police behaviour have been established to investigate allegations of impropriety or to help police and governments maintain control of the police accountability policy agenda by creating the illusion that governments are actually doing something when in reality the status quo is being maintained. In such circumstances they are often used to take the heat off governments or, as AP Herbert suggests, "not so much for digging up the truth, as for digging it in" (Herbert 1961 quoted in Prasser 1994, 11). Herbert's suggestion is particularly applicable when a police service has been politicised, for when that happens it is in the government's interest to maintain the status quo.

Regardless of why inquiries are established, they do have some type of policy function. As Ransley (1994, 29) points out, even those established to investigate allegations of wrongdoing make recommendations about how to deal with that wrongdoing, and recommendations are "clearly of a policy nature". While this is true, the decision to act on policy advice remains with government and there are many examples of governments ignoring inquiry recommendations in relation to the police.

Even if an inquiry is established to genuinely investigate allegations of police impropriety in the hope of achieving more effective accountability, when the report is brought down governments have to weigh up the benefits and costs of implementing the recommendations. The government's reluctance to act in many instances may be influenced by what Friedrich (1940) described as "the rule of anticipated reactions" which is explained by Ham and Hill (1993, 69) as possibly operating "when a community group fails to mobilise because it anticipates an unfavourable response by decision-makers, or when decision-makers themselves do not act because they expect opposition from key actors".

There is evidence of governments preferring to sacrifice accountability in order to avoid a confrontation with police, but governments cannot do so forever. As inquiry after inquiry reveals the same set of problems, governments, through public and media pressure, are forced to act.

Incremental effect of commissions of inquiry

Despite the sometimes dubious reasons for establishing inquiries and the reluctance of some governments to implement their recommendations, the literature shows the incremental but nevertheless influential effect commissions of inquiries have had on the introduction of civilian oversighting bodies, particularly in the United Kingdom, Toronto and Australia.

United Kingdom

Alderson (1992) and Lambert (1986) make the link between highly publicised happenings involving police in the 1950s in London and the establishment of a royal commission into the police in 1960. One of the terms of reference of this inquiry related to "the relationship of the police and the public and the means of ensuring that complaints by the public are effectively dealt with" (Alderson 1992, 23). The majority decision rejected the idea of civilian participation but a minority did recommend independent, civilian involvement in the form of a Commissioner of Rights. The majority decision, which formalised the internal system by taking the discretion over whether to investigate a complaint or not away from chief constables, did not satisfy the public. It failed to treat the cause of public concern or to adequately address police accountability problems. It can best be described as a symbolic attempt by government to be seen to be doing something while at the same time allowing the police to maintain their control of the complaints against police process. At this stage in

Britain it appears as if the closed policy community was still in control of the police accountability agenda. However, as with many symbolic policies, the problem remained and eventually resurfaced. Influential individual actors then became involved and the issue was back in the political spotlight.

In 1973 Philip Whithead MP presented a Private Member's Bill to parliament asking for the introduction of a police complaints tribunal to review decisions by chief constables and the Director of Public Prosecutions involving "no action" to complaints. Whithead agreed to withdraw the Bill on the condition that the home secretary establish a committee to report on the handling of citizens' grievances against the police (Lambert 1986; Robilliard and McEwan 1986). The Police Complaints Board (PCB) for England and Wales, Britain's first attempt at external, independent, civilian oversight was in large part the result of the home secretary accepting recommendations made in *The Handling of Complaints Against the Police: Report of the Working Group* (Russell 1978; Robbilliard and McEwan 1986). However, the structure and functions of the Board were influenced by the police using their political power to gain concessions.

The extraordinary overt use of power by police federations in the Philadelphia and New York City experiments with civilian oversight had "no parallel in Britain" (Loveday 1987, 12). But that is not to say that opposition by police in England and Wales was not intense; it just occurred in a more subtle manner. Police chose to bargain rather than bully. Humphry (1979), referring to the police federation's insistence that the internal system did not need reform, argues that strong union opposition was tempered by "a classic piece of 'horse trading'".

The Police Federation warned that it would not accept the new Police Act unless it was given the right "to sue malicious and reckless complainants for libel or defamation" (Humphry 1979, 44), a right they had been campaigning about for years. The Federation also argued successfully that the investigative stage of the process should remain with the police, that police should not be subjected to double jeopardy and that the Director of Public Prosecutions role should not be altered (Robilliard and McEwan 1986). The double jeopardy concession caused the Police Complaints Board considerable problems. Lambert (1986, 66-67) points out how the negotiated interpretation very often translated into no jeopardy. Police maintained the right to have the criminal standard of proof, beyond reasonable doubt, applied in respect to disciplinary hearings. The Police Federation also won the right for its members to see the full complaint and to take civil action against vexatious complainants. These concessions, plus an officer's ability to use Federation funds for lawsuits (Humphry 1979, 51), helped the Federation to sell the new system to rank and file members. Between the publishing of the Police Bill and its receiving Royal Assent, there was little criticism by the Federation about the proposed Police Complaints Board. As Humphry (1979, 57) explains, "it 'kept its head down' most of the time convinced – rightly as it transpired – that the real bargaining had been done before the Bill appeared".

However, the police hierarchy continued to object to the Bill, arguing that it interfered with the (unwritten) constitutional position of chief constables and the commissioner of the metropolitan police by reducing their disciplinary powers. For the first time since the establishment of the "new police", non-police people would have some authority over the lower ranks (Humphry 1979, 46), a situation which was completely untenable to some.

The introduction of the Police Complaints Board led to the resignation of the reformist Police Commissioner Sir Robert Mark. According to Mark, he did not resign because he was against the concept of an independent element being introduced into the complaints process but rather because the PCB would undermine the chief officer's responsibility for discipline and he had no desire to operate under such a system (Humphry 1979; Reiner 1983). But as Reiner (1983, 134) points out, "to have an effective review that does not weaken chief constables' sole disciplinary power is as impossible as squaring the circle".

In his final interview as Commissioner of the London Metropolitan Police, Mark showed the depth of his animosity toward the government for daring to go against the police commissioner's beliefs about how an independent element should be constituted (Humphry 1979, 47). Mark condemned the government saying that:

> I believe the Police Act was drawn up by Jenkins' (the then Home Secretary) backroom boys, an intellectually arrogant crew who consulted no one about the Bill, certainly not the Met, nor I believe the Chief Inspector of Constabulary at that time. I am appalled that the Complaints Board will consist of political nominees. Quite apart from its largely unnecessary procedural absurdity and cost it will have the effect of allowing political nominees to exercise control over police discipline, a sadly retrograde step (*Sunday Times* 13 March 1977, quoted in Humphry 1979, 53)

Mark's public criticism of government policy was symptomatic of a growing trend in Britain in the 1970s for police to become publicly embroiled in the political fray. Reiner (1983, 146) sees this trend as a "bid for unilateral power" by the police. However, as he argues, "policies that have profound political implications should be undermined by a supposedly neutral and technical 'professional' expertise". Policing, Reiner believes, "is too important to be left to policemen" (Reiner 1983, 146).

The objections by the police hierarchy and police unions to the introduction of an independent element into the complaints process in Britain, while resisted by police, was certainly done in a more muted fashion than the campaigns waged in Philadelphia and New York. The different reactions between the two countries can be explained, in part, by different historical, cultural and political traditions. But it can also be explained by the different approach by government to the introduction of what was then a highly controversial policy. By placing a report between it and the policy decision, the British Government was able to distance itself from the recommendations while at the same time have them placed on the agenda for discussion. This also allowed the police the opportunity to bargain. While this approach is more helpful to police-government relations, it does not necessarily translate into an effective oversight body.

The Police Complaints Board's lack of powers eventually led to its demise. It took the "Brixton riots" and the subsequent inquiry by Lord Scarman before the government was prepared to introduce a more powerful civilian oversight body, the Police Complaints Authority.

Criticism and condemnation of the Police Complaints Authority, particularly from the Police Federation, was frequent and strong. In 1989 the Federation unanimously passed a vote of no confidence in the Authority. However, it failed in a legal attempt to stop PCA members attending formal interviews of officers the subject of supervised investigations (PCA 1995, 10).

Toronto

Even though the civil rights movement was instrumental in highlighting the problem of police behaviour in Toronto, and with the assistance of the media of placing complaints about police on the political agenda, the establishment of the Office of Public Complaints Commissioner (OPCC) in Toronto (later changed to the Office of the Police Complaints Commissioner) resulted from the recommendations of a series of inquiries. In six years there were five inquiries into various aspects of police-community interactions (Watt 1991). Arthur Maloney QC was appointed to examine the police complaints system in 1975. He recommended the appointment of an independent civilian commissioner of complaints. Recommendations for an independent element were echoed in three subsequent studies conducted in the 1970s: the 1976 Morand Royal Commission into Metropolitan Toronto Police Practices, the 1977 Pitman Inquiry into Race Relations and the 1979 study by Sidney Linden QC, commissioned to examine possible ways of introducing a civilian component into the handling of complaints against police. Also in 1979 a study on police-minority relations was undertaken by a catholic cardinal at the behest of the Metropolitan Toronto Council. He too recommended civilian involvement in the complaints process (Lewis, Linden and Keene 1986, 117-21). All inquiries looked, to varying degrees, at the resolution of public complaints against the police (McMahon and Ericson 1984; McMahon 1988; Lewis 1991).

Recommendations from report after report supporting the concept of an independent, external civilian element eventually had some effect on government policy. Governments could no longer ignore what had the potential to develop into a crisis situation. In 1981 a public complaints commissioner was appointed as a temporary measure in what has been described as "a three year pilot project" (Lewis, Linden and Keene 1986, 121). This temporary measure became permanent in 1984 and, in 1990, the jurisdiction of the OPCC was extended beyond Toronto to include the whole of Ontario (Landau 1994).

The introduction of a civilian element in the complaints process in metropolitan Toronto went ahead with the consent and cooperation of the police department and the police association who were consulted throughout the policy formulation stage of the process. However, Lewis (1991) suggests that their consent and cooperation was forthcoming because the police did not believe that any officer would be seriously disciplined for misconduct without the police first believing the discipline was warranted. However, the powers given to the Office of Public Complaints Commissioner allowed a board of inquiry to override a penalty imposed by the chief of police. This power was invoked by the public complaints commissioner and led to an attack on the Office by the police association (Lewis 1991).

The incident which prompted the union attack occurred in 1985. The police commissioner (used in the North American sense of the word) had dismissed a complaint against an officer. The OPCC disagreed with the decision and ordered a tribunal hearing into the matter. The tribunal found misconduct by the officer and ordered that he resign or face dismissal. The police association reacted by vowing to dedicate its energy and significant resources to the destruction of the public complaints system. It turned its attentions to delaying, obstructing and defeating the policy of civilian oversight. It used the forced resignation or dismissal to mount a legal challenge to the validity of the *Metropolitan Toronto Police Force Complaints Act*. The Divisional Court upheld the Office of Public Complaints Commissioner's decision. The association appealed to the Ontario Court of Appeal but the Court denied them leave and the officer was forced to resign.

Having lost its case through formal legal channels, the police association resorted to the type of intimidatory tactics adopted by the New York police. They were determined to ensure that everyone knew of their dissatisfaction with a process which allowed "one of their members [to lose] his job at the hands of civilians" (Lewis 1991, 166). Mass meetings were called and it was decided to partially withdraw police services until the officer was reinstated and the OPCC destroyed. Police brought their cause to the attention of the public by wearing slogans on their caps calling for the destruction of the Office of Public Complaints Commissioner and to the attention of the government by refusing to summons traffic offenders. The police association failed to gain media, judicial or public support. However, it continued to try to have the officer reinstated and in 1987 the then president of the association made known the feelings of its members when he said, "The Association fervently believes that the only good external complaints system is a dead complaints system" (Walter cited in Lewis 1991, 167).

The police association strategy of legal challenge followed by an overt display of power designed to bring the oversight body to heel captured public attention, but not in the way the association had perhaps hoped. Many organisations came to the defence of the external, independent, civilian system. The public reaction to the association's campaign in Toronto may be symptomatic of the community's growing lack of faith in any profession's ability to oversight the conduct of their members in a fair and impartial manner and for them to bring down penalties commensurate with community standards.

It may also have been an indication that, at that time, the power of the police was on the wane. The evidence suggests that the public was losing confidence in the police. This was brought about in large part by growing dissatisfaction with police behaviour and the lack of redress for complainants. Therefore, there was no logical reason why the citizens of

Toronto would want to risk a return to the closed system of the past by supporting the police against the oversight body.

Nor was there a logical reason for the government to support the police. Having taken so long to respond to citizens' demands for a more open and just complaints system, it would have been politically unwise for it to then close down the external civilian oversight body so soon after it was established. The nature of the police campaign left the force momentarily isolated.

But it seems that the Ontario police may have learnt that behind the scenes negotiations with government can be more effective than publicly trying to bully it into submission. In 1997 the government of Ontario closed the Office of Police Complaints Commissioner, disbanded boards of inquiry and returned the power to discipline officers to police chiefs. The sole remaining independent civilian oversight body, the Ontario Civilian Commission on Police Services, has less power than the disbanded OPCC. For example, it only becomes involved in the complaints process if a complainant is dissatisfied with the outcome of the police chief's decision, whereas the OPCC could investigate in its own right from the initial stage of the complaints process.

The government claims that the new system will modernise, streamline and simplify the oversight process and make it more responsible and accountable to the complainant (Ontario Ministry of the Solicitor-General and Corrections 1997, "Amended Police Services Act Introduces Taxpayer Fairness", Media Release, January). However, commentators and human rights groups, such as the Canadian Civil Liberties Association, the African-Canadian Legal Clinic and the Urban Alliance on Race Relations disagree. They have expressed their dissatisfaction with the new model and describe it as a retrograde step in the move toward more open and transparent accountability processes. The discussion on models in Chapter Four supports their claim.

The negotiation process, which took place between police and government before any formal announcement that the complaints process was to be reviewed, indicates that the decline in police power experienced in the early to mid 1980s was only temporary.

A confidential report obtained by the *Now* journal reveals that the Ontario Association of Chiefs of Police (OACP) met with Ontario's Assistant Deputy Solicitor-General Fred Peters, on eight occasions in the months leading up to the government's announcement that it would be reviewing the current system for oversighting complaints against police. In a letter, written three weeks before the Assistant Deputy Solicitor-

General was formally asked to conduct the review, a director of the OACP advised the head of the Association that their organisation's position was being accepted by the government and other stakeholders. The correspondence also made it clear that the letter should not be shown to the media (*Now* 5 Dec 1996, 17).

A senior spokesperson for the solicitor-general rejected suggestions that "the fix was in", maintaining that the final decision about civilian oversight in Ontario rested with cabinet. Proposals by the Ontario Association of Chiefs of Police which formed part of the McLeod Report[3] into civilian oversight in Ontario, found their way into legislation (*Now* 5 Dec 1996, 17).

It seems that police-government relations are strong again in Ontario and that the police have regained their ability to influence government policy in respect to important civil liberty issues.

Australia

In Australia the suggestion that there ought to be some form of independent, external civilian oversight of police conduct emanated from the first Australian Law Reform Commission's (ALRC) Report, *Complaints Against Police*, in 1975.[4] This report was commissioned to look at ways of dealing with complaints against police in a proposed new national police force.[5]

The Commission's recommendation that an "independent element be introduced into the investigation and determination of complaints against members of the Australia Police" (Australian Law Reform Commission 1975, 71) was largely accepted by the Commonwealth Government and was included in the Australia Police Bill 1975. However, when parliament was dissolved in November 1975, the Bill lapsed. When the new Liberal-National Party Coalition Government took office it did not proceed with the amalgamation. But in light of a number of developments in this area in

3 *A Report and Recommendations on Amendments to the Police Services Act Respecting Civilian Oversight of Police*, 21 Nov 1996, Toronto, Ontario.

4 In Australia, each of the six States and two Territories has responsibility for its own general-purpose police force. The Australian Federal Police, which come under the Federal Government's jurisdiction, is not a general purpose police force. However, it does contract out a general purpose policing function for the Australian Capital Territory.

5 The Whitlam Government proposed amalgamating the Commonwealth Police, the Northern Territory Police, the Australian Capital Territory Police and certain parts of the Department of Customs and Excise.

Australia and overseas (Australian Law Reform Commission 1978), the government requested that the ALRC review its 1975 findings and produce a supplementary report. The ALRC's 1978 report also recommended the introduction of an independent element.

The 1975 report drew on evidence from Britain and United States about their internal investigation systems and the 1978 report noted negative experiences with internal investigation systems in two Australian States – Victoria and Queensland. It also referred to the establishment of Britain's independent external civilian oversighting body, the Police Complaints Board, and to the passage of the Commonwealth *Ombudsman Act 1976* which conferred *ex post* powers on the Commonwealth Ombudsman in relation to the Commonwealth, Northern Territory and Australian Capital Territory police forces (Australian Law Reform Commission 1978).

These ALRC reports raised the complaints against police issue in a relatively non-confrontational manner and the proposals outlined in the reports were largely accepted by the Commonwealth, Northern Territory and Australian Capital Territory police (Australian Law Reform Commission 1978, 5). But as the following section will show, the States' police forces resisted their governments' introduction of such a policy. Australian police tended to follow the "horse-trading" tactics used by the British police and, like their British counterparts, their bargaining power was such that they were able to influence the final shape of the oversight body. The following examples from South Australia and Western Australia support this argument.

South Australia

The South Australian police hierarchy and police union objected to several provisions in the Bill to establish an external, independent, civilian oversight body, the Police Complaints Authority. Part of the union's tactic was to threaten strike action. The threat was used as a bargaining tool to reduce the power of the PCA and to win concessions for the police; it was never actioned (Goode 1987).

Negotiations between the police hierarchy, police union and government lasted some six months. Initially, the police association rejected the draft Bill and the police hierarchy expressed dissatisfaction with some of its provisions. Objections raised by the police were rebutted by the Council for Civil Liberties who publicly supported the Bill (Goode 1987, 64). The issue dominated question time and debate on the Bill was postponed. The minister met with the police association's executive for further discussions.

In November 1984 the police association met again and "resolved to continue its negotiations with the government for another week". The day before the next association meeting, its secretary announced that the provision compelling answers to questions was still unresolved but that the government had agreed to "a privilege against self-incrimination in relation to criminal offences but not disciplinary offences". At this stage the police commissioner announced his satisfaction with the legislation (Goode 1987, 64).

In late November 1984 a further meeting of the association was held and a letter from the minister was tabled which stated that the government would postpone further debate until early February 1985. A meeting of the police association resolved to continue the fight in respect of the investigative powers of the proposed Police Complaints Authority, but agreed to defer industrial action while further negotiations took place (Goode 1987, 64).

On 2 January 1985, while negotiations between the government and police association were ongoing, the government announced that legislation would be introduced to dramatically increase the "penalties for assaulting police, hindering police, disorderly behaviour and bribing police". The police association "welcomed" this announcement (Goode 1987, 65). By now it was obvious that the union was using its power to trade for concessions from the government.

Throughout February 1985 negotiations continued. The police association met and repeated its call for the Bill to be withdrawn and renewed its threat of industrial action if the full membership were not shown the Bill before it being introduced. The Attorney-General introduced the "coincidental" bill which vastly increased penalties in relation to offences against police and increased police powers to allow them to stop and search people without a warrant and to detain suspects for questioning. The police association welcomed this legislation. However, a less powerful pressure group, the Criminal Lawyers Association, condemned it complaining that the government had only undertaken "token consultation" with their Association (Goode 1987, 65).

The government again introduced the Complaints Bill. The Police Complaints Authority's powers had been further limited in the following manner: it could not examine people on oath; it would need a search warrant to conduct a search; anonymous complaints would only be investigated in special circumstances; and police, and their close relatives, would have privilege against self-incrimination. With these compromises in place the police association agreed to the Bill. It was passed on 4 March 1985 (Goode 1987, 65).

Western Australia

On the same day that the Police Complaints Authority in South Australia began operations, the Western Australia Parliamentary Commissioner for Administrative Investigations (PCAI) had its jurisdiction extended to cover complaints about police conduct, rather than simply those which dealt with police administrative matters.

Before the extensions of the PCAI's jurisdiction, a Complaints Against Police Bill, modelled on the Commonwealth *Complaints (Australian Federal Police) Act 1981*, was introduced into the Western Australia parliament. The Bill set out in detail the procedures to be followed by the commissioner of police in respect to the receipt, investigation and handling of complaints about police officers, and the review procedures to be conducted by the PCAI. The Bill met with strident opposition from the police union and was the subject of much debate in the parliament. Some 20 months of negotiations, several meetings between the police union and the Labor Government and the government's willingness to agree to the union's request for at least six changes to the Bill did not satisfy the union. Like their South Australian counterparts, they threatened strike action. They also passed a vote of no confidence in the Police Minister, the Premier and the government. Then police minister, Carr, obviously frustrated with police intransigency on the issue, reported to the parliament that the union had indicated that even "if we took out every clause in the Bill and left the staples stapling together blank pages [they] would not accept the Bill if it was called the Complaints Against Police Bill" (*Western Australia Legislative Assembly Parliamentary Debates* 14 November 1984, 4052).

The Bill passed through the legislative assembly but did not make it through the legislative council. In its place an amendment to the Parliamentary Commissioner's Act was passed. The amendment allowed the parliamentary commissioner to investigate complaints against police officers and members of the police department, but only after the police commissioner had first been allowed a reasonable opportunity to carry out his or her own investigation. Not being able to investigate a complaint from the outset is a basic weakness in any oversight body's capacity to be effective (see Chapter Four).

The examples used in this chapter demonstrate the lengths to which the police and the police unions were prepared to go to try to preserve their control of the complaints against police process. It appears that even if police are consulted at the planning stage, which was the case in Toronto in the early 1980s, their cooperation and consent can be conditional upon everyone playing by their standards. In Britain and Australia confrontation between police and government was not so blatant as in Philadelphia and New York but that does not mean that police action did not cause government some concern about the political damage that could arise from a drawn-out confrontation with the police. In order to avoid that confrontation they were prepared to sacrifice police accountability on the altar of pragmatism.

The privileged position of police

The literature deals with the establishment of commissions of inquiries and their findings in relation to complaints against police. However, it does not adequately explain why liberal democratic governments took so long to act in the face of mounting and damning evidence about police malfeasance, including police brutality, police corruption and their apparent disregard for due process. Why did governments, who supposedly have as a basic tenet the protection of the rights of the individual, continue to ignore the recommendations of the commissions they established? In summary, why have external, independent, civilian oversighting bodies been the policy of last resort in many instances?

One possible explanation may be found in Davis et al's (1988, 8) argument that "Underlying all public policy choices are political interests. No matter how much decisions are proposed by experts, legitimated by learned tribunals or justified on the grounds of technical rationality, policy is about politics".

Thus, important police accountability decisions have often been made on the basis of political expediency. In other words, faced with the dilemma of antagonising the police which does, in some instances, mean the combined power of the police department and police union, or placating opposing civil rights pressure groups, governments have often found it expedient to favour the seemingly more powerful police groups. The police are a solid, permanent and essential body, whereas few citizens groups are.

Governments' reluctance to act against the wishes of the police can also be explained in terms of the "privileged position" of police. When

Lindblom (1977, 170-88) was talking about the "privileged position of business" he was referring to their economic power and the fact that government must consider the business position in order to run its economic policies. Clearly, the privileged position of police is not the same as that referred to by Lindblom, as business can legitimately make economic decisions independent of and contrary to the wishes of the state. The police do not enjoy the same type of freedom. Even though they have discretion and a degree of operational independence which gives them the ability to make choices, and it can be argued they are a more cohesive group than business, the bottom line is that police are the coercive arm of government created by an Act of Parliament.

But there are other sorts of privileged positions in terms of policy than those which are enjoyed by business. As the enforcement arm of the state, the police are indeed privileged as they are essential to the state's very existence for, without the power to coerce, governments cannot govern. Even though clashes between police and governments can at times be fierce, the symbiotic nature of their relationships means that divorce is out of the question.

This is not to suggest that the privileged position of police gives them omnipotent power. Just as with business, governments will act in the interests of the broader community (Miliband 1977) and against the police when they consider it is important enough to do so. Even though governments are mindful of police power, the privileged position they occupy in society and the reciprocal nature of police-government relations, the bottom line is that police power is limited and the nature of the relationship between police and governments varies according to the particular issue under consideration.

That having been said, while police have not been able to prevent the establishment of civilian oversight bodies and the growing trend toward this form of accountability, they have used their privileged position to influence the form civilian oversight has taken. As mentioned previously, this has often been at the expense of effective accountability.

The move to civilian oversight

The New York and Philadelphia experiences did little to encourage other American cities to embrace this new form of police accountability. During the 1970s the trend toward civilian oversight in the United States was only "minimal" (West 1991, 387). By the end of the 1970s seven of America's 50 largest cities had some form of civilian involvement in the complaints against police process, although not all could be classified as external, independent organisations.[6] By 1991 this figure had grown to 30 (Walker and Bumphus 1991, 2) and in 1995 Walker and Wright identified 66 bodies that involved civilians in the handling of complaints against police in the United States (1995, 1).

In 1976 the Police Complaints Board, Britain's first attempt at civilian oversight, was established. It was replaced by a more powerful body, the Police Complaints Authority, in 1985. The first Australian civilian oversight body was established in 1976 and by 1985 all Australian State and Territory police services were oversighted by a civilian body. Even though Canada did not introduce this form of police accountability until 1981, its growth since then has been substantial.

Given police opposition to the concept, their success in bringing about the demise of civilian oversight bodies in the 1960s and in some instances the public acceptance of the police's view as evidenced in the New York referendum, how can this steady growth pattern be understood? Obviously, particular explanations will be more applicable in one jurisdiction than another, and there is always the exception to the rule. Nevertheless it is possible to identify some common elements which help to explain the gradual introduction of this form of police accountability and the reluctant acceptance of it by police departments and police unions.

During the 1970s and 1980s there has been greater social awareness among the middle classes about the injustices done to minority groups by the state in general and by its coercive arm, the police. By contrast, in the 1950s, citizens appeared indifferent to allegations of police abuse and, hence, indifferent to calls for a more open system of handling complaints against police (Terrill 1991). Increased community support for civilian oversight can be seen as one way of trying to right the wrongs of the past.

Politicians, responding to the mood of the electorate, demonstrated a greater commitment to improving police accountability. Often that commitment was superficial or, as Loveday (1987, 16) says, "little more than palliatives designed to provide a limited solution to an immediate political problem". Nevertheless, there were indications of a shift in terms of the debate. At least politicians were no longer ignoring minority and civil

---

6 Chicago, for example, has civilian investigators in the Office of Professional Standards but they report to a superintendent of police. While the Office receives and registers all complaints, it can only investigate those which involve excessive force. All other complaints are referred to the police department's internal affairs division (Loveday 1987).

liberty groups' complaints about police abuse or playing Santa Claus to the police with the closure of a civilian oversight body as the present.

There are also interesting distinctions between the tactics used by governments in the 1950s and 1960s and those of the 1970s and 1980s. It appears that governments within the United States and in other liberal democratic societies learned some valuable lessons from Philadelphia and New York. Instead of enforcing new policies on the police without much explanation or consultation, civilian oversight has been introduced more "carefully and considerately" after negotiations with police departments and police unions (Brown 1985a; West 1991, 387). By adopting a more conciliatory and consultative approach, governments have avoided putting the raw, naked power of the police to the test the way they did in New York. This has also helped to prevent the issue becoming the "political football" it was in the 1960s (West 1991, 387).

A gradual change in attitude by the senior echelon of the police service has also assisted the growth of civilian oversight bodies. In 1960 the International Association of Chiefs of Police opposed the concept (Terrill 1991, 301). However, by the 1980s senior management in many police departments were beginning to appreciate that external, independent, civilian accountability institutions could help police gain and maintain the respect and cooperation of the community. This was important to the image they were trying to create through community policing (Bayley 1991). Senior police also recognised that the information generated by oversight bodies was a valuable management tool. In some jurisdictions commissioners of police are now openly supporting the concept. For example, in Australia, Queensland's Police Commissioner Jim O'Sullivan has publicly supported that State's external independent civilian oversight body, the Criminal Justice Commission (*Courier-Mail* 8 April 1996, 9).

Possibly the most significant contributing factor to the growth of civilian oversight has been a change in tactics by several police unions. Perhaps sensing (a) the change in citizens' reactions to police misconduct and (b) the government's response to that change, police unions have turned the inevitability of civilian oversight to their advantage by winning important concessions from government. This chapter has already cited several examples to demonstrate the nature of those concessions. One further example will suffice here.

In Detroit an external, independent oversight body, the Board of Police Commissioners (BPC) was established in 1974 but it was not until 1978, following an Executive Order by the mayor, that it became operational. The four-year delay was the result of "intense and effective opposition" to the BPC by the chief of police and the police unions (Loveday 1987). However, realising that it was probably only a matter of time before civilian oversight became a reality, the union negotiated successfully for concessions. Beside the right to legal representation and the requirement that officers receive 72 hours' notice before an interview for non-criminal investigations, it re-established the right of the accused officer to have the case automatically arbitrated. Loveday (1987, 30) explains that:

> There is some likelihood that the agreements negotiated by the union have served to insulate police officers from civilian investigation and police disciplinary procedures. As one commentator has argued, to the problem of discretionary powers of police in law enforcement and the issues of the "blue curtain" of police solidarity, must now be added the collective bargaining agreements negotiated by police unions which constitute a major impediment to the control of police misconduct.

As well as gaining concessions that in some instances appear to protect police rather than expose them to vigorous external scrutiny, civilian oversight bodies have not proved to be the repressive, draconian institutions that the unions predicted. No firm evidence has been presented to support union claims that police morale suffers because of the establishment of oversight bodies, that police do not act in operational situations for fear of a complaint being lodged against them or that resignation rates increase when civilians become involved in the complaints against police process (CH Lewis 1994 pp 99-100; Criminal Justice Commission 1996c, 10).

As civilian oversight has become a more common part of the accountability landscape, some police unions have appeared to accept that these institutions can actually benefit rather than hinder police. Shortly after the OPCC was established in Toronto the police association seemed to accept that increasing community involvement in the complaints process could assist in lessening public hostility towards police. Opening up the complaints process provided the opportunity for a credible "system of checks and balances". Even though it forced police to reveal their handling of complaints, thereby advantaging those making a complaint, the "open" process also advantaged the police[7] (Lewis 1991, 161-62).

---

7 This acceptance and support is often only temporary. Events surrounding the closure of the OPCC indicate that the police will take advantage of situations that allows them to regain control of the complaints process.

The benefit civilian oversight can offer rank and file police was also acknowledged by the former president of the Queensland Police Union Senior Sergeant John O'Gorman. He is on record as saying that:

> While the Criminal Justice Commission exists it enables us [the union] to say to people who want to make allegations against police, to score points – if you have the evidence, the facility is there to have it investigated, that facility is the CJC.
>
> The union has quite deliberately supported the CJC, quite actively supported it. I have said on a number of occasions that any attempt to dismantle the CJC will be actively and energetically resisted by this union. (cited in CH Lewis 1994, 103).

One of the reasons O'Gorman gave for supporting Queensland's external, civilian oversight body was that it provided an independent place for citizens to register their complaints. This, he appreciated, helped to enhance police-community relations. O'Gorman also accepted that the CJC provided the mechanism whereby any systematic criminal behaviour by police would likely be detected and acted on before it got "the toe hold that it did prior to the Fitzgerald Inquiry" (cited in CH Lewis 1994, 103).[8]

The change in attitude by some police unions also may have been prompted by the fact that civilian-controlled tribunals/boards are often proving to be more lenient on police than police are on their own. That does not mean that without civilian oversight the police attitude and approach to complaints against other officers would not revert to what it was before external civilian involvement in the complaints process (see Chapters Two and Three), but it does mean that when disciplinary matters are dealt with by the police hierarchy and referred to a civilian board or tribunal in the appeal process, the oversight body often overturns the decision of senior police by dismissing the charge or lessening the sanction imposed (Kerstetter 1985, 162, 163; Loveday 1987, 13; CH Lewis 1992).

One explanation for the quashing or lessening of charges may be that senior police did not arrive at the right decision in the first instance for, if they had, their decision would have withstood the scrutiny of the

8 Union support, however, is dependent on the attitude of the executive, in particular the president. Since O'Gorman stood down as president of the Queensland Police Union of Employees, the new president has displayed what can be described as a 1960s' rather than a 1990s' attitude to police accountability. Among other things he has actively campaigned to have the Criminal Justice Commission's jurisdiction over police limited to "serious criminal offences only". This issue is one of several raised in a memorandum of understanding between the police union and Queensland's National-Liberal Coalition Party when it was in opposition (see Chapter Nine).

civilian tribunal/board. This view is supported by Perez's (1994) finding that civilian review is fairer on accused police officers in that there are more procedural safeguards to protect police than in the internal police disciplinary systems. Put another way, it could be argued that internal systems ignore procedural fairness which is what many accused police officers do when dealing with the public. Indeed, this is the reason many find themselves the subject of disciplinary charges. This suggests that a basic problem for police, at the managerial level and on the street, is the application of procedural fairness.

Another reason may be the different perspectives of those in charge of maintaining discipline within an organisation and those who review that decision. The chief police officer has responsibility for the professional standards of the department as a whole and for its status in the community. These are, and should be, important considerations in the internal disciplinary process. Civilian tribunals/ boards, on the other hand, focus on the rights of the individual and view sanctions in terms of how they affect the individual. Indeed, the appeal process is based on the premise that the individual has been treated unfairly by the organisation. These somewhat opposing views may never be reconciled.

Whatever the reason for the trend toward civilian oversight, a cursory look at the powers given to most civilian oversight bodies shows that their mandates have been severely limited as a result of the power of the police. In many instances police-government negotiations have often resulted in the "least meddlesome", least obtrusive form of civilian involvement. This is reflected in the legislative frameworks of many civilian oversight bodies and is raised in the following chapter which deals with civilian oversight models.

The trend to civilian oversight does not undermine the argument that police occupy a privileged position in society and, thus, are able to exert considerable influence over police accountability policies or that police power has been negated. Rather, it shows that after recognising the inevitability of a political decision, police decided to use their considerable power to achieve different ends.

Conclusion

The first three chapters of this book have given an account of the origins of civilian oversight and described and analysed the sometimes volatile but largely negotiated path which led to the establishment of external, independent, civilian bodies. They also looked at the way in which the police used their power to weaken the legislative framework of these relatively new accountability institutions. The next chapter analyses the alternative models which have emerged out of the negotiation process and the restrictions placed on many oversight bodies which limit their ability to be effective.

4

MODELS OF COMPLAINTS SYSTEMS: THE NEED TO MOVE ON

Introduction

Methods used to deal with complaints against police theoretically can range from an exclusive police-controlled model, still used in the overwhelming majority of United States police jurisdictions (Walker and Wright 1995, 1), to a system in which the receipt, investigation, determination and discipline of police is the exclusive responsibility of an external independent, civilian agency. Between these two extremes are a plethora of models, which to varying degrees use civilians to monitor, supervise, review and/or investigate complaints and, in some instances, to recommend disciplinary action and impose sanctions.

Scholars writing about the different models agree that it is impossible to identify, in any clear and precise terms, what constitutes a "typical" civilian oversight body. It appears that there are nearly as many variations to size, role, functions, powers and status as there are jurisdictions which have adopted this form of accountability. While each jurisdiction has its own distinctive spin, it is possible to loosely group models according to certain criteria (see, for example, Kerstetter 1985; Loveday 1987; West 1988; Goldsmith 1988, 1991b; Petterson 1991; Terrill 1991; Walker and Bumphus 1991; Bayley 1992b; Perez 1994; Walker and Wright 1995).

A literature has developed which primarily explores the extent and point of civilian involvement in the complaints process with the models described by Kerstetter in his 1985 article, *Who Disciplines the Police? Who Should?*, being repeatedly used as reference points by other authors. Because of their prominence in discussions about civilian oversight, this chapter begins by briefly describing Kerstetter's three models. Other writers have refined the categories in a way that is arguably more useful. Goldsmith's six "ideal types", for instance, allow for greater insight into the scope of variation. For this reason, and because Goldsmith's (1988) classification system is relatively uncomplicated, his work is used to identify problems which arise out of the various categories.

The growing trend toward external civilian oversight (Goldsmith 1991a) has highlighted limitations in existing models and raised questions about their adequacy. For example, do they reflect the contemporary situation or do other factors need to be incorporated into the models? What, if any, additional matters need to be taken into account when assessing the effectiveness of such bodies? This chapter addresses these points and suggests that there are fundamental factors which existing models seem to ignore.

Kerstetter's models

There are competing dilemmas in the civilian oversight of police conduct. On the one hand is the desire of professional organisation to keep its own house in order (professional autonomy); on the other is the community's right to be involved in keeping the coercive arm of the state publicly accountable for its actions. In an attempt to respond to this dilemma and suggest which was the most "balanced system", Kerstetter appraised the different ways in which civilians can be involved in the complaints process. He identified three principal models: Civilian Review, Civilian Input and Civilian Monitor. They are briefly described below.

Civilian review

In Kerstetter's Civilian Review model, which he classifies as the most powerful and controversial form of civilian oversight, the external oversight agency has the authority to investigate, determine and recommend punishment. The recommendation is usually done by way of an advisory opinion to the police chief. In some jurisdictions the oversight body can monitor the policies and procedures of the police department. Kerstetter reports that the positive aspect of this model is its potential to enhance the legitimacy of the review process and the police in the eyes of the community (Kerstetter 1985, 64).

Civilian input

The Civilian Input model creates more limitations on the oversight agency. It confines civilian involvement to the receipt and investigative stage of the complaints process. The complaint is received by a civilian investigator who "acts as an independent source of the facts" (Kerstetter 1985, 160) for the police hierarchy. Several variations to the model are possible. In some instances the civilian who receives and investigates the complaint is a member of the police agency and therefore is not independent of the police. If the civilian is a member of an independent agency, he or she reviews the police investigation and can request additional information. After the review process is complete, the civilian body prepares a report recommending disciplinary action to the police hierarchy. The adjudication of complaints and the disciplinary process remains under the control of the police.

Civilian monitor

The Civilian Monitor model, favoured by Kerstetter, is based on the Ombudsman concept. The police, usually through an internal affairs division, investigate allegations of police misconduct and decide whether the complaint is sustained. The imposition of discipline and sanctions remain with the police. In essence, the external oversight body's role is to examine whether the police investigation process was thorough and the discipline imposed fair and just. In some jurisdictions broader, systemic issues relating to police policies and procedures can be addressed by the oversight body.

Other variations

These are, of course, broad categories which can be further defined. They demonstrate how the debate has developed. Kerstetter himself makes reference to variations that can occur within each of his three categories. Walker and Bumphus (1991), Walker (1992), Walker and Wright (1995), West (1988, 1991) and Perez (1994) who, to varying degrees draw on Kerstetter, note further modifications. While Loveday (1987) does not use Kerstetter, some of his models include other variations. Petterson (1991), who cites Kerstetter, Goldsmith and West's models, adds a tier to the Civilian Monitor category by making a distinction between "audit" and "monitor". An auditing function, he argues, is confined to reviewing the "fairness and thoroughness" of the procedures used by police with a view to improving the system, whereas the monitor model is concerned with individual cases.[1] It would be a pointless exercise to try to explore all of the ways in which these models differ as the variations are numerous but often limited and the language used to define key issues is diverse.

A most useful and straightforward development of Kerstetter's model is by Goldsmith (1988). In an article which, *inter alia*, looks at some developments in the area of police complaints procedures, Goldsmith identifies six "ideal types" which highlight some of the different forms police complaints procedures may assume. He does this to draw attention to the main themes and areas of divergence in the legislative frameworks of civilian oversight bodies and to try to conceptualise in an area which, as he points out, has traditionally been concerned with pragmatic matters (1988, 63). Because Goldsmith's categories are easier to comprehend than some others that describe tiered models with different levels within the tiers, and because it is possible to more easily fit (albeit loosely) Kerstetter's and other researchers' models into Goldsmith's six "ideal" types, his work is used to provide a starting point for understanding how the literature explains and interprets the civilian oversight debate.

Goldsmith's "ideal" types

Goldsmith's types can be set along a continuum. His first model, described as the "Benchmark", reflects the traditional paramilitary bureaucratic approach used by police organisations for decades. There is no external or internal civilian involvement. Police investigate and supervise the handling of the complaint; disciplinary matters and sanctions are also determined by senior police. Goldsmith notes that a variation to this model occurs when police from other districts are assigned to undertake the investigation. He uses the Benchmark to identify the main areas of departure in other models.

Using Petterson's (1991, 274-83) idea of a theoretical spectrum to identify the degree to which the complaints against police process is independent of the police, the Benchmark model would sit on the extreme left hand side of a continuum and an external, independent, oversight agency, comprised entirely of civilians with the power to investigate,

1 This point is open to debate as Kerstetter does note how Civilian Monitor models can examine systemic issues relating to policy and procedural matters. He classifies it as a variation rather than as a tier.

monitor, review, determine and impose all disciplinary sanctions would be placed on the extreme right hand side.

X	X
exclusive control by police – no external input	exclusive control by civilians – no police involvement

Goldsmith's other five models (and those of many other researchers) fit somewhere between these two extremes. The greater the involvement by civilians, external to and independent of the police, the further to the right the model would sit.

Goldsmith's second model, which he labels "Civilian In-house", has most of the characteristics of the Benchmark model. The important distinction is that the police department employs civilians "to investigate and/or monitor how police handle citizens' complaints". Discipline and sanctions remain the responsibility of the police but in some instances civilians can recommend penalties. This model is similar in many respects to Kerstetter's Civilian Input model.

"Civilian External Supervisory" is Goldsmith's third category. It is at this stage that the independent nature of the process becomes evident. Police are still responsible for the initial investigation and senior police determine and impose discipline but an "organisationally distinct civilian agency" monitors[2] the complaint process. Even though the independent agency has the power to direct that charges be laid, the responsibility for determining the outcome and deciding on sanctions remains with the police hierarchy. As Goldsmith notes, the military/bureaucratic approach is largely preserved with civilians being "fairly narrowly confined" to a monitoring or supervisory role. There are similarities between this and Kerstetter's Civilian Monitor model.

In Goldsmith's fourth example, the "Civilian External Investigatory" model, as well as monitoring and handling the complaint, civilian participation is enhanced through their involvement in the investigative stage. The oversight body's power to investigate may be exclusive or done in conjunction with the police internal investigation unit but discipline remains solely with the police hierarchy. In practice, the civilian agency's ability to investigate is usually confined to serious matters. In some

2 Goldsmith defines monitoring as ranging from "reading all complaints forms", "accompanying investigators", suggesting particular lines of inquiry, suggesting a particular disciplinary action or directing that the chief of police lay charges (1988, 64).

instances it may be restricted to the period after the police have investigated.

In the fifth model, the "Civilian External Investigatory/ Adjudicative", civilians play an important part in the monitoring, investigation and adjudication phase of the complaint process. Civilian involvement in the adjudication and penalty stage signifies an important "symbolic" departure from the military-bureaucratic approach, in that the authority of those who head the police service is no longer "sacrosanct" in terms of complaints against police. The model shares many characteristics with Kerstetter's Civilian Review model.

Goldsmith's final model is classified as an "External Civilian Agency". Police conduct the investigation of all complaints on behalf of the oversight agency and civilians participate in the monitoring process and the final disposition of the complaint. As Goldsmith points out, this model addresses Bayley's proposition that police need to be part of the disciplinary process, but does not go as far as the fifth model in addressing citizens' concerns about police investigating police.

Although Goldsmith talks about ideal types, it is interesting to note that he does not include a category which would sit at the extreme right hand side of the theoretical spectrum: a model in which every phase of the complaints process is handled and controlled exclusively by civilians. This may have been deliberately omitted because in the complaints against police debate it is assumed that police will be involved at some stage of the process.

Goldsmith's categories help to explain the form the more commonly used models take and, placed on a spectrum, they show the evolving nature of the concept in terms of civilian involvement. But simply describing them can be a somewhat sterile exercise unless the information is used for some kind of evaluative purpose.

Considering Goldsmith's categories

Models are not intended to either prescribe or describe; rather they create ways of examining problems. Nevertheless, by using them as measuring sticks against which to assess actual performance, it can be asked which model provides the greatest insight into an organisation's likely chance of success. On the basis of what has been considered so far, questions arise about how effective the models are in holding police accountable for their actions, which model has the most chance of success and what problems there are in practice. It is to these issues that this chapter now turns.

Benchmark model

It has already been clearly demonstrated in Chapter Two that the internal, police-controlled Benchmark model, which is still widely used in the United States, has been discredited as an effective form of police accountability. Indeed, it is argued that according to either standard of proof, the balance of probabilities or beyond reasonable doubt, there is overwhelming testimony that misconduct investigations which have been the exclusive domain of the police have almost always failed, by legal and community standards, to keep police accountable for their actions.[3]

Civilian in-house

Because of its closeness to the Benchmark, the Civilian In-house model experiences many of the same problems in that the complaints against police process is still firmly under the control of the police. When civilians are employed by the police department and accountable to senior police, they are not independent. Perez (cited in Kerstetter 1985, 165), Brown (1985a) and Goldsmith (1991b) identified problems with this arrangement. Civilian investigators, they argued, can often become captured by the police to the point where they become defensive of police and cynical about complainants. This model suffers the same credibility problem as the previous one in that any investigation conducted in-house by people employed by a police department (sworn or non-sworn) is not considered independent and therefore credible in the eyes of the community (Goldsmith 1991b, 36-38).

Civilian external supervisory

The Civilian External Supervisory model is, as Goldsmith says, an important first step conceptually on the road to external, independent, civilian oversight. However, in practical terms this model has little chance of being effective as the oversight body is denied investigatory powers. As Brown (1985a) notes, the inability of an oversight body to conduct a truly independent investigation is at the heart of the debate about external, independent civilian oversight. It is a crucial issue and relates to weakness in the Benchmark, Civilian In-house and External Supervisory models.

---

3 There is, of course, the exception. Perez (1994) cites the Oakland Police Department's Internal Affairs Section as an example of an exemplary internal system .

A Civilian External Supervisory model is based on a *post hoc facto* review process which is mostly confined to a paper review of the police investigation. This approach was criticised by Lambert (1986, 82) who makes the point that "No system, however elaborate, which concentrates on supervision and *ex post facto* review of police investigations will satisfy the demand that justice will only be seen to be done when the investigation of complaints against the police is taken out of the hands of police themselves".

A *post hoc facto* review arrangement existed in New South Wales between 1978 and 1983 and was criticised by the then Ombudsman George Masterman (1985, 38) who told the first International Conference on Civilian Oversighting of Law Enforcement that:

> A civilian oversighting body which does not extensively utilise direct questioning itself but relies on paper statements taken by police officers, is deluding itself and the public. Such a body is a charade and a dangerous one at that. It deceives the public into believing that there is an effective watchdog or review body [when] there is not.

The Police Complaints Board in the United Kingdom proved to be a charade. Established in 1976, it relied solely on police investigations and exercised a limited review power in terms of complaints. Over the years the public lost confidence in the Board's ability to effectively perform its oversight function. This lack of confidence was referred to in the Scarman Report which, as mentioned in Chapter Three, inquired into the cause and effect of the April 1981 Brixton riots. Scarman found that the Police Complaints Board did not have the confidence of significant sections of the population (Scarman 1986, 179-87) and that one of the reasons for this was that it lacked "a sufficiently convincing independent element" (Police Complaints Authority 1995).

The public query whether the police should be part of the crucially important investigative stage at all. Critics of the idea claim that if police are involved in the investigation of a complaint, at any level, it means that police are still investigating police (Lambert 1986; Police Complaints Authority 1994b, 15). In response to the police argument that only police have the necessary investigative skills, critics point out that the ability to conduct an investigation is not a God-given talent, rather it is a technical skill which can be taught. Therefore, with the proper training, civilian staff can become skilled investigators and over time can learn about police procedures.

Although police are more comfortable with the idea of civilian oversight in 1999 than they were in 1969, many still object strongly to anyone other than police conducting an investigation. In defence of their argument, they claim that only police know their way around police systems and procedures and only another officer understands the way a police person thinks and operates. This ongoing debate about police involvement in the investigative stage of the process is far from resolved.

Civilian external investigatory

The Civilian External Investigatory method is an important step forward in a practical sense as non-police become involved in the crucially important investigative stage. However, this power is often qualified. Some oversight agencies cannot use their investigatory powers until after the police have conducted the initial investigation. While this is an improvement on not being able to investigate at all, it is a limited improvement. From a practical point of view, not being able to investigate from the outset means that by the time the oversight agency becomes involved in the investigation of a complaint, evidence has been necessarily disturbed by police conducting the initial inquiry and in some instances exhibits have deteriorated. The oversight body's ability to interview witnesses is also delayed and as any police officer knows, for a statement to be credible it must be taken as soon after the event as practicable. Other oversight bodies with investigative powers can only exercise them in relation to a particular class of complaint, usually those of a serious nature or those involving very senior police. Not being able to conduct an investigation from the crucially important initial stage of the complaints process or having investigations restricted to serious allegations can hinder an oversight agency's ability to deliver the standard of independent, external police accountability that the community expects and wants.

Another weakness in the Civilian External Investigatory model is that civilians lack input into the discipline phase and, as was seen in Chapter Two, when police have total control of the discipline and sanction process their decision about what is an appropriate penalty does not always parallel community expectations. When the oversight body has no right to appeal against what it considers is a blatantly inappropriate sanction, it is constrained in its watchdog role.

Civilian external investigatory/adjudicative

It is Goldsmith's fifth model which allows significant civilian input into all facets of the complaints against police process. Even though there is a "statutory presumption" that police will undertake the investigative stage of the complaints process through their internal investigations unit, the oversight body does have the power to take over a police investigation or conduct its own investigation using its civilian investigators. Unlike the Civilian Internal Investigatory model, civilians are also involved in the adjudication and disciplinary stage of the process. This is usually through a board of inquiry which can hear evidence against police the subject of a complaint, arrive at a decision and impose sanctions that can range from a reprimand to dismissal.

The range of powers available to the oversight body in this model can help to reassure the public that an impartial and independent agency can, if necessary, investigate a citizen's complaint. These powers can also result in a fairer and more thorough police investigation as police are aware that an inadequate or unfair investigation, or one that appears to be taking an unreasonable amount of time, can be taken over by the civilian oversight agency.

External civilian agency

It is somewhat difficult to assess this model as it is unclear whether the police conducting the investigation are seconded to the oversight agency and therefore accountable to its civilian chief officer, or whether they are working in the police department and accountable to the chief of police. It is also unclear in what capacity civilians are involved in the final disposition of the complaint. These distinctions are important in terms of how the community perceives the objectiveness of the complaints process. If the police are accountable to the police chief and civilian input into the final disposition is only advisory, the external civilian agency may be seen as simply a variation on the police investigating police process.

Effectiveness of models

When trying to compare the effectiveness of the various models, two thorny questions arise: (1) how to measure effectiveness; and (2) how to assess for whom the system is effective – the complainant, the police officer or the community.

Measuring effectiveness

The number of exogenous variables in the complaints against police process makes any comparative statistical analysis about the effectiveness of various models virtually meaningless. The author's experience in trying to compare complaints statistics across Australian jurisdictions proved to be a near impossible exercise. When trying to ascertain a relatively simple statistic like the number of complaints received in the various Australian jurisdictions, it was found that different approaches were used by State and Territory authorities. Some States compile their statistics according to complaints received while others deal with allegations received. One complaint can contain several allegations. In other States both these figures are available. However, one State refers to approaches made while another talks about cases. Cases may contain more than one complaint or allegation.

When attempting to compare the numbers of matters finalised in any one year, it was noted that these figures can relate to allegations, complaints, actions or cases. One State explained that many allegations categorised as finalised may have involved the opening of a file for administrative purposes. Another State was unable to give an accurate account of this figure until 1994 as before then it did not record the outcome of complaints dealt with by the police. Yet another pointed out that unlike other jurisdictions in Australia its Act did not provide for the receipt of oral complaints.

The time taken to finalise complaints is all but impossible to compare. In most States the body which oversights complaints against police also has responsibility for oversighting complaints against other public servants. One jurisdiction did not differentiate between complaints about police and other public officials until 1993. The introduction of informal resolution or conciliation greatly affects this figure. Even though most States have adopted these speedier forms of dispute resolution, it was found that commencement dates differed widely.

Another problem related to the way some States kept their own statistics over the five-year period initially examined (1990-95). It seems that a change in senior personnel can mean a change to the way statistics are complied and it is often difficult, if not impossible, to make the necessary link between the two different approaches. Some States have changed the format for compiling statistics without there being a change in personnel. This was usually the result of a change in powers but, again, there were often only tenuous links made between the old and new methods for compiling statistics.

Other variables, such as the number of police employed, the average age of police officers, significant increases or decreases in the resources of the oversight agency and any changes to their powers and functions would also need to be taken into account when comparing complaints against police data. The above experience highlights some of the difficulties encountered when trying to compare complaints statistics in Australia. The futility of trying to attempt any international comparison that was based on quantitative data quickly became apparent.

Similar difficulties have been shared by other writers including Perez (1994) who found that trying to evaluate the effectiveness or legitimacy of civilian oversight systems by examining complaints statistics is "an illusory endeavour at best".[4]

Often the effectiveness of investigations (internal and external) are linked to substantiation rates. However, this method does not take account of the fact that the overwhelming majority of complaints against police

4 Perez (1994) did attempt to evaluate the effectiveness of three different models: Internal Review, Civilian Review and the Civilian Monitor by (a) participant observation (although the amount of time spent in agencies varied significantly); (b) police officer surveys; and (c) complainant attitudinal surveys. Perez attempted to evaluate the various systems in terms of their integrity, legitimacy and learning (capacity to change police behaviour). In terms of integrity, he found that "all three models do a similarly effective job of fairly, competently and objectively handling individual complaints" (1994, 231). This finding seems to contradict overwhelming evidence from numerous commissions of inquiries and government reports and from other researchers about the fairness and objectivity of internal systems. It may be explained in part by Perez's choice of one particular police department for examining internal review systems. As he said, the Oakland Police Department's Internal Affairs Section is "known throughout the law enforcement and academic worlds as the most rigorous internal operation"'. Consequently, it may not be representative of the majority of internal review systems across the United States of America. Also, because of the inordinate amount of time spent with that organisation as opposed to the other organisations he studied, Perez found that "the role that I chose for myself was different from the one I assumed at other organisations. I had time to develop a rapport and a trust with Oakland Police Department officers and investigators that I could not obtain elsewhere" (1994, 279). In effect, he became "one of the boys" (Perez 1994, 280). This may also account, in part, for his findings.

In relation to legitimacy, the internal systems did not fare so well and had the least amount of acceptance by the community who felt that the secrecy surrounding internal affairs processes was particularly disturbing. In terms of learning, influencing the behaviour of police officers on the street, Perez found that internal review systems had the most powerful deterrent effect on police behaviour but that external review systems can also have a deterrent effect when they focus on policy issues which can benefit the community, individual police officers and the police department (1994, 244).

concern incidents which involve the complainant and a police officer. In other words, in circumstances which there are no independent witnesses to corroborate either party's account. Even if there are police witnesses the code of silence means that officers will nearly always support other police. Thus, as Chevigney (1995, 92) points out substantiation rates are related to the evidence available to prove or disprove allegations, "So whether complaints are sustained or not is almost haphazard in relation to the number and seriousness of actual abuses".

Other problems that arise when trying to measure effectiveness concern an increase or decrease in complaints received. Does an increase in complaints indicate a rise in police abuses or does it mean that the community has faith in the civilian complaints systems and is therefore more willing to report allegations of misconduct? In the reverse, if complaints decline is that because of a decrease in police misconduct or lack of faith in the civilian oversight body?

The issue of how to measure the effectiveness of civilian oversight bodies needs further attention. Researchers such as Samuel Walker (United States) and David Brereton (Australia) are starting to undertake studies in this important but largely neglected area.

Effective for whom?

In terms of "effective for whom", Perez's research reveals that a complainant's opinion on the legitimacy of a particular complaints system is often based on the outcome of their grievance. If it is unsubstantiated and there are no findings against the police officer, the complainant is usually dissatisfied with the system. If the reverse proves to be the case, the complainant is invariably satisfied. Police officers, Perez (1994, 73) found, "are often too defensive about their own conduct and that of their fellow officers to objectively evaluate review systems".[5]

Given that the impetus for civilian oversight was the growing disquiet about police misconduct and the lack of public confidence in the police-controlled methods for handling complaints against police (Goldsmith 1991a; Lewis 1991; Terrill 1991), the same criteria could be used when trying to assess which of Goldsmith's models is most likely to address those concerns. As a matter of logic this would be the system which gives the civilian oversight body the maximum opportunity to be

5 Detailed studies on the attitude of complainants have been undertaken by Landau (1994) and Maquire and Corbett (1991).

involved in the complaints process: the Civilian, External, Investigatory/Adjudicative model. This conclusion is supported by an earlier study by Perez (cited in Kerstetter 1985, 161-62) who found that this type of model was considered objective, thorough and fair by citizens and by Hayes (1997) who reviewed the police complaints system in Northern Ireland. Hayes's study found that 83 percent of people surveyed indicated a preference for non-police investigators who worked for an independent oversight organisation.[6]

Police, however, have expressed their opposition to the Civilian, External, Investigatory/Adjudicative model. The police hierarchy claims it creates difficulties for them as it undermines their authority over the force, and the police rank and file maintain that it lowers morale and prevents them from performing their law and order and peace-keeping roles for fear of being accused of wrongdoing. However, as mentioned in the previous chapter, they have yet to present any rational, objective evidence to support these claims.

The difference in perceptions of fairness by police and the community has been a common feature throughout the civilian oversight debate. Given the "them against us" adversarial syndrome and the often opposing views held by police and citizens about the need for due process, it is unlikely that the gap will ever be fully bridged. Nevertheless, in relation to Goldsmith's six ideal types, the Civilian, External, Investigatory/ Adjudicative model, which allows for maximum civilian involvement, would best seem to meet citizens' concerns about the need for an independent, fair and impartial oversight system. Whether it is the most effective in terms of changing police behaviour as opposed to placating community concerns has still to be proven.

Deficiencies in the models

The models outlined to date serve a useful purpose in that they group common features, the powers and functions of oversight bodies, and help the reader to understand the degree of civilian involvement in the complaints against police process. It needs to be remembered, however, that the practices for the handling of complaints against police, then developed into theoretical models, are not the product of rational, long term planning. Rather they are compromises produced after negotiations

---

6 Hayes surveyed 295 people who had made complaints against police. 82 people replied which represents a 28 percent response rate. As his report notes, care has to be taken not to read too much into the findings from such a small sample.

between governments, supposedly representing the wishes of the people, and the police. It is not surprising, therefore, that there are weaknesses in all of them. Leaving detailed specifics aside, two general weaknesses are evident:

- some important functions are either not included in any of the models or are only alluded to and therefore do not receive the attention they deserve; and
- the models are too internally focused; they do not take sufficient account of political and other external environment issues.

The second point, external environmental issues, is taken up in the following chapter. In terms of the first weakness, some neglected but important functions of the civilian oversight process will now be considered. They include complaints by police about the conduct of other police, and proactive, preventive issues. They illustrate the need to extend the matters covered in the traditional models.

Complaints by police about other police

A deficiency in the legislative framework of many oversight bodies is their inability to investigate complaints against police made by other police. In Australia, for example, the Commonwealth Ombudsman, who has jurisdiction over the Australian Federal Police, does not have this power.[7] Until recently the Victorian Deputy Ombudsman (Police Complaints) could not investigate complaints made by police about the misconduct of other officers. In May 1997 the *Police Regulation Act* was amended to strengthen the Ombudsman's powers in this regard. However, the Ombudsman's jurisdiction is limited to matters of serious misconduct, which means that police wishing to report the alleged misconduct of other police still have to go through the internal system except for the gravest instances of misconduct. The South Australian Police Complaints Authority also lacks this power in respect to complaints lodged with the

7 There is an administrative agreement with the Commissioner of the Australian Federal Police which allows the Ombudsman to interpret the definition of conduct more broadly. However, the Ombudsman's jurisdiction is on shaky ground as the arrangement is not ratified by legislation. This leaves the Ombudsman's actions open to challenge in the courts. It also means that a change of commissioner, or a change of heart by the current commissioner could see the end of this administrative arrangement. As well, the administrative arrangement restricts the Ombudsman to "on duty" matters. Consequently, if the conduct being complained about occurred while the officer was off duty, the Ombudsman can not investigate. In such circumstances the police officer making the complaint is forced to complain to the police.

police department, but it can act if a police officer lodges a complaint directly with the PCA.

The lack of independent, external oversight of complaints by police against other police has enormous consequences for individual officers and for the police as an organisation. To begin with, such a policy is discriminatory. Depending on the legislative framework of the civilian oversight body, complaints lodged by civilians are investigated, monitored and/or reviewed by an impartial body. Police, on the other hand, are denied this vitally important independent facet of the accountability process. They are forced into a situation of having to complain to a police-controlled internal process, a method of accountability which, as Chapters Two and Three demonstrate, has been totally discredited by a succession of royal commissions, commissions of inquiry and reports.

This policy also means that if honest police have no faith in their internal investigation section which, it is argued, was the case in Queensland before the Fitzgerald Inquiry (Fitzgerald 1989, 205), they have nowhere to go with their concerns. Through no fault of their own they are forced to remain loyal to a code which protects immoral and illegal behaviour and to turn a blind eye to the misconduct, violence or corruption of some police officers. This unjust and unsatisfactory situation only serves to strengthen the "blue curtain of silence", a well-documented cause of sustained endemic police corruption and abuse (Goldstein 1977; Reiner 1992; Skolnick and Fyfe 1993). By maintaining such a policy governments run the risk of allowing the ethical standards of the police organisation to be set according to the "lowest common denominator" principle. When a scandal erupts, as it inevitably does under such conditions, the community tends to judge the entire force on the basis of those standards and is often faced with having to fund yet another commission of inquiry into police misconduct. To try to avoid this happening again in Queensland, the Fitzgerald Report recommended that the Criminal Justice Commission have jurisdiction over complaints by police about the alleged misconduct of other police. The following evidence suggests that it is one of the strengths of the CJC model (detailed in Chapter Eight).

The number of officers reporting other police (excluding the commissioner) has risen dramatically since the CJC was established. In 1990-91 the figure was 3.2 percent of all complaints received; by the year 1993-94 it had risen to 14.2 percent. In 1994-95 the figure stood at 16.7 percent (Criminal Justice Commission 1996c, 4) and in 1995-96 at 14 percent. In 1996-97 the number of police reporting other police dropped to 12 percent but in 1997-98 the figure rose again and stood at 13.6 percent (Criminal Justice Commission 1998, 27).[8] Several factors have contributed to the somewhat unusual phenomenon of police reporting other police in Queensland. They include a change in the rules governing the reporting of misconduct, a change in police attitude, specifically at the management and supervisory levels of the service, and the existence of the external, independent Criminal Justice Commission.

The pre-Fitzgerald Inquiry police rules required police to report known misconduct. They did not provide for the reporting of suspected misconduct, a limitation which was exploited by many police. Section 7.2 of the post-Fitzgerald *Police Service Administration Act 1990* makes it an offence for police not to report the "known or reasonably suspected misconduct" of other officers. The fear of disciplinary action for failing to comply with Section 7.2 may be greater for some officers than fear of reprisal from other police. This was confirmed in a research project conducted by the Centre for Crime Policy and Public Safety, Griffith University, on behalf of the CJC (see Brereton and Ede 1996, 7-8). While there was broad agreement that police were now more likely to report other officers among the sample interviewed, the prime motivating factor, particularly by supervisors, was concern about what could happen to them if they failed to report suspected misconduct (Brereton and Ede 1996, 7). While this may not be an ideal reason, it is at least a start in breaking down the code of silence and is, therefore, preferable than officers not reporting police misconduct at all. It is also not the only reason.

The CJC's independent status, its ability to investigate in its own right, rather than having to rely on a police internal investigation unit, and its capacity to receive complaints by officers about the alleged misconduct or criminal conduct of other officers has helped give some police the confidence to report the misconduct of other officers.

The ability to report the suspected misconduct of other police to an independent and impartial oversight body could prove to be an important starting point in addressing the code of silence and the "them against us" syndrome common to all police departments throughout the world. However, it is not taken up in the discussion on models, descriptive or functional. The other weakness referred to above, policy and procedural

8 These figures "do not include those incidents which police officers are obliged to report to the CJC irrespective of whether the reporting officer suspects any other officer of misconduct, for example, high speed motor vehicle pursuits, deaths or attempted suicides in custody or any serious injury resulting from police action" (Criminal Justice Commission 1996c, 4).

matters, is covered in the literature but not to the degree that it deserves. This issue is canvassed later in this chapter where it is argued that the combined reactive-proactive approach offers the greatest opportunity to address the cause as well as the symptoms of police misconduct and, as such, it is worthy of greater attention. But before moving on to discuss the need to widen the focus of civilian oversight bodies, it is worth remembering that some agencies which oversight the complaints against police still do not have the necessary powers to carry out important reactive functions.

Core reactive functions

As seen in the previous chapter, the power of the police can have a significant effect on a civilian oversight body's enabling legislation. So too can the nature of the problem(s) which led to civilian involvement in the first place. While circumstances differ in each jurisdiction, this form of accountability has been in operation long enough to argue that there are certain core features which a civilian oversight agency needs to effectively oversight the complaints against police process. Many of these features relate to the reactive aspect of civilian oversight. An ideal reactive model would need to include the power to:

- receive complaints from police about the behaviour of other police;
- be the central receiving point for all complaints against police;
- assess and classify all complaints;
- monitor, review and/or supervise investigations about police conduct which are in the first instance investigated by police;
- investigate complaints from the initial stage of the complaints process;
- appeal a police-imposed disciplinary sanction;
- refer serious matters to an independent tribunal;
- have own motion power; and
- receive and act on anonymous complaints.

Any civilian oversight agency with the full complement of these powers has a better chance of effectively fulfilling its reactive police oversight role than one which does not. The advantages such powers bring to the oversight function will now be discussed.

In terms of core, reactive functions an external, independent, oversight body must be the central point for receiving citizens' complaints against police. As Petterson (1991, 272-73) argues, many people with alleged grievances about police behaviour would not lodge a complaint if it had to be done through a police department. He cites fear of police retaliation as the reason. Petterson's judgment is supported by Perez (1994, 231) who found that "at the intake level, there is not much debate. Put simply, other than police locations are always preferable". Hoffman and Crew (1991, 10) also believe that complaints should be lodged with a civilian oversight agency. Their rationale is based on the community's confidence in the independence of the oversight system.

Any complaints received by a police department/agency should be forwarded to the oversight agency and it should undertake the assessment and classification phase of the process. This includes misconduct of a minor nature which police consider is suitable for informal resolution/ conciliation. Civilian involvement in the assessment and classification phase is important because it is at this stage of the complaints process that decisions are made in respect to whether an investigation is warranted or if informal resolution is appropriate. In some instances it is also possible to decide if the complaint can or cannot be sustained. Hoffman and Crew's reason for being able to lodge a complaint with an independent agency is also applicable at this stage, for the public would not have confidence in a system that allowed the police to decide the direction a complaint should take.

If an oversight agency decides that an allegation appears to be minor in nature, it would almost certainly refer it to the police for investigation. Nevertheless, it should have the right to review the police department's investigation before a final determination is made and before the complainant is advised of the outcome. The oversight agency may also refer more serious allegations to the police for investigation. However, it should have the power to monitor and/or supervise the police investigation or to recall it if progress is not satisfactory. At the assessment and classi fication stage, or when an oversight body is reviewing monitoring or supervising a complaint, it needs to be able to request additional information from police and the police should be obliged to supply it. Coupled with the receiving, assessing and classifying of complaints, these powers allow the oversight agency and not the police to have control of the complaints process.

It is essential that any external, independent civilian oversight body has the ability to investigate in its own right and from the initial stage of the complaints process and is able to receive complaints from police (minor or serious). The rationale for these powers has been discussed already.

Another necessary power is the right to appeal a police-imposed disciplinary sanction which the oversight agency considers is inappropriate by community standards. It is highly likely that if an oversight body had this power it would rarely be used, but that is not the point. The knowledge by police that such a right exists could act as a safeguard against the inappropriate sanctions which were common when police controlled the process and still occurs in jurisdictions where oversight bodies do not have this power. This power was recently granted to Queensland's Criminal Justice Commission. But not before two disturbing complaints resulted in "ludicrously inadequate" penalties being imposed by police.[9]

"Own motion" power allows an oversight body to act on a matter without having to first receive a formal complaint. This power is needed, for example, when an investigation reveals a serious breach of conduct separate from the complaint under investigation; when an incident is of high public interest and concern; and when snippets of information, which indicate serious misconduct, are passed to the oversight agency. Without this power there would be occasions when a civilian oversight agency would be unable to investigate suspected misconduct.

The capacity to deal with anonymous complaints is also an important reactive power. Even though anonymous complaints are more difficult to investigate and can sometimes amount to nothing more than a malicious attempt to try to "get even" with a police officer, it is important that an oversight body has the ability to respond to them. Some complainants fear police retaliation if they lodge a complaint and would not report alleged misconduct if they had to identify themselves. For example, there have been occasions when anonymous complaints lodged with Queensland's Criminal Justice Commission have been found to have substance and clearly the information would not have been given if the complainants had to identify themselves (interview with senior civilian employee, Official Misconduct Division, Criminal Justice Commission).

To help overcome the problem of this class of complaint being lodged for malicious and/or vexatious purposes, Queensland's *Criminal Justice Act* has been amended to restrict the CJC's ability to investigate anonymous complaints unless independent corroboration is possible. In other words, anonymous complaints, whether by letter or telephone, need to contain information which can be readily checked and proven to be of

---

9 The two incidents are commonly referred to as the "Paynter Case" and the "Pinkenba Six" incident (see Queensland Council for Civil Liberties 1994, 21; Criminal Justice Commission 1996c, 15-17; Parliamentary Criminal Justice Committee 1995).

substance. If this is not the case then no action can be taken. This proviso not only goes part of the way to allaying police concerns, it also helps to reduce the waste of valuable resources which can occur from the investigation of some anonymous complaints.

Many of the core reactive features discussed here can be found in Goldsmith's Civilian External Investigatory/Adjudicative model and Kerstetter's Civilian Review model. Variations of this ideal reactive model have been implemented for example in Toronto, Manitoba and Queensland.

While some of these reactive powers may seem excessive to police, experience has shown that the more controversial ones, such as the right to investigate from the initial stage of the complaints process, the power to refer serious matters to a disciplinary tribunal and the power to appeal police disciplinary sanctions are rarely exercised. Nevertheless, any organisation which acts as the community's independent watchdog over the alleged excesses of the coercive arm of the state should be able to operationalise them when necessary. These powers also have preventive value. Knowing that an oversight body has them may dissuade some police from imprudent, sloppy or improper investigative practices. For example, the ability to monitor, supervise and/or review a police investigation into allegations of misconduct and to recall a complaint can help to improve the general quality of police investigations into other police. Most importantly, by giving an oversight body these powers the public can have confidence that, should the circumstances warrant it, rigorous police accountability methods can be applied by an independent civilian agency. Also when governments are prepared to grant an oversight body the necessary reactive powers it needs to be effective, it indicates to the community that, in terms of government policy, upholding the individual rights of the citizen takes precedence over police demands that they be allowed to control the complaints against police process.

While reactive powers are essential and go to the heart of an oversight body's existence, on their own they only deal with problems after the event. They are a necessary but not sufficient ingredient in the effective oversight of complaints against police. As argued on page 73, civilian oversight models need to be extended to include proactive, preventative issues.

Proactive, preventive issues

Proactive, preventive issues are addressed in the literature, but with a few notable exceptions, they do not receive the attention they warrant. Brown

(1985a, 27) makes reference to the fact that some oversight agencies are unable to influence police behaviour beyond the handling of the particular complaint. Under such circumstances the complaint is handled as an "isolated" incident and it is "but a pious hope" that the external, independent civilian oversight agency will be able to change police behaviour to any great degree. This issue has been canvassed by Petterson (1991) in his "auditor" tier and Walker and Bumphus (1992) who note that some supporters of civilian oversight argue that complaints data can be used in conjunction with other data to monitor or formulate police departmental policy and help improve police performance. When describing what he thought would be an ideal police review system, Perez (1994) addressed the proactive dimensions of civilian oversight and argued that data generated from complaints should be used in the modification and formulation of policy. It is worth noting that the police hierarchy should be obliged to respond to a civilian oversight body's recommendations in writing, and within a particular time frame, otherwise they may never be acted upon.

David Bayley (1992b) also addresses the inability of some oversight bodies to become involved in police policy issues, in other words to be proactive. He discusses civilian oversight in the context of police brutality but his arguments are applicable to complaints about police in general. Rather than concentrate on the degree of civilian involvement in the process, Bayley (1992b, 6-7) uses two models – a "Deterrence" model and an "Evaluation" model – to ascertain the possible effect each may have on police behaviour. The differences between the two are a matter of emphasis.

Deterrence	**Evaluation**
Focuses on the individual	Focuses on ineffective policies
Individual officer held responsible for misconduct	Organisation held responsible for officer's behaviour
Those involved in civilian oversight are responsible members of the public	People involved in the oversight function are expert civilians
Civilians involved in oversighting act as a jury of peers	Civilians oversighting complaints bring canons of science, social science and scientific evidence to bear
Challenges police monopoly on complaints handling and discipline	Power of police is not challenged. Leverage is obtained through power of publicity and public dialogue

The traditional, reactive "Deterrence" model which holds an individual police officer responsible for his or her actions has quasi judicial features and focuses exclusively on the "rotten apple" approach to police misconduct. In this model, Bayley argues, there are basically two stages in the handling of a complaint: investigation and discipline. Traditionally police did it all. However, with the advent of external oversight bodies, civilians have become involved in three ways: they review the police investigation; they can supervise the police investigation and tell police what to do or they can make an independent investigation of the complaint. In some instances they may also have a role in the discipline stage in that they can recommend sanctions but the determination is left to the police.

Bayley believes policy makers have to look toward using an evaluative approach to police misconduct issues and one which does not exclude the police. His "Evaluation" model focuses on policy issues. It concentrates on identifying defective policies and exposing inadequate management practices which, he says, are also responsible for failing to keep police behaviour in check. The "Evaluation" model also attempts "to bring pressure on the barrel to fix the barrel and not just root out the rotten apples" (1992b, 7). It therefore adopts a broader more systemic approach to the problem of police misconduct and places pressure on police to put their own house in order.

Bayley raises the question of whether, in the oversighting of police conduct, all of the focus should be placed on the "deterrent basket" (1992b, 8). The debate on civilian oversight, he maintains, has to explore in greater depth, and in public, how managerial inadequacies contribute to low standards of police behaviour. He does not advocate the adoption of an either/or approach. Rather he advocates that both are needed to help change policing organisations and the police culture.

Bayley's argument is persuasive. If the problem of police conduct is to be addressed, a combined deterrence-evaluation approach is needed. The police hierarchy's emphasis on punishing individual conduct after the event, to the virtual exclusion of looking at the policies which are supposedly designed to act as a guide before and during an event means that without a change in emphasis old problems will remain. The police hierarchy's attitude seems to be reflected in the legislative framework of many oversight agencies which concentrate on punishing the rotten apple. The change of emphasis being advocated by Bayley provides a difficult challenge for police organisations which cling to the paramilitary structure. Rank demands obedience even when an order and/or a policy is inappropriate or just plain wrong.

Beyond recommendations – an integrated approach

The debate about external, independent civilian oversight bodies has in the main focused on the reactive aspect of the complaints process. The crucially important proactive, dimension is only starting to be addressed in theory and practice and then usually only in the context of the ability to make recommendations to the police department/agency on administrative and procedural issues. But, ideally, preventive functions should go beyond those suggested by Bayley and Perez. They also need to include:

- a discrete corruption prevention function; and
- the capacity to undertake independent, police-related research.

For when proactive and reactive functions are used in an holistic way long-term change is possible. The structure of Queensland's Criminal Justice Commission enables it to adopt an holistic strategy.

As well as an Official Misconduct Division (OMD) that deals with the reactive aspect of complaints against police, the Criminal Justice Commission has a Research and Prevention Division which concentrates on proactive, preventive issues.[10] Having these two divisions within the one organisation allows the CJC to adopt an integrated reactive-proactive approach to police misconduct issues. This is in contrast to the more traditional police oversight models described by Goldsmith, Kerstetter and other researchers which, because of their structures, only allow for a peripheral ad hoc approach to preventive issues.

Increased opportunities

The following brief overview of some Criminal Justice Commission programs highlights (a) the range of opportunities an holistic approach offers to the civilian oversight process and (b) the advantages of a division

---

10 Corruption prevention initially formed part of the Official Misconduct Division's responsibilities. In the early days of the OMD's operations it became apparent that reactive matters were continually taking preference over proactive issues. To try and remedy the situation it was decided in 1992 to quarantine the resources of the corruption prevention unit by making it a division in its own right. In July 1998 the functions performed by the Corruption Prevention Division were amalgamated with those of the Research Division and a new division, the Research and Prevention Division was formed. Research and prevention functions were combined to reflect the CJC's goal of achieving better synergy in these areas and to facilitate increased opportunities for research into corruption prevention matters. The amalgamation is also in line with the recommendations of the Lester Parliamentary Criminal Justice Committee's three-yearly review of the CJC (Criminal Justice Commission 1998, 56).

devoted to prevention strategies being part of the same organisation as a reactive investigative division.

Because of its location within the CJC, the Research and Prevention Division is able to formulate many of its programs on the basis of data generated by the Official Misconduct Division's Complaints Section, and is alerted to matters arising out of investigations which indicate a particular behavioural trend is developing. For example, a research project into watch-house related issues was directly stimulated by complaints received by the OMD.

The Research and Prevention Division's task is enhanced by being able to easily approach the OMD for practical support on research projects. Easy access to this type of data proved invaluable when the Research Division compiled its five-volume report on police powers and no doubt contributed to favourable public comments regarding the report, such as "excellent work"; "thoroughly researched and well based"; and "thorough going and extremely useful" (Parliamentary Criminal Justice Committee 1993b, 10; 1993c, 14, 15).

In the reverse the Research and Prevention Division can greatly assist the work of the Official Misconduct Division. Research and Prevention undertook an in-house survey of complainants who expressed dissatisfaction with the complaints process. The findings were used by the OMD to establish new procedures. This project is ongoing and has been broadened to include all complainants (as opposed to those who have expressed dissatisfaction) to see if further improvements can be introduced to increase client satisfaction. Research and Prevention has also conducted research into the police discipline and complaints process and has compiled data from assault allegations to identify patterns of behaviour and environmental factors which, if addressed, could reduce complaints. The research findings are of particular benefit to the OMD which has responsibility for this aspect of the CJC's functions.

There have been suggestions that the CJC's prevention function should be undertaken by an external body. However, an external prevention body would not enjoy the same degree or ease of access to information from investigations as an internal division. Thus, many of the lessons to be learned from complaints investigations could be lost forever. Even if a formal arrangement could be achieved between an external agency and an independent, civilian oversight body, it is highly unlikely that the same frankness in exchange of information would be forthcoming. Bureaucratic politics and all the attending problems often result in "demarcation disputes" (Davis et al 1993) and even though such disputes can occur within an organisation, they would probably be more acute between organisations, especially one with the type of secrecy provisions attached to the Criminal Justice Commission.

Direct benefits for the police

The integrated, holistic approach that the CJC model allows is of direct benefit to Queensland police. Staff of the Research and Prevention Division work with police training officers helping to devise preventive policies which focus on strategic intervention. For example, when it was a division in its own right Corruption Prevention was involved in the Queensland Police Service's Constable Development Program, specifically the *Ethical Decision Making* module. This module is now an integral part of the Service's recruit training curriculum. Besides maintaining on-going input into this area, Research and Prevention Division staff are also involved with the Service's Competency Acquisition and Management Development Programs (Criminal Justice Commission 1998, 58).

CJC research reports have practical relevance for police. The report *Ethical Conduct and Discipline in the Queensland Police Service: The View of Recruits, First Year Constables and Experienced Officers* (Criminal Justice Commission 1995b), was the catalyst for the Queensland Police Service introducing a service-wide ethics education program. This in turn led to the establishment of the Service's Ethical Standards Command. CJC and Command staff have worked together on several projects, including the complaints investigation process, integrity testing programs, procedures for protecting staff making public interest disclosures, and strategies for monitoring how newly acquired police powers are operationalised (Criminal Justice Commission 1998, 15). From time to time the division also undertakes joint publications with the Police Service. In 1997-98 the police and its oversight body worked together on the following reports: *The Physical Requirements of General Duties Policing; Clustering Evaluation*; and *Guide to Problem-Oriented and Partnership Policing*. (Criminal Justice Commission 1998, 11-24).

By working with police to design and implement police-related projects, the division has been able to suggest alternative approaches to problems and to demonstrate to police that the Commission's recommendations are practical. Significantly, many of the Research and Prevention Division's recommendations have been adopted by the QPS (for examples, see Criminal Justice Commission 1998, 22). This type of "partnership" with police also helps to address the police-civilian oversight body dichotomy and strengthens the professional approach to policing which many police departments are striving toward.

Membership of committees and advisory boards such as the Police Education Advisory Council, Queensland Police Education and Training Committee and the QPS Crime Prevention Working Group has allowed the Criminal Justice Commission to have meaningful input into policy formulating bodies and, where practicable, to align its research projects with the concerns of these bodies. Membership of other committees, such as the Operation Skills and Equipment Committee, Policing Strategies Steering Committee, Police Powers Implementation Steering Committee and the QPS Corporate Services Review assists the Commission to gain valuable insight into practical policing issues which, in turn, can be incorporated into research and prevention programs.

As part of its statutory obligation to monitor the progress of the police reform program and the overall performance of the Service, the Research and Prevention Division conducts regular surveys of recruits, first year and other constables, to gauge their opinions on the education and training system. The results of these surveys are relayed to the Police Education Advisory Committee (PEAC) and the police academy so they can be used to help improve the quality of education and training policies.

The division conducts surveys to measure the Queensland community's confidence in its police service. This allows the Commission to monitor any change in the public's attitude to the QPS. By doing this on a regular basis, the independent CJC, the QPS, government and the parliament are kept informed about public concerns. If necessary, police policies and procedures can be modified before unintended consequences manifest themselves into complaints against police. The surveys also send a message to the community: that their opinions matter to the police service and its independent watchdog.

By having discrete corruption prevention and independent research functions, the Criminal Justice Commission is not seen as simply wielding a big stick over police. It is also seen as the provider of impartial, expert and relevant advice which assists police to prevent complaints occurring. The value of this kind of input has been acknowledged by the Queensland police hierarchy (*Courier-Mail* 8 April 1996, 9). When the police hierarchy publicly supports the independent, external, non-police oversight body, as the Queensland Police Service has, an important message is sent to the public: the police as an organisation is slowly changing. It is willing to listen and act on independent, well researched and relevant advice from its oversight body. Also, because the CJC's research reports on policing issues are independent of government and available to the public, the QPS is seen to be more open and accountable to the community it serves. Over time this may help to address problems associated with the "them against us" syndrome spoken about earlier.

Oversight bodies which are deprived of the ability to introduce integrated reactive-proactive policies can not be expected to achieve long-term change in police behaviour. A reactive only approach results in missed opportunities. These missed opportunities need to be given a much higher profile in debates about the effectiveness of civilian oversight.

Conclusion

Reactive functions are an important aspect of the civilian oversight process. However, to change police behaviour in the long-term, policy makers need to rethink their approach. The benefits to be gained from incorporating the proactive features outlined by Bayley (1992b) and Perez (1994), plus a discrete corruption prevention unit and independent research function need to be considered.

The holistic nature of this approach could help to enhance community knowledge and understanding of the policing function which in turn, could assist in lessening the destructive, "them against us" syndrome. It could also help to change the police and community's perception of oversight bodies. Given the opportunity, civilian oversight bodies could move from being purely punishing institutions to organisations that help to initiate and facilitate police reform programs. This shift in focus could be the first step toward building a new relationship between oversight body and police, one based, in part at least, on partnership and consensus rather than conflict. However, this cannot happen unless governments act, for it is governments which are responsible for the powers granted to civilian oversight bodies.

But as the following chapter shows, even if oversight bodies are given the necessary proactive and reactive powers needed to be effective they can be prevented from using them to maximum advantage by government intent.

5

GOVERNMENT INTENT AND SUPPORT

Introduction

It seems that once police watchdog bodies are established, the privileged position of police, as discussed in Chapter Three, is not the only obstacle they encounter. Governments can also hinder effective oversight. Having responded to an immediate political problem and satisfied citizens' demands for an external civilian body to oversight police misconduct, many governments then tend to ignore the independent agency's need for adequate resources and/or amendments to its enabling legislation. Terrill (1990) argues that a government's lack of commitment to civilian oversight is demonstrated by its "inactivity and inattentiveness" which severely hampers the organisation's ability to be effective. This problem was also noted by Brown (1985a) when he spoke of the lack of "unequivocal support by government" toward oversight bodies. But why do governments react in this manner? Do they deliberately set these bodies up to fail or is the answer more complicated? The literature on statutory authorities provides a partial answer.

Theoretically, statutory authorities are created so an organisation can be free from the day-to-day political control experienced by government departments. As such, they modify traditional lines of accountability, particularly in systems which adhere to the Westminster system of responsible government (Jaensch 1991). While this can be an advantage for governments in that they can distance themselves from responsibility for the activities of the statutory authority, as Warhurst (1980) explains, it can also create its own set of dilemmas. This is particularly so in the case of controversial statutory authorities such as independent civilian oversight bodies as they compound the dilemma by creating a new set of problems. For organisations which are established to oversight police misconduct are not an attempt to remove a layer of accountability as most statutory authorities are; rather they are set up to add an additional layer. Governments are creating an independent body to oversight one of its own activities, while at the same time trying to maintain normal lines of accountability in terms of police commissioner-police minister or police chief-mayor, city administration relations.

To examine Terrill's and Brown's inactivity, inattentiveness and lack of support argument further, examples from various Australian States over the past ten years are used. They are grouped loosely under the headings "limiting activities" and "lack of resources". This book has already acknowledged that different political, cultural and historical factors influence the nature of civilian oversight bodies in different countries. They can also influence the relationship which exists between oversight agencies and governments. However, the following examples are by no means exclusive to Australia.

Australian examples

Limiting activities

The trend in Australia has been to create agencies which primarily review investigations carried out by police internal investigation units and monitor/supervise police investigations into the more serious allegations of police misconduct (Criminal Justice Commission 1995c). The majority closely resemble Goldsmith's Civilian External Supervisory or Civilian External Investigatory models. Some, such as the New South Wales Ombudsman, have evolved from the former to the latter. However, not all Australian oversight agencies have the ability to conduct their own investigation from the initial stage of the process.

For example, for over four years the Parliamentary Commissioner for Administrative Investigations in Western Australia repeatedly asked Western Australian governments for this power. The Parliamentary Commissioner has also been requesting the power to supervise police investigations from the outset. In December 1992, toward the end of the Lawrence Labor Government's term of office, the PCAI was hopeful that the necessary legislation was imminent. However, a change of government in February 1993 resulted in the process having to be restarted. The Court Liberal Government did not respond to requests until October 1996. When it did, the government did not widen the PCAI's powers, it chose instead to add another layer to the police accountability process. Allegations of police corruption and serious misconduct are now referred to the Western Australia Anti-corruption Commission in the first instance. It can, after consultation with the PCAI, refer a matter to the Parliamentary Commissioner for investigation. Under these circumstances, the legislative requirement that the police be given 42 days to investigate before PCAI involvement is negated.

The Commonwealth Ombudsman, who has jurisdiction over the Australian Federal Police (AFP), also believes that allegations involving serious misconduct, violence or abuse should be investigated independently by her/his office in the first instance (Commonwealth Ombudsman 1995, 157). Under the current legislation complaints are usually investigated by the AFP's Internal Investigation Division (IID). If this is not appropriate because the complaint concerns IID staff, practices or procedures, a special investigator is assigned. The special investigators are usually members of the AFP but are independent of the complaint. They often report directly to the Ombudsman. With the agreement of the commissioner of police, special investigators can be persons from the Ombudsman's office.

The Commonwealth Ombudsman's office does have the power to re-investigate IID investigations if it is not satisfied with the findings but as it pointed out, "the time that has usually elapsed often makes these investigations ineffectual – we only re-investigated one case in 1994-95" (Commonwealth Ombudsman 1995, 158).

As noted in the 1995 *Annual Report*, the AFP commissioner has agreed to let the Ombudsman's office supervise serious and sensitive complaint investigations and the two parties worked together to establish guidelines for the supervision of such complaints. But this agreement is dependent on the police commissioner's approval not on the Ombudsman's discretion (Commonwealth Ombudsman 1995, 158).

Deficiencies in the legislation governing these oversight bodies highlights the inadequacy of government policy in the area of complaints against police. A situation should not exist whereby a police oversight body is dependent on the goodwill of a police commissioner to effectively fulfil its citizens' watchdog role. If governments are serious about effective police accountability, legislation should be introduced which responds to legitimate requests by oversight bodies to have their functions broadened. These requests are based on experience and are designed to remedy proven shortcomings in the legislative frameworks of these accountability organisations.

Lack of resources[1]

But powers by themselves are not enough. Even if oversight bodies are granted the authority they need to effectively fulfil their public interest function, they are unable to do so without adequate resources. While this may appear to be stating the obvious, the following evidence from several Australian States over the past nine years shows that at various times governments have tended to ignore what is axiomatic.

In 1990 the Commonwealth Ombudsman reported that if he was to effectively carry out a major part of his statutory function, to conduct his own investigations into allegations of police misconduct, his office would have to be better resourced (Commonwealth Ombudsman 1990, 63). The following year the government and parliament were again warned that effective external scrutiny without additional resources would be impossible to achieve (Commonwealth Ombudsman 1991, 100). By 1995 there had been no change to the need for extra resources. In her 1995 *Annual Report* then Ombudsman Phillipa Smith noted that lack of resources meant that her office was restricted to supervising only a small number of complaints each year. By 1997 the situation had become so critical that she devoted an entire chapter of her 1997 Annual Report to the issue (1997, 105-15). Statistics were presented which showed a dramatic 19 percent increase in complaints received and a corresponding 19 percent cut in the Ombudsman's budget. An inevitable consequence has been a large increase in the use of the discretionary power not to investigate. According to Smith, this has had the effect of arbitrarily constraining a "key mechanism for ensuring public accountability and redress for individuals" (1997, 114).

In 1991 then New South Wales Ombudsman David Landa complained that his office was being hampered by government-imposed budgetary constraints which, if not alleviated, would threaten the independence of the Ombudsman (New South Wales Ombudsman 1991, 25, 26). He was so concerned about the consequences of his inadequate budget that he submitted a detailed 40-page special report to parliament: *The Effective Functioning of the Office of the Ombudsman.*

The purpose of the report was "to inform the Parliament of the Ombudsman's inability to carry out his statutory functions and the charter

1 Some of the information in this section is drawn from Lewis, Colleen 1996, Independent Oversight of Complaints Against the Police: Problems and Prospects, Research paper No 30, January, Centre for Australian Public Sector Management, Griffith University, Brisbane.

of the Office of the Ombudsman due to budgetary constraints imposed on the Office" (New South Wales Ombudsman 1991b, 1) and to advise the parliament that unless additional funds were received he would be unable to "maintain services to the public of New South Wales" (New South Wales Ombudsman 1991b, 38). In support of his request for additional funding, the Ombudsman pointed out that his Office was "demand driven" and, as such, had no control over the number of complaints received. When asked by the author what the government's response to the report had been, Landa replied "thundering deafness, voluminous, ear-splitting deafness" (interview with David Landa, former Ombudsman for New South Wales).

In his 1992 *Annual Report* Landa reinforced the message about the consequences of insufficient resources by noting that in the previous two years complaints against police had risen by 42 percent without any increase in funds to handle the additional load (New South Wales Ombudsman 1992, 27). This problem, shared by most oversight agencies, seems to be ignored by governments when decisions about funding are considered.

The New South Wales Ombudsman's Office did receive a capital grant to upgrade office equipment and a "modest increase" in recurrent funding (Landa 1994). Obviously the increase in recurrent funding was too modest for in his 1994 *Annual Report* the Ombudsman complained that insufficient funds were preventing him from fully utilising his powers. As he so correctly put it "The reality is that powers without necessary resources are not true powers" (New South Wales Ombudsman 1994, 22).

The former Police Complaints Authority in South Australia, Peter Boyce, has been most trenchant in his criticism of government policy in relation to resourcing the Authority. In March 1995 he wrote that for:

> [T]he past five years, the Authority has effectively operated in an environment of uncertainty as to its resources and ultimately, its future direction. I can only comment that the patent neglect which occurred in attempting to resolve the Authority's difficulties is inexcusable. The . . . incapacitation of a vital watchdog is an indictment on all involved. (South Australia Police Complaints Authority 1995, 3).

According to Boyce, the South Australian Government was "maintaining a body which [was] inadequate and ineffective as an independent oversight agency of complaints against police" (South Australia Police Complaints Authority 1995, 4). The South Australian Government's solution to the Authority's chronic under-resourcing problem was to suggest that the extra funds needed by the PCA should come out of the police budget. The police objected and who could blame them, particularly since they were facing the prospect of significant budget cuts themselves (South Australia Police Complaints Authority 1995, 12). Surely the government did not expect the police to agree to a further cut to top up their oversight agency's budget? But a much more important issue is at stake here – oversight agencies must be independent of police not reliant on their goodwill for the additional funds needed to carry out their statutory obligations. The government's response to the Authority's funding crisis can be described at best as unwise.[2]

In 1994 the Tasmanian Ombudsman reported that he had spent the previous year trying to maintain an adequate standard of service with limited resources. He also recorded his suspicions that "the number of complaints I record as unsubstantiated does not accurately reflect the degree to which there have been administrative deficiencies in the public sector" (Tasmania Ombudsman 1994, Introduction).

In Western Australia the situation is no different. The PCAI has made the telling point that the existing system had been suffering "for several years from the effects of woefully inadequate resources" which, among other things, have caused "lengthy delays in dealing with some complaints" (Western Australia Parliamentary Commissioner for Administrative Investigations 1993, 33).

Most of these agencies are not dedicated police complaints bodies but in all but two jurisdictions (Tasmania and the Commonwealth) complaints against police form the majority of their work. Anyway, if the South Australia Police Complaints Authority's plight is an example, there may be no financial advantage in being a dedicated police complaints body.

It is appreciated that government resources are finite and that many publicly funded organisations can legitimately claim that they are not adequately resourced. However, the sometimes chronic lack of resources experienced by these and other accountability organisations over a number of years has serious consequences for the public, the oversight agency and the police.

---

2 The ongoing saga surrounding the funding crisis which afflicted the PCA is outlined in more detail in the combined 7th, 8th and 9th Annual Report of the South Australia Police Complaints Authority.

Consequences of under-resourcing

The credibility of a police oversight body can be destroyed when its independence is threatened by unreasonable budgetary constraints. As former Commonwealth Ombudsman Professor Dennis Pearce (1993, 17-18) notes, "Every time the Ombudsman tells a member of the public that assistance cannot be provided because of lack of resources or expertise, a part of the standing of the office in the community is foregone". Also when resources, and not the nature of a complaint, dictates the police oversight body's course of action it is no longer fulfilling its statutory watchdog obligation to the public.

The police are also victims of inadequate funding to police oversight agencies. Delays in attending to complaints, brought about because of demand continually outstripping the oversight body's ability to supply, creates a backlog which places undue pressure on a police officer's career. It also frustrates complainants and can result in both players losing confidence in the system. Given the growing trend toward the use of civilian oversight in the handling of complaints against police, oversight bodies may be able to harness the power of the police in their campaign for increased resources to reduce backlogs.

Having to cease public awareness campaigns because of inadequate funding, an issue raised by the then New South Wales Ombudsman David Landa in his 1991 special report, is counter-productive. There seems little point in establishing an independent police watchdog if public awareness of its existence has to be severely limited because of government-inflicted financial difficulties; unless of course the government does not intend that its role and functions should be promoted to the community.

Obviously, when there is not enough money to adequately perform reactive functions, it is almost impossible for a police oversight body to pay the necessary attention to broader systemic issues or to engage in any meaningful proactive activities. This is detrimental to police reform and to police-community relations. It can also adversely affect the relationship between the oversight agency and the police as it forces the oversight body to become solely a punishing institution.

But starving police oversight bodies to (hopefully) prevent them from exposing misconduct by a government employee is also a somewhat blinkered response. It ignores the very real possibility that the community is more willing to accept that misconduct will happen within a police service from time to time, than it is to accept attempts by governments to play down or hush-up the true situation. Evidence suggests that previous attempts by governments to deny problems relating to police misconduct have made the community cynical and distrustful of governments and the police and, under particular circumstances, have had adverse electoral consequences (Goldstein 1977, 156-86; Fitzgerald 1989).

Inadequately resourcing an oversight body which has discrete reactive and proactive units can cause internal divisions within the organisation. Competition for too scarce resources creates conflict not consensus, and it is usually the unit which deals primarily with preventive policies which suffers the most. This means that proactive policies (the future for long term cultural change) are forced to take a subordinate position to the "big stick", reactive approach.

Some reasons why governments starve oversight bodies

Theoretically, oversight bodies are established "to secure individual justice in the administrative state" (Seneviratne 1994, 12), to improve rules and procedures in the public service and to reassure citizens that decision-makers can be made to justify their decisions before an independent arbiter (Pearce 1993). Yet, in practice, liberal democratic governments often starve police oversight bodies of resources and restrict their powers.

Pearce (1993, 15), making the observation that the ability to control budgets is the most powerful weapon that the executive has over oversight bodies, touched on the essence of the problem when he said:

> It must never be forgotten that review bodies do not have access to funds independently of those supplied by the executive. Even a Parliament is dependent upon an appropriation of government funds. So it becomes a political issue how an Ombudsman is resourced – as it is with all other review bodies.

What then are some of the political issues which encourage governments to adopt an aggressive even hostile attitude toward oversight bodies?

Gary Sturgess (1994, 127), one of the architects of the New South Wales Independent Commission Against Corruption (ICAC), believes that politicians have "mixed feelings" about independent watchdogs. As the representatives of the people they understand why the community supports and appreciates the role such bodies play in cleaning up public administration but they also "fear" them. Governments fear the political damage that may occur from the public airing of the shortcomings of a government department, particularly one which embodies the coercive powers of the state. This is especially so in countries such as Australia which has adopted the Westminster system of responsible government and all that it entails in terms of ministerial responsibility (Davis et al 1993).

The nature of an oversight body's role contributes to the often difficult relationship between it and government. The former Ombudsman for Saskatchewan made the point that:

> The cumulative effect of appearing to be constantly in search of change and remedies for the public, and finding it necessary to air differences with the government in public several times each year, must put this relationship in some jeopardy. Sooner or later, there is a tendency to shoot the messenger when governments don't like the message (quoted in New South Wales Ombudsman 1990b, 4).

In the case of police oversight bodies in Australia, the most common ammunition used to shoot the messenger is an inadequate budget. This method of control is more subtle and politically safe than attacking an oversight body's findings (New South Wales Ombudsman 1994) or abolishing the body.

The uneasy relationship between independent watchdogs and governments also occurs because the watchdog is perceived to be the bearer "of only bad news" (Pearce 1993). This may be true of reactive bodies but need not be the case if an oversight body has a meaningful proactive function which enables it to work with the police to increase community confidence in the Service. Governments should consider the advantages that can flow from an oversight body having a dedicated corruption prevention function and the ability to undertake independent research into police-related matters (as discussed in the previous chapter) rather than concentrating exclusively on what may be the negative political consequences arising from the exposure of police misconduct.

A government's attitude toward funding an oversight agency may also relate to its multiple coverage, particularly when it extends to politicians. Many governments establish these watchdog agencies to do more than simply deal with police conduct matters. For example, an Ombudsman has responsibility for complaints against police and for monitoring, reviewing and/or investigating complaints against other public servants. For some oversight bodies the multiple coverage extends to politicians. The Independent Commission Against Corruption in New South Wales and the Criminal Justice Commission in Queensland have the power and responsibility, under certain circumstances, to address the conduct of elected officials. There is little incentive for governments to adequately fund and generally support a body which has the potential to find fault with all government departments, but there is even less incentive if that body has the ability to find fault with the behaviour of politicians. Therefore, an oversight body's ability to attract adequate funding may be dependent on a government's assessment about whether greater political damage could result from being seen to under-fund an oversight body than from any possible future exposure of misconduct by public servants including politicians. The dilemma for a government is that for political reasons it may not wish to emasculate the oversight body but also it does not want it to go too far. How it resolves that dilemma is usually influenced by the standing and the credibility of the oversight body in the eyes of the community.

The issue of multiple coverage and the effect it may have on an external, independent civilian body's police oversight role is worthy of greater attention. For example, does multiple coverage create a whole new set of problems for the oversight agency and, if so, how does it impact on its police oversight function? Steps are taken to address this issue in Chapter Nine.

The importance of relationships

Tensions in relationships are not confined to government and oversight body. As seen in Chapters Two and Three, they can also exist between oversight body and police, particularly the police union, and between police and government, often when discussions about the powers and functions of the oversight body are being negotiated. The consequence is a set of tensions. These tensions are institutional rather than personal; in extreme circumstances they can lead to the closure of the oversight body.

In New York the demise of the CCRB had its origins in tensions between police and government over the establishment of a civilian oversight body. In Victoria, Australia, the problem was not the introduction of civilian oversight. Before the establishment of the Victorian Police Complaints Authority, the Ombudsman oversighted complaints against police and when the PCA was closed down the function returned to the Ombudsman's office with the position of Deputy Ombudsman (Police Complaints) being created. In the Victorian situation the Police Complaints Authority's demise can be directly attributed to tensions between police and oversight body.[3]

3 See Freckleton 1988a, 1988b; Freckleton 1991; Freckleton and Selby 1987; Freckelton and Selby 1989.

The Victorian experience highlights the importance of an oversight body establishing a professional working relationship with police. It seems that in this regard the PCA was not successful. It is not expected that police should like an oversight body but unless they have a respect (albeit begrudging) for the quality of the oversight body's work and, perhaps even more importantly, for its attitude toward police, they may refuse to cooperate with it. When this happens an untenable situation is created which governments inevitably have to resolve. In Victoria it was resolved by disbanding the PCA.

The matter of relationships is important. The relationship between police and oversight body and police and government have been explored in this book, and in the literature on the handling of complaints against police. However, as previously argued, the relationship between government and oversight body, which is crucial to the success of any oversight body, has not received sufficient attention. Besides addressing the core reactive powers needed to effectively oversight complaints against police, and the proactive dimensions required to deal with broader preventive issues, the important issue of relations, particularly government-oversight body relations, needs to be analysed and taken into account when evaluating the success or failure of the civilian oversight process. In other words, it is necessary to recognise the need for a new model.

The need to move on

Much of the literature on models needs to advance beyond Kerstetter's 13-year-old pioneering work. By continuing to try to group new models under Kerstetter's categories, or even Goldsmith's more expansive classification system, the exercise runs the risk of not only becoming messy and confusing but also enclosed and limited.

Over the past 20 years, in particular, external, independent civilian oversight bodies have become a more accepted and recognised part of the police accountability landscape. They have also become more experienced and hence more knowledgeable about what powers they need to effectively perform their watchdog role. Oversight bodies themselves are campaigning for additional powers and in some jurisdictions Ombudsmen have won the right to conduct their own investigations from the initial stage of the complaints process. This means that some are no longer simply *post hoc facto* review bodies. They have moved further to the right of Petterson's theoretical spectrum and beyond Goldsmith's Civilian External Supervisory and Kerstetter's Civilian Monitor models.

Since 1989 there has been a new model of civilian oversight in Queensland Australia, the Criminal Justice Commission. The CJC combines a reactive, proactive, holistic approach to the issue of police conduct. It looks at the "rotten apple" and "the barrel" and assists police to devise policies that will help to insulate the service from those who seek to contaminate it.

The proactive functions of the CJC's discrete Research and Prevention Division need to be taken into account when discussing models of civilian oversight. But more important than simply acknowledging new categories, the literature needs to explore in greater depth the way in which the proactive and reactive functions can feed into each other, thereby allowing for a more integrated approach to police misconduct. In other words, any analysis needs to go beyond simply adding proactive dimensions to the existing core reactive functions. What is required is for links or, as Perez (1994) says, "loops" to be made between the proactive and reactive functions of oversight bodies.

However, even if existing models are tidied, new ones created or, in the case of West's (1988) functional typology, new proactive functions added, problems will remain. Taking account of proactive functions is a necessary but not sufficient step. The modified models and typologies will still imply some notion of self-containment in that they assume the framework of the debate centres around the creation of a body with particular functions and powers. What is largely neglected when attempting to evaluate the effectiveness of this form of police accountability is the relationship between civilian oversight body and government. The literature talks almost exclusively about supervisory relations between police and oversight body and to a lesser extent the relationship between police and government, particularly at the policy formulation stage of civilian oversight. But relations between government and oversight body are an important consideration.

Therefore, in addition to the core reactive roles discussed by Kerstetter and Goldsmith, plus the addition of proactive roles and functions addressed by Bayley and Perez and expanded on in the CJC model, a further dimension needs to be added. This crucial dimension is oversight body-government relations, the nature of which can significantly influence government intent and hence the level and type of support (or otherwise) an oversight body receives from government.

A useful starting point for trying to develop some notion of what would be required in any model which incorporates government intent is to give a descriptive account of some of the problems which need to be solved. Chapters Six to Nine of this book, which present two case studies from the Australian State of Queensland, offer a contribution to that body of knowledge.

Queensland has had two civilian oversight bodies: the Police Complaints Tribunal and the Criminal Justice Commission. They offer vastly different perspectives on government intent. The Criminal Justice Commission's relationship with governments is dealt with in Chapter Nine. The Police Complaints Tribunal, which is the subject of the next chapter, shows, among other things, how governments will sometimes use the civilian oversight process in the same way they do royal commissions – as smokescreens to blur their true intentions. It also includes the ingredient of a politicised police force, which adds yet another dimension to the important issue of relationships.

6

THE POLICE COMPLAINTS TRIBUNAL – QUEENSLAND [1]

Introduction

Queensland's first attempt at civilian oversight of complaints against police was a dismal failure. Theoretically, the Police Complaints Tribunal was established to enhance accountability. In practice, the power of the police and government intent combined to create an oversight body which for much of its life deflected criticisms and shielded police from responsibility for their imprudent and illegal actions. As Fitzgerald (1989, 290) found:

> The Police Union, the Police Department and the Government have developed attitudes and policies dominated by political considerations. The Police Complaints Tribunal, like the Internal Investigation Section, from both a conceptual as well as practical viewpoint, has had the effect of masking rather than dealing with police misconduct.

From 1976 until the start of the *Commission of Inquiry into Possible Illegal Activities and Associated Police Misconduct* (the Fitzgerald Inquiry) in 1987, the situation existed where a closed policy community, comprised of the police commissioner, the police union, the executive, and from mid-1983 to 1987 the Police Complaints Tribunal, dominated the complaints against police policy arena. This arrangement meant that none of the usual tensions between police and oversight body, oversight body and government and government and police existed. Indeed the reverse was true.

---

1 A part of the information in this chapter is drawn from Lewis C, 1988, Police accountability: Queensland Style, unpublished Honours thesis, Griffith University, Queensland.

The police commissioner had willingly allowed the police service to be politicised.[2] This strengthened the power of the police and greatly enhanced their privileged position with government. The loser from this arrangement was the Queensland community because it occurred at the expense of police accountability.

Before examining why the Police Complaints Tribunal failed to deliver effective accountability, this chapter will examine the nature of police-government relations in Queensland before the establishment of the PCT. By placing the advent of the PCT in the appropriate historical context, it is possible to analyse the "why" and "how" surrounding what, for the Queensland community, proved to be a most unsatisfactory experience with the civilian oversight process. It also serves to contrast the political environment surrounding the establishment of the PCT and CJC and the consequences it can have for effective oversight.

This chapter begins by looking at the nature of the relationship between the police and government from 1970 to 1976 when Ray Whitrod was commissioner of police and how it changed to the National Party Government's advantage when Terence Lewis was catapulted to the police commissioner's position in 1976, a position he held until he was stood down during the Fitzgerald Inquiry by then Deputy Premier Bill Gunn. It concludes by analysing the PCT and explaining why it was doomed to failure.

1970-1976

Ray Whitrod became commissioner of the Queensland Police Force in September 1970. As an outsider (a non-Queenslander), his appointment was not welcomed by the police force and was openly resented by the Queensland Police Union. The union vehemently and publicly fought against the introduction of most of Whitrod's reforms, which included the establishment of a police academy, a police arts and science course, a tamper-proof examination process, promotion by merit, the civilianisation of administrative functions and increased accountability, particularly in relation to police misconduct and corruption.

2 In the context of this book, the term "politicised" is based on Finnane's definition of the concept. He explains that a police service is compromised when the executive has an improper influence on policing decisions and/or the police themselves play an improper role in policy formulation and law-making. The yardstick used to determine the extent of the politicisation is the constitutional position of British police which is based on an officer's original powers and constabulary independence as discussed in Chapter One.

Allegations of corruption within the force were brought to Whitrod's attention on the day he arrived in Queensland. Senior Constable Hogget warned him of serious corruption within the Criminal Intelligence Bureau and identified some of those involved. Hogget's information was confirmed the following day by then senior constable, now Assistant Commissioner Greg Early[3] (*Courier-Mail* 25 June 1988, Weekend 1, 8).

During the Fitzgerald Inquiry, Whitrod explained how Hogget and Early had told him that former Police Commissioner Frank Bischof "had recruited three bright young detectives to act as his 'bagmen' – the collectors of bribes" (*Courier-Mail* 25 June 1988, Weekend 1, 8). The alleged bright young detectives were identified at the Fitzgerald Inquiry as Glenn Hallahan, Tony Murphy and Terence Lewis (Fitzgerald 1989, 41, 75).

To add to Whitrod's problems throughout his term as commissioner, he also had a difference of opinion with then Premier Sir Joh Bjelke-Petersen over the independence of police in operational matters and the degree of accountability needed within the Force. The different expectations between Premier Bjelke-Petersen and Commissioner Whitrod are demonstrated in the following two examples.

In Brisbane in July 1976 a student was struck on the head by a policeman using a baton during a protest march. Having viewed filmed evidence of the event, Commissioner Whitrod ordered an inquiry into the incident. But the Premier had other ideas. He intervened and announced that "cabinet, not Whitrod, would decide whether an inquiry would be held" (Hogg and Hawkner 1983a, 164). The inquiry was quashed. Even though the police commissioner thought that the police should be held accountable for their actions, it seems that the Premier did not.

The decision by Premier Bjelke-Petersen to quash the inquiry confirmed what many in the community were coming to believe: that he was attempting to politicise the police force and accountability was to be one of his bargaining tools. The usually conservative *Courier-Mail* newspaper echoed the sentiments of many when it reported, "Clearly the Police Commissioner has not only the right but the duty to order investigations into complaints against members of the police force . . why on earth has the Premier decided that he must get into the act? . . . There is no justification for political interference" (quoted in Hawker 1981, 74).

---

3 On the day Lewis was appointed commissioner of police, Early became his personal assistant and remained in that position throughout all of Lewis's 11 years as commissioner.

Shortly following this event the police commissioner and the Premier were at odds again. This time the issue concerned a raid on a "hippie commune" at Cedar Bay where it was reported police had destroyed the settlement by setting fire to dwellings. Despite widespread criticism from many quarters about police behaviour, including from the government's Liberal Party coalition partners, the Premier refused to hold an open inquiry into alleged police misconduct. His response to calls that the matter should be investigated was to denigrate those who complained and claim that the criticism was "all part of an orchestrated campaign to legalise marijuana and denigrate the police" (Communist Party 1977, 16). The continued refusal by the Bjelke-Petersen Government to make police accountable for their actions prompted the media to ask if Queensland had been brought to the position were complaints against police were ignored (*Courier-Mail* 5 Oct 1976).

Without the government's knowledge, and contrary to its wishes, Whitrod conducted an inquiry into the alleged misconduct at Cedar Bay (Hogg and Hawker 1983a). In this instance Whitrod chose to exercise his original powers and uphold his sworn duty to enforce the law. At a press conference the following month he announced that as a result of his investigations charges would be brought against four officers. At the same press conference he announced that he would be resigning as police commissioner.

The continual undermining of his authority by the Premier was a factor in Whitrod's decision to resign, but the primary reason was the announcement in early November 1976 that Terence Lewis, a junior inspector at Charleville (a country Queensland town) would be promoted to assistant commissioner. Lewis's name had not been put forward by either the Commissioned Officers Association or the police commissioner.

Whitrod was enraged by the Lewis appointment, not only because the government's action had undermined his position as police commissioner but more importantly, according to Whitrod, because of cabinet's particular choice. Whitrod told the Fitzgerald Inquiry that he was "flabbergasted at cabinet's decision", as cabinet was aware of allegations that Lewis was supposedly one of the former Police Commissioner Frank Bischof's bagmen. When Whitrod questioned then Police Minister Newbery about the rumours surrounding Lewis, and hence his suitability to be an assistant commissioner, Newbery is reported to have said: "Oh, but that was when he was a detective sergeant. He is now an inspector and he wouldn't do that sort of thing now" (*Courier-Mail* 3 March 1988, 1).

Whitrod believed the reason Sir Joh promoted a junior inspector to assistant commissioner was that the Premier wanted to seize control of the force. With Lewis as an assistant commissioner, Whitrod felt that Sir Joh would have "taken away control of the police" from the commissioner. He would have been able to deal directly with Lewis and "countermand" or "nullify" any of Whitrod's instructions. This, Whitrod said, would have left him in the position of being nothing more than a front man, a shield for what might, and indeed did, develop (*Courier-Mail* 4 March 1991, 1). This situation was untenable to Whitrod.

The question of police-government relations was a crucial factor in Whitrod's resignation. He told a packed press conference once his resignation had taken effect that:

> I am not claiming that there ought to be a complete independence of action for the Commissioner. All I assert is that there ought to be a minimum of interference by the political authority. This is essential if members of the community are to believe that the enforcement of the law is being carried out in a manifestly impartial manner. It needs therefore to be shielded from even the appearance of politically motivated interference. . . The Commissioner of Police cannot be just another public service adviser to a Cabinet Minister. He is the head of a large body of police officers, each one under oath to personally enforce the law . . . (RW Whitrod, statement to a press conference, Brisbane 29 November 1976, 1, quoted in Wettenhall 1977, 20-21).

Ray Whitrod had spend his six years as commissioner struggling against attempts to politicise the Queensland police force. His fight was in vain.

1976-1987

Following Whitrod's resignation, cabinet chose not to appoint an acting commissioner whilst advertising the position of commissioner. Instead it promoted the very recently appointed Assistant Commissioner Terence Lewis, who had no senior level administrative or management experience, to the position of commissioner. In doing so, cabinet left itself open to allegations of having made a partisan political appointment.

Mystery still surrounds the reason behind the Lewis appointment. Perhaps the most plausible explanation for his sudden rise to power was given by the first wife of Allen Callaghan, Bjelke-Petersen's press secretary and close aide for many years. She claimed that "The decision to appoint Terry Lewis in 1976 was totally Allen's. . . He said he [Terry

Lewis] would be perfect for the job [as police commissioner]. He said he would be a Premier's person" (*Courier-Mail* 26 January 1988).

Whatever the reason behind Lewis's extraordinary promotions, the unsatisfactory situation existed whereby all promotions above the rank of senior sergeant needed cabinet approval. Whilst cabinet had ultimate control over such appointments, the danger existed for an exchange of favours between police and politicians. The prospect of promotion to commissioned officer rank is a strong inducement to comply with government wishes. So too, perhaps, is a knighthood.

With Mr (later Sir) Terence Lewis heading the force, the Premier escalated his confrontationist law and order policies. Secure in the knowledge that many police were on-side, and those who were not would not break ranks, the government used the police to break up demonstrations against uranium shipments and banned political street marches. The right to appeal the denial of a street march permit was moved from a magistrate to a superintendent of police (Hawker 1981, 78-79). Police were also used during an electricity industry picket in 1985 to implement draconian legislation. It appears that little, if any, police discretion was exercised as members of parliament and the clergy who protested peacefully against this legislation were arrested.

By this time the government was not even pretending that the police should be operationally independent and the police commissioner was publicly supporting the government. In a speech delivered at the police academy shortly before the 1983 state election, Lewis stated that "The people of Queensland and the police force owe the Premier a very deep gratitude. The free enterprise policy of the Bjelke-Petersen Government has been responsible for Queensland's tremendous growth" (quoted in Whitton 1989, 84).

Such a statement from any Australian senior public servant is unusual to say the least, but in the lead up to an election it is extraordinary. The fact that it was made by the police commissioner is particularly disturbing as it indicates an improper relationship between the government and its coercive arm, the police.

Inappropriate police-government relations

The Lewis diaries, which were exhibits at the Fitzgerald Inquiry, confirmed the extent to which the government had become involved in the day-to-day operations of the police force, and the way in which the police commissioner had become involved with the parliamentary and administrative wings of the National Party.

The diaries showed that for years Terence Lewis, the head of the Queensland Police Force, had been directly involved in mainstream National Party politics. The police commissioner was telephoning another minister, a former policeman, to talk about the actions of the police minister; the commissioner discussed with a National Party trustee and power broker, senior government appointments, electoral redistribution and the honours list; Lewis and Bjelke-Petersen discussed internal party promotions within the government; government members phoned the commissioner seeking favours and Lewis sought investment advise from a National Party trustee; the commissioner phoned a parliamentarian about the Liberal Party conference and Lewis and the Premier discussed who may be the next premier and deputy premier of Queensland. These "examples only" from Lewis's diaries indicate an improper relationship between the police commissioner and the government. They clearly demonstrate that the Queensland police force was not being run in accordance with the principles underpinning police-government relations in liberal democratic societies.

Further confirmation of the less than arm's-length relationship between Lewis and the government came in a 42-page submission Lewis gave to the Fitzgerald Inquiry in which he categorised his friends. "Special friends" included Premier Sir Joh Bjelke-Petersen who Lewis claimed was "a special friend with whom I could discuss any matter in confidence" (*Courier-Mail* 12 October 1988, 4). The former National Party trustee and power broker Sir Edward Lyons was another very "special friend"; so too was former National Party Minister Don Lane and the former chair of the Police Complaints Tribunal and District Court Judge Eric Pratt (*Courier-Mail* 12-13 October 1988, 1, 4).

The situation existed where there was an improper exchange of political influence between the police and members of the government and as Clifford (1981) has argued, political influence is a "fairly obvious contributor to police corruption". This certainly proved to be the case in Queensland.

Police malfeasance

Very early on in the life of the Fitzgerald Inquiry it became evident that the network of corrupt activities within the Queensland police force went far beyond the theory that corrupt police were the rare few "rotten apples" at the bottom of the barrel. This theory, which was often relied on by former Premier Sir Joh Bjelke-Petersen and a succession of police ministers when confronted with allegations of police corruption, has been discredited. For example, Justice Lusher, in his report into the New South Wales Police in 1981, found that "In an organisation such as the police force where signs of corruption are perceived the 'rotten apple' theory as a control measure should be firmly rejected" (Lusher 1981, 631-32).

The Fitzgerald Inquiry laid bare a system of corrupt activities in relation to organised crime and its links into prostitution, gambling and starting price bookmaking. It also revealed the extent to which the actions and inactions of the police force had assisted the growth of criminal activities in Queensland and, in many cases, how the police themselves instigated, controlled or were involved in a variety of illegal activities including car theft rackets, false identification cards, prostitution and illegal gambling.

The Inquiry also heard how police blatantly falsified evidence and perjured themselves in order to secure convictions. Corrupt former policeman Jack Herbert, a key figure at the Inquiry, admitted that it was his usual practice to tailor his evidence within the Queensland police force, "When we first arrested anybody we would sit down at the typewriter and it would be a matter of . . . 'once upon a time there were three bears and there's thousands'. This was the attitude. You would make up the story as you went along" (*Courier-Mail* 2 September 1988, 1).

As Whitton (1989, 181) explains perhaps the most alarming part of Herbert's evidence was that, "Justice and the rule of law were virtually a dead letter: fabrication was endemic in the force. The danger this poses for the liberty of the subject is incalculable; we do not know how many enemies of the regime, or persons who simply annoyed police, were routinely verballed into prison" (Whitton 1989, 181).

Corrupt former policeman Noel Kelly, who received an indemnity for corruption but not for perjury, claimed that verballing was a common practice among detectives. Starting price (SP) bookmakers told the Inquiry of careers, some spanning 20 years, during which time they were rarely questioned, let alone prosecuted by police (*Australian* 29 May 1988, 8). Corrupt police in the licensing branch protected SP bookmakers by ensuring that at least one corrupt officer who was in on the "joke"[4] was on duty every shift (*Courier-Mail* 11 September 1988, 4).

4 The "joke" was the term used by corrupt officers to refer to their corrupt activities.

Members of the licensing branch regularly drank alcohol in massage parlours whilst on duty or visited them after work for drinking sessions. A constable whose first posting as a plain clothes officer was to the licensing branch, told the Inquiry that many police spent their shifts travelling from brothel to brothel accepting free alcohol and sex (*Courier-Mail* 21 October 1987).

Self-confessed corrupt former policeman Harry Burgess, who served in the licensing branch from 1979-1985, told the inquiry that one of the two groups who ran Brisbane's brothels were paying police more than $10,000 a month for protection (*Courier-Mail* 29 October 1987, 4). Anne Marie Tilley who, with her partner Hector Hapeta controlled a string of massage parlours, escort agencies and sex shops in Brisbane and the Gold Coast, testified that corrupt police assisted the growth of her brothel empire so they would receive larger protection payments (*Australian* 21 June 1988, 3).

By the time the Fitzgerald Inquiry was established in May 1987, police malfeasance in Queensland extended from the Gold Coast to Cairns, and covered many facets of police work. But how did the Queensland police get away with such brazen misconduct and for such a prolonged period of time? Evidence suggests that three factors were significant in the breakdown of police accountability in Queensland: the blue curtain of silence, the government's wilful blindness and the failure of the system of complaint investigation. The code of silence has already been referred to in this book (see Chapter Two).

The wilful blindness on the part of the government, which was a product of the politicisation of the police service, contributed significantly to the breakdown in police accountability. The government saw only what it wanted to see, and apparently it did not wish to see anything that might upset the status quo. It defended the police against allegations of misconduct and corruption and denigrated those who dared to criticise. Sir Joh Bjelke-Petersen even continued to defend and denigrate after the Fitzgerald Inquiry had been operating for some three months. Rather than acknowledge the obvious, he chose to question the character of some Fitzgerald Inquiry witnesses. Sir Joh told the Queensland parliament to "just think of the people who are making these accusations, the type of people they are – the type of people they associate with. These ladies and others that have been talking down there in the way they have, naming this fellow and that" (*Courier-Mail* 11 September 1987, 1).

The Bjelke-Petersen Government's policy toward police misconduct reflected the attitude of the premier. It seems that ministers who wished to maintain their ministerial status complied with Sir Joh's wishes. While it is not intended in any way to excuse either existing or former corrupt police for their actions, the evidence suggests that before the Fitzgerald Inquiry a large part of the blame for the lack of police accountability in Queensland rests squarely on the shoulders of the executive, and former Premier Sir Joh Bjelke-Petersen. The government was ultimately accountable to the people for the efficient and effective running of the police service, yet for years they protected police. The more they did so the more brazen the police became. This dangerous situation caused a member of the then Labor Party opposition to warn that, "because of the Government's attitude, some police officers think they can do no wrong. . . To the detriment of the State's Police Force, the number of police officers who think they have the complete protection of the minister and the Government is growing" (Queensland, Legislative Assembly 1982, *Debates*, 1 April, 5542). The situation had been reached where the government had traded police accountability for police compliance.

A third factor contributed to the breakdown in police accountability. No one guarded the guardians. The remainder of this chapter explains why.

Rationale for establishing the Tribunal[5]

The idea that Queensland should have a Police Complaints Tribunal was made in response to allegations by two former police officers[6] that some police were involved in corrupt activities. These allegations were made on the Australian Broadcasting Corporation's *Nationwide* programme in March 1982. Even though then Police Minister Russell Hinze's response to the program was to describe it as a "soap opera on par with 'General Hospital'" (quoted in Dickie 1989, 102), he simultaneously announced

---

5 Before proceeding with any analysis of the PCT, a distinction needs to be made between its pre- and post-1988 years of operation. During the Fitzgerald Inquiry (1987-1989), the position of chairperson changed twice. Both His Hon Judge Morley QC (1988-1989) and His Hon Judge McGuire QC (1989-1990) were appointed for a limited period in a "caretaker" capacity pending the Fitzgerald Inquiry's findings and recommendations. They have been praised for their efforts in dealing with the backlog of complaints and for attempting to make police accountable for their actions (Fitzgerald 1987, 292; Queensland, Legislative Assembly 1990, *Debates*, 10 May, 1333). Also, there has been no adverse comment about the Tribunal in its formative year of operations under the chairmanship of Judge William (Bill) Carter QC.

6 The allegations were made by two officers who had been members of the Licensing Branch: Kinglsey Fancourt and Bob Campbell (Dickie 1989, 101-102).

that he would seek cabinet's approval to establish a permanent police complaints tribunal. This apparent contradiction by Hinze is clarified somewhat when it is understood that improved police accountability was not the primary reason for establishing this oversight body.

The rationale underpinning the setting up of the tribunal was twofold. The first was to relieve pressure on the police minister, the government and the police department. Indeed, the desire to shift the spotlight from allegations of police misconduct was such that the Police Complaints Tribunal Bill was rushed through the planning and drafting stage and presented to parliament for debate some two weeks after the criticisms commenced (Queensland, Legislative Assembly 1982, *Debates*, 1 April, 5519). The second rationale was outlined by Police Minister Hinze, during the second reading of the Police Complaints Tribunal Bill. He explained:

> For as long as I have been a member in this house, police have been made fair game for anyone who wanted to make non-specific and sensational allegations with malicious political intent. . . The Government will no longer tolerate open-slather criticism of our Police Force by people who lack the necessary evidence to back up their claims. The proposed tribunal will provide a permanent and independent forum for the hearing of allegations against our police force. . . Throughout Australia there seems to be a general trend towards attacking police by making unsubstantiated allegations that capture the headlines and then refusing to supply specific information. The proposed tribunal will put an end to that. Individuals who make allegations against the police will be encouraged to bring those allegations forward for investigation by the Internal Investigations Section, whose record of efficiency is undisputed. If individuals feel that their allegations are not properly looked into, they will be able to take them to the Police Complaints Tribunal (Queensland, Legislative Assembly 1982, *Debates*, 1 April, 5548).

It appears from Hinze's comments that the establishment of the Police Complaints Tribunal had more to do with protecting police from so-called "unsubstantiated allegations" of police misconduct and "undesirable interests" (Dickie 1989, 102) than holding police accountable for their actions. This assessment is substantiated by the provision in the Act which provided for imprisonment for people who made vexatious complaints and custodial penalty for registering a complaint which a complainant was subsequently unable to substantiate to the very high standard of proof required, which was beyond reasonable doubt (Queensland, Legislative Assembly 1990, *Debates*, 10 May, 1347).

Structure of the Police Complaints Tribunal

The structure of the tribunal also raises doubts about how effective the government wanted the Police Complaints Tribunal to be. The PCT originally consisted of three members: a district court judge (chairperson), a solicitor and stipendiary magistrate and the president of the Queensland Police Union. The size of the tribunal was described as "farcical" by Labor opposition member Bob Gibbs. Such a small membership, he argued, did not allow for a broad scope of opinion (Queensland, Legislative Assembly 1982, *Debates*, 1 April, 5521). In 1985 the Act was amended to create the position of deputy chairperson and to increase the membership to four. The deputy chairperson's position had to be filled by a stipendiary magistrate. All appointments were on a part-time basis and the term of appointment, for one year, was renewable.

The former president of the Police Union of Employees Senior Sergeant Colin Chant was a member of the tribunal from its inception in 1982 until April 1989. There is a blatant conflict of interest in such an appointment. As president of a police union, Chant's first loyalty was to the members of the union. Yet these members were the people whom, in the overwhelming majority of cases, the tribunal was investigating.

The "untenable" situation such a tribunal member would face, in having to find union members guilty of misconduct or corruption, was also addressed by Gibbs who argued that, "no thinking person in Queensland could be convinced of the need to have a representative of the union appointed to the Tribunal. Within a very short time the government will find that the Police Union representative on the Tribunal will be placed in a very compromising invidious position" (Queensland, Legislative Assembly 1982, *Debates*, 1 April, 5522-23).

The conflict of interest situation Chant was placed in became evident early in the life of the PCT. Police Minister William Glasson announced that he wanted to stamp out prostitution and illegal gambling because they caused the public to be suspicious that police received bribes. The president of the police union and member of the Police Complaints Tribunal Col Chant's over-sensitive reaction was to say that, "Police are shocked that Mr Glasson should make a statement like that". He added that the Police Complaints Tribunal had "not even heard a whisper about corruption" (quoted in Dickie 1989, 102) and warned that unless the police received an apology from the police minister they would bypass him and deal directly with the Premier. The Premier became involved saying that "Mr Glasson must be more careful in the way he expresses himself. I will be talking with him on the weekend. He has to be discreet". There was a meeting between Police Commissioner Lewis, Police Minister Glasson and Premier Bjelke-Petersen, after which Glasson announced that, "If there is corruption in the force it's very minimal" (*Sydney Morning Herald* 13 Oct 1987).

Events such as these helped to ensure that no one, including honest police and citizens, would take the Police Complaints Tribunal seriously. A former police officer Nigel Powell[7] told the Fitzgerald Inquiry that he did not take his suspicions of police corruption to the tribunal because of reservations about its composition. In particular, he expressed concern about a union representative's ability to be totally independent when investigating allegations of police misconduct (*Courier-Mail* 16 Oct 1987, 4).

Other appointments to the Tribunal have also been criticised.[8] Noted Australian researcher on police matters Mark Finnane (1987, 76) criticised the composition of the PCT by querying whether a judge, a stipendiary magistrate, a police union president and a former solicitor-general qualified it to be classified as a civilian body.

Fitzgerald (1989, 209) condemned its composition saying that:

> The Police Complaints Tribunal has structural deficiencies. It is dominated by a police representative and a former public servant which is quite unsatisfactory. It is also unsatisfactory for magistrates, who regularly have to decide questions of police credibility in the courts, to be members of the Tribunal.

The composition of the PCT calls into question the intent which underpinned this police accountability policy. So too does the method of appointment. Officially, the decision over appointments rested with the executive. In practice, the influence of the police commissioner was commonplace.

Method of appointment

The second chairperson of the tribunal was Judge Eric Pratt QC of the Queensland District Court and a former Victorian police officer. Entries in Lewis's diaries indicated his interest in Pratt's career and his appointment to the Police Complaints Tribunal. Pratt stated that the entries were "innocuous or incorrect" (quoted in Dickie 1989, 104). The references included an entry in December 1979 which stated that "Eric Pratt phoned

---

7 Nigel Powell was instrumental in helping to expose police corruption in Queensland.

8 The criticisms about appointments to the tribunal relate to the positions the members held outside the Tribunal. They are not intended as personal criticisms.

re QC appointment. Phoned Hon Lee (Minister for Administrative Services) re same". Pratt became a Queen's Counsel on 31 January 1980. Another entry revealed that Lewis had spoken to Pratt and a former Queensland Special Branch police officer, then Transport Minister Don Lane about Supreme Court vacancies (Dickie 1989, 104). An entry on 12 May 1983 explains that "Sir Edward Lyons phoned re speaking to Premier re Pratt". On 22 May another entry attests that Lewis "phoned Judge Pratt re complaints tribunal". An entry on 30 May reveals that "Hon Lane phoned re Judge Pratt for tribunal".

Judge Eric Pratt QC was appointed as chairperson of the Police Complaints Tribunal on 7 June 1983, an appointment he held until 1988. Dickie (1989, 104) notes that Pratt's term as chairperson was "controversial" and that many tribunal decisions were criticised by the legal profession and the media. Dickie further notes that entries in Lewis's diaries suggest that he and Pratt "discussed cases before the tribunal or incidents likely to become the subject of complaint" (1989, 104). Pratt denied that he was involved in any improper action (Dickie 1989, 104).

Lewis's diaries also indicated a strong friendship between him and Judge Pratt (see Dickie 1989, 104). In a statement to the Inquiry, Lewis claimed that Pratt was one of his "special friends" with whom he "could discuss any matter in confidence" (Lewis 1988, Submission to the Fitzgerald Inquiry, 11 Oct).

While a friendship does not in itself constitute misconduct, it does suggest that there was not an "arm's length" relationship between the head of the Police Complaints Tribunal and the head of the police force the tribunal was supposed to be oversighting. Given the key roles each was supposedly playing in maintaining police accountability, their special friendship was inappropriate.

The Police Complaints Tribunal formed part of the legal and administrative structures established to make police accountable. Its role in the chain of accountability was to independently oversight the complaints against police process. The police commissioner should not play an instrumental role in selecting Tribunal members. For the government to allow him to do so makes a mockery of the notion of the Tribunal as an impartial accountability institution. The membership of such a body is fundamental to its performance and to how the public perceive the quality of that performance. Lewis's involvement in appointments to the Tribunal ensured that it soon became part of the closed police accountability policy community.

The head of the organisation being scrutinised was helping to arrange the membership of the scrutinising agency. As a result, community involvement was virtually non-existent. There was no community consultation process and no community representatives on the PCT. This helped to minimise the risk that more effective methods for handling complaints against police would be placed on the political agenda.

Lack of resources

Inadequate resources also helped to ensure that the Police Complaints Tribunal would fail as an effective accountability institution. Despite the fact that the tribunal technically had the power to conduct its own investigations in practical terms it did not have the ability to do so. As the first chair of the PCT His Hon Justice Carter explained, "A lack of resources was absolutely, quite definitively a major problem. We were just three individuals, a district court judge, a magistrate and a policeman constituting a tribunal to entertain complaints. A secretary, a couple of stenographers and a room, that is what we had" (interview with His Hon Justice William Carter QC, former chairperson, Police Complaints Tribunal). At its initial meeting on 7 May 1982 the tribunal had little choice but to resolve that matters brought to its attention would be referred to the police commissioner for investigation.

In effect, the tribunal was forced to rely on the police Internal Investigation Section (IIS) to conduct investigations on its behalf. Consequently it was tied to the quality of those investigations. In the case of the PCT, this proved fatal. The Fitzgerald (1989, 289) Inquiry found the IIS's investigation techniques were crude, relevant witnesses were not always interviewed and the interrogation of police officers was "pleasant, ineffectual and feeble". He further reported that it:

> [L]acked commitment and will, and demonstrated no initiative to detect serious crime. . . The Section's effects have been token, mere lip service to the need for the proper investigation of allegations of misconduct. [It] has provided warm comfort to corrupt police. It has been a friendly, sympathetic, protective and inept overseer. . .

Adequate resources would have allowed the PCT to by-pass the now discredited Internal Investigation Section.

Judge Pratt's term as chair ended in February 1988. His position was filled by Judge Morley QC. In April 1989 Judge Morley's Tribunal reviewed the state of the PCT's resources and found them to be "unacceptable". Morley's Annual Report detailed how an under-resourced

Tribunal was "a misrepresentation to the public". The report also noted that even though the legislation which governed the Police Complaints Tribunal could be improved it did not constitute a major problem. The principal problem confronting the PCT for Judge Morley was inadequate resources (Police Complaints Tribunal 1989, 33).

The following appraisal of the formal powers of the PCT highlights how inadequate resources widens the gap between theoretical powers and practices in the civilian oversight process.

Police Complaint Tribunal's powers

The Police Complaints Tribunal was empowered to receive complaints made against the police, to consider matters of public knowledge involving allegations of misconduct, improper conduct, or neglect of duty by any member of the Queensland Police Force, and to keep under review every entry registered in a Central Register of Complaints, which the commissioner of police was obliged to maintain.

The tribunal's review powers in terms of the Register included the power to reconsider the subject matter of any entry and to investigate all matters pertaining to the entry and to give only such weight as the tribunal considered fit to conclusions recorded by the commissioner of police against any entry. After making the necessary inquiries, the tribunal could determine whether further action was necessary. If that proved to be the case, it had the power to decide the nature of that action. The PCT was also obliged to report once a year to the police minister on the activities of the Tribunal (*Police Complaints Tribunal Act 1982*).

The PCT could investigate anonymous complaints and had the discretion to decide which matters or complaints it would investigate. This included the discretion not to investigate matters regularly brought to its attention. The tribunal could conduct its own investigations or cause investigations to be conducted on its behalf. It could direct the commissioner of police to carry out investigations or make further investigations and to report his or her findings to the PCT. Other powers included the power to decide if any material before it should be published. The tribunal could compel the attendance of witnesses, compel the production of documents, carry out inspections, take views, receive evidence on oath or affirmation and do all other things necessary to enable it to discharge its functions (*Police Complaints Tribunal Act 1982*).

If the PCT was dissatisfied with the final result of a matter it had dealt with, it could determine whether a public statement should be made about its dissatisfaction. The tribunal could recommend that a prosecution ought to be considered in relation to a complaint or matter and then adopt a "watchdog" role in terms of whether or not prosecution occurred. If it felt strongly enough about a prosecution decision, it could report publicly and explain its dissatisfaction to the community (*Police Complaints Tribunal Act 1982*).

In terms of the necessary features an ideal oversight body should have (outlined in Chapter Four), the Tribunal did lack:

- the ability to receive complaints from police about the alleged misconduct of other police;
- the ability to be advised of all complaints lodged with the police;
- the power to appeal any disciplinary sanction imposed by the police;
- the right to monitor and supervise any investigations the police were conducting into complaints against police; and
- the ability to refer serious matters to a disciplinary tribunal.

But even if the PCT had been granted all of these powers, it would not have been possible to exercise them without adequate resources.

Failure to detect corruption

But the problems surrounding the PCT did not stop with structure, composition and adequate resources. Other reasons which help to explain its failure as a police accountability institution can be found in the Annual Reports from year ended 30 June 1984 to 30 June 1987. During that period it appears that the tribunal had been co-opted by the police accountability policy community and, like the government, had become an apologist for the police. For example, in 1984 it reported that "The Tribunal feels that the number and nature of the complaints does suggest that a high standard of police behaviour and adherence to regulations is being kept in Queensland" (Police Complaints Tribunal 1984, 72).

In relation to complaints about insensitivity and incivility, the Tribunal suggested that "many times, it would appear that the officer may have been careless in his selection of words or the complainant may have misinterpreted the police officer's intention". When discussing complaints about a police officer not abiding by the law and providing his or her name on request or giving an "incorrect" name, the tribunal explained that "At times misunderstandings have arisen and names given have been distorted by traffic and/or other noises. In some instances, the complainant has merely not heard or forgotten the officer's name". The list of excuses for police incivility or misconduct continues. When addressing the number of complaints received in respect to constables who had only been police officers for a few years and the cynicism they displayed when dealing with the community, the tribunal suggested the explanation was "the constant stress of dealing with law-breakers, combined with the stress of modern living [and the] personal toll [it takes] on members of the Force" (Police Complaints Tribunal 1984, 73).

In its 1985 *Annual Report* the Tribunal found it necessary to make the point that, "Members are satisfied that the picture sometimes painted, suggesting the Queensland Police Force is generally corrupt, overly aggressive or covers up misdemeanours by its officers, cannot be supported by the facts and figures. The Tribunal takes the view that the contrary is the case" (Police Complaints Tribunal 1985, 85).

Given the extent of police misconduct revealed at the Fitzgerald Inquiry, it is obvious that the network of corruption which reached into the highest echelons of the force was flourishing for much of the life of the Police Complaints Tribunal. However, despite repeated allegations of police corruption by Labor opposition members in the parliament and by the media, between 1983 and 1988 the Tribunal repeatedly rejected suggestions of widespread corruption within the Queensland Police Force and that the force had been covering-up misconduct. The public and police distrust of the tribunal was such that not one substantial complaint of corruption was ever lodged with it and, despite the PCT's ability to do so, it never attempted to initiate any investigations into allegations of corruption and misconduct. As the Labor opposition member Rod Welford explained, the tribunal "was seen as a political device to suppress what would have been genuine inquiries into serious allegations of misconduct" (Queensland, Legislative Assembly 1990, *Debates*, 10 May, 1348).

Perhaps the most celebrated case to come before the Police Complaints Tribunal was the Barry Mannix case. Barry Mannix was charged with the murder of his father in July 1984 and, in October of the same year, was committed for trial and remanded in custody. However, on 8 November three other people were charged with the murder. On 15 November Barry Mannix lodged a complaint with the Police Complaints Tribunal, alleging six breaches of the *Criminal Code* by police. They included: deprivation of liberty, assault, threats to compel a confession to murder, fabrication of evidence and perjury. On 16 November he sought and was granted bail. On 21 November a fourth person was charged with his father's murder. On 6 December the Attorney-General filed a "No True Bill" with respect to the charges against Mannix. Mannix's complaint to the PCT alleged that he was held by police for 12 to 13 hours, during which time he was subjected to threats and assaults by police and, when physically and mentally exhausted, had made two untrue written confessions in relation to the murder of his father. Mannix implied that he made these confessions because he was subjected to ill-treatment by police (Police Complaints Tribunal 1986b). The Police Complaints Tribunal found no charges against any police officer. With much irony, Labor Party opposition member Tom Burns described the Mannix Report as "the showpiece of the Tribunal's reports; the most remarkable document ever compiled by a police review authority" (Queensland, Legislative Assembly 1987, *Debates*, 14 Oct, 3178).

Findings such as these added to the growing distrust of and lack of respect for the tribunal. So too did the fact that tribunal reports (excluding Annual Reports) did not have to be tabled in parliament. Indeed, the police minister did not even have to admit whether or not he had received a report.

Lessons to be learned

As the evidence presented in this chapter suggests, several factors contributed to the ineffectiveness of Queensland's first external civilian oversight body. The government established it for the wrong reason: to create an illusion that complaints against police were being properly investigated rather than to ensure that they were. As Judge Morley explained, over time the "tribunal was identified by the public as not the standing civilian Commission of Inquiry which its Act created, but as an agency of the Police Force" (Police Complaints Tribunal 1989, 4).

Its membership, initially three and subsequently four part-time members, was inadequate for the task. Some appointments were entirely inappropriate. The longest serving member of the tribunal, the President of the Police Union, was in a conflict of interest situation throughout his seven year tenure. The longest serving chairperson, Judge Eric Pratt, was described by the then police commissioner as a "special friend" and it appears the commissioner of police used his influence with government in the selection of some members. In theory the Tribunal may have been independent of the police. In practice it was not. Because the government failed to adequately resource it, it had to rely on what was an inept police internal investigation section to investigate all complaints against police.

Nor was the Police Complaints Tribunal independent of the government. It was responsible to the police minister rather than the parliament or a parliamentary committee.

Another factor which led to the inevitable failure of the PCT was the politicisation of the policing function. A politicised police force brings the power of the police and police-government relations into play in a way that has negative consequences for accountability. Police power is increased when the Force receives almost unconditional backing from government. Even if an oversight body is dedicated to ensuring effective oversight, when its aims conflict with the mutual objectives of police and government it will find it extremely difficult to deliver effective accountability.

However, it seems that for most of its life the PCT was willingly captured by the police and government. The problem was not counterproductive tensions in the relationship between oversight body and government and oversight body and police but rather the consensual nature of the association between all three players. This association led Fitzgerald (1989, 290) to describe the Tribunal as "an illustration of an administrative body with the superficial trappings of quasi-judicial impartiality and independence set up as a facade for government power". It was, he said, "regarded by corrupt police as impotent . . . [had] lost all public confidence [and was] seen as an apologist for the Police Force" (1989, 292). Furthermore, it was "ineradicably tarnished with a deservedly poor reputation" which had "almost certainly" reduced the number of complaints made to it (1989, 292). He recommended that it be closed down.

Conclusion

This case study of the Police Complaints Tribunal shows how the politicisation of the policing function skewered government intent toward protecting police at the expense of effective accountability. Under these circumstances, external civilian oversight bodies are used as a smokescreens to blur the difference between theory and practice. Governments grant the oversight body many of the core reactive powers outlined in Chapter Four but deny it the resources to operationalise those powers. They also undermine the oversight agency's ability to be effective by the people appointed and re-appointed as members.

But what happens when the power of the police is negated and the government is virtually forced, through electoral pressure, into establishing a new and innovative external, independent, civilian oversight body, a body which reports to the parliament, not government, is adequately resourced, has the capacity to be both proactive and reactive in a meaningful way, and whose personnel are not only independent but are perceived by the community to be so? These questions are addressed in the following three chapters which present a case study of Queensland's second attempt at civilian oversight of the complaints against police process: the Criminal Justice Commission.

The next chapter analyses the unusual set of conditions which facilitated the establishment of this unique and powerful external, independent, civilian oversight body, and Chapter Eight provides a mainly descriptive account of its structure, powers and functions. This is done, in part, to offer a more complete understanding of the consequences of oversight body-government relations which are analysed in Chapter Nine.

7

CREATING THE CONDITIONS

Introduction

Impediments to effective civilian oversight can often be traced to the compromises reached between police and government at the formulation stage of the policy process. They include resources, powers, coverage and support. Queensland's second attempt at civilian oversight, the Criminal Justice Commission was (initially) not subjected to these problems. They were overcome by the extraordinary *Commission of Inquiry into Possible Illegal Activities and Associated Police Misconduct* (The Fitzgerald Inquiry). It not only recommended the establishment of an external, independent, civilian oversight body, it also provided a detailed blueprint of the model to be implemented.

The Fitzgerald Inquiry was established in May 1987 to respond to allegations by former and serving officers that the Queensland Police Force had been ignoring, condoning and profiting from criminal activity. The allegations were made on the nationally broadcast *Four Corners* program, *The Moonlight State.* In the absence of the Premier Sir Joh Bjelke-Petersen, the Deputy Premier and Police Minister Bill Gunn, agreed to establish an inquiry, which it was suggested would sit for six weeks. Ultimately it lasted for two years. Its effect went far beyond any other inquiry into police-related issues in Australia.

The Fitzgerald Inquiry altered the nature of police-government relations, the power of the police and the police union. It also effected the results of an election and the policy agenda of an incoming government. This chapter describes and analyses this unprecedented outcome. It does so because the Fitzgerald Inquiry went beyond recommending extensive reform of the police force and the establishment of a powerful and new form of civilian oversight body, the Criminal Justice Commission. It also established the conditions that allowed for its creation.

The Fitzgerald Inquiry and police-government relations

Queenslanders could be forgiven for thinking that nothing much would change as a result of the Fitzgerald Inquiry. Over the previous 25 years there had been four inquiries into police, all of which proved to be illusions of action.[1] They did nothing to improve police accountability processes; but then they were not designed to. Rather, they typified what Prasser (1994, 13-14) claims are an array of responses developed by governments "to control inquiries and effectively neutralise them". These tactics include limiting the terms of reference, ignoring recommendations and establishing bureaucratic committees to examine suggested reforms.

The unsatisfactory and unproductive outcomes of the previous inquiries made the community, the legal profession and honest police sceptical about yet another attempt to deal with police malfeasance. So too did Police Commissioner Lewis's initial reaction to the *Four Corners* program, which was to claim that, "neither I nor any of my senior officers believe the Queensland Police Force is corrupt . . . since the inception of the [Police Complaints] Tribunal in 1982 not one complaint of police corruption about an officer has been lodged" (quoted in Whitton 1989, 123). Many people decided to adopt a wait-and-see approach to the Inquiry. However, it showed signs of being different from the start.

Mr Gerald Edward (Tony) Fitzgerald QC agreed to head it, on the proviso that he be given adequate resources, the ability to widen the terms of reference, indemnities for informants and independence from the bureaucracy (Whitton 1989, 125). Deputy Premier Gunn agreed to these conditions and the government honoured his commitment. For the duration of the Inquiry resources were adequate. The terms of reference were widened on two occasions and indemnities were granted which helped to weaken the code of silence. Those police, who for years had

---

1 The four inquiries into police-related issues in Queensland between 1963 and 1985 were:

The Royal Commission into Rumours of Police Misconduct in Relation to the National Hotel (The Gibbs Inquiry) 1964, Brisbane (see Dickie 1989; Whitton 1989 and Fitzgerald 1989).

Inquiry into Allegation of Police Misconduct in Relation to SP Bookmaking at Southport (The O'Connell Inquiry) 1977 (report not released). For further details on the Southport Betting case, see Fitzgerald 1989, 38-41; Dickie 1989, 52-54.

Committee of Inquiry into the Enforcement of Criminal Law in Queensland 1977 (The Lucas Inquiry) (see Fitzgerald 1989).

Sturgess Inquiry into Sexual Offences Involving Children and Related Matters 1985 (The Sturgess Inquiry) (see Wanna 1991; Dickie 1989; Fitzgerald 1989).

demanded so-called loyalty to the code from other police, were quick to abandon the principle to protect their own self-interest.

Public sittings commenced on 3 July 1987. The first person called was Commissioner Lewis. After reading from a prepared statement, which extolled the virtues of the Force, Lewis dropped "the first bombshell". He explained how he had received verbal instructions from successive police ministers and the Premier that police were to give a low priority to brothels which were run in "a tolerable manner". He further explained that "uniformly the policy as to prostitution has been put on the basis that prostitution was to be contained and controlled" (Dickie 1989, 193-94). Former and serving ministers immediately tried either to distance themselves from Lewis's allegations or refused to comment (*Courier-Mail* 28 July 1987). The Commissioner's remarks may have been designed to unite the fortunes of the government and its police force. However, they had the opposite effect – "a serious rift" started to develop (Dickie 1989, 194).

A crisis, in the form of the Fitzgerald Inquiry, was splitting the previously cohesive and closed policy community. For the first time since Lewis's appointment as commissioner, key members of it started to disagree publicly about whether there had been an agreed agenda in relation to the policing of vice. More public disagreements were to follow.

The Commissioner was followed into the witness box by Deputy Commissioner Ron Redmond. He confirmed Lewis's assertion that there was a government policy to contain and control prostitution. He then dropped his own bombshell by adding that Police Minister Bill Gunn had said that brothels served a useful purpose. To counter Redmond's statement, Counsel for the Queensland Government Ian Callinan QC suggested that the police minister's comment related to the role brothels played in helping to gather criminal information, and that Gunn may have gained that impression from the police commissioner. Callinan also managed to get an admission from the deputy commissioner that neither the law nor the police oath of service allowed for a control and containment policy (Dickie 1989, 195-96). The implication was that police were operationally independent when enforcing the law, therefore, the way in which they chose to deal with prostitution laws was their decision, it had nothing to do with the government. The government's counsel also tried to convey the impression that the police department, in particular the police commissioner, had misled police ministers and the Premier over the true state of vice in Queensland. This may have been true. Nevertheless, given the history of police-government relations during the Lewis-Bjelke-Petersen era (1976-1987), it was not going to be easy for the police administration to try to shift the blame by saying it had simply been enforcing government policy, or for the government to argue that it had only acted on the best advice of the commissioner of police. Neither party had maintained a proper arm's-length relationship with the other.

Over the next few months several indemnified police, mainly connected to the Licensing Branch, admitted to receiving corrupt payments from SP bookmakers and Queensland's brothel operators. As the Inquiry started to uncover the organised, vertical nature of police corruption there were calls for the police commissioner to resign. When indemnified Assistant Commissioner Graeme Parker admitted he was corrupt, the calls for Lewis's resignation increased. On 21 September 1987, four months after the Fitzgerald Inquiry commenced public hearings, Commissioner Lewis was stood down for the duration of the Inquiry. The government was now in damage control mode.

The last person to take the stand at the Fitzgerald Inquiry was Sir Joh Bjelke-Petersen.[2] He gave evidence that at no time did he suspect elements of the police service or its commissioner were involved in corrupt activities. Nor did he draw any connections between corruption within the force and a politicised police force. His evidence also revealed that Sir Joh did not appear to understand the principles of the doctrine of the separation of powers. Indeed, he seemed to be ignorant of the concept.

By the time the Inquiry's public sittings had finished, it was not only the politics of mutual admiration between police and government which had come to an end. Fitzgerald exposed a system in which crime and corruption ranged across activities including prostitution, the running of sex parlours and brothels, illegal gambling, SP betting, bribery, the rorting of ministerial expenses,[3] protection rackets and money laundering (Coaldrake 1989b, 156). However, before all of the crime and corruption had been exposed, the National Party decided to change leaders. The change in leadership from Sir Joh Bjelke-Petersen to Mike Ahern may have had unintended consequences for some National Party parliamentarians. It

---

2 Sir Joh Bjelke-Petersen was initially charged with one count of official corruption and one count of perjury, but the Crown elected to proceed with only the perjury charge. The perjury related to evidence he had given to the Fitzgerald Inquiry about monies given to Sir Joh by an Asian business man (see page 89 of the Fitzgerald report for a brief summary of events surrounding the incident). The jury deadlocked and the Director of Public Prosecutions decided not to hold another trial because of Bjelke-Petersen's age and the belief that overseas witnesses would not return for a retrial (*Sun Herald* 21 Feb 1993, 28).

3 Four former ministers in the National Party Government were subsequently found guilty of corrupt activities and served time in jail.

ensured that unlike the four previously mentioned inquiries into police conduct, the Fitzgerald Inquiry's recommendations would be fully implemented.

The Fitzgerald Report

When he took over as Premier, Ahern inherited all of the difficulties surrounding the Fitzgerald Inquiry, an inheritance which constituted a continual threat to his leadership and the National Party's electoral chances (Cribb 1991, 116). Despite this Premier Ahern, to his great credit, wholeheartedly supported the Inquiry and all that it was trying to achieve (Coaldrake 1989b, 160; Cribb 1991, 116). However, he was panicked into promising to implement the recommendations of the Fitzgerald Report "lock, stock and barrel", a promise he made *before* the report had been completed.[4] Ahern's commitment reflects the status which the Fitzgerald Inquiry had gained, but also the desperation of the National Party to stay in power. It also meant that the leaders of Queensland's other political parties were forced to give their unequivocal commitment to implement Fitzgerald's recommendations. Such were the somewhat bizarre politics of the time. Bizarre because in the lead-up to a state election all political parties were locked into implementing the recommendations of a report which was still in the process of being written.

When the report was presented, it was venerated by Queenslanders and seen as the bible for a new era of police, public sector and political accountability (Wanna 1991, 209). Fitzgerald's report emphasised the need for innovative, proactive, long-term measures to try and change police and political culture. This contrasted sharply with the traditional big stick, quick fix approach to misconduct issues.

The tight time frame between the tabling of the report (July 1989) and the state election (December 1989) did not allow the government the opportunity to distance itself from its politically damaging findings which, inter alia, found there was corruption, impropriety and mismanagement within the police department; that the police union had a disproportionate influence on government policy; and that an improper relationship between police and government existed which allowed such conditions to flourish. The report also identified shortcomings in Queensland's

---

4 In fairness to Ahern, it should be mentioned that the "lock, stock and barrel" promise was originally made by a member of Ahern's staff. But when journalists questioned him about it, his advisers thought it would do more political damage to vary the pledge than it would to go along with the staff member's comments.

parliamentary process, a lack of external controls or internal supervision in relation to ministerial expenses, and the need for major improvements in the area of administrative law and human rights.

In the first few months following the release of the Fitzgerald Report, Russell Cooper successfully challenged Mike Ahern for the leadership of the National Party. Initially Cooper tried to distance his government from having to fully implement all of Fitzgerald's recommendations. He announced the establishment of a special committee, the Premier's Independent Commission for Change and Reform (PICCAR) to "supervise" the Fitzgerald reform process. Public reaction to the setting up of PICCAR was swift and hostile. There were allegations that it was a "sham" and a "farce of the highest order and worthy of a *Yes Minister* script" (*Courier-Mail* 27 Sept 1989). The public outcry which followed the announcement of PICCAR left Cooper and his party in little doubt that to continue down a path which deviated from the prescribed reform agenda would be electoral suicide (Cribb 1991, 123; Wanna 1991, 214).

Cooper's premiership only lasted some two-and-a-half months. After 32 years in the political wilderness, the Labor Party swept to power. But much of its policy agenda had been set for it by the Fitzgerald Report. Two new important institutions, the Electoral and Administrative Review Commission and a Criminal Justice Commission had already been established, with their frameworks and agendas being set by Fitzgerald and not the government.

Inheriting from a commission of inquiry a comprehensive policy agenda in the politically sensitive area of criminal justice, which included wholesale reform of the police force and the establishment of an important accountability institution which had jurisdiction over the conduct of police, other public servants and politicians, had consequences for the relationship which developed between the CJC, and government. This issue is dealt with in Chapter Nine.

The circumstances surrounding the establishment of the CJC were exceptional in terms of the policy process. But other factors also contributed to the conditions which facilitated the setting up of this powerful and unique external, independent civilian oversight body. These were the power of the police and the police union's attitude to Fitzgerald's recommendations.

Power of the police

The fact that the Criminal Justice Commission was the direct result of a recommendation from a commission of inquiry is not unusual. Many other oversight institutions in the United States, Britain, Canada and Australia have been established by a similar ad hoc approach to accountability. But invariably police have been able to successfully bargain with governments to lessen the civilian accountability institution's legislative powers. So what was different in Queensland in 1989? The Criminal Justice Commission is a very powerful independent, external civilian oversight body and, in terms of its structure and functions, is unique in the world. Why was there virtually no resistance to the establishment of the CJC by the Queensland police hierarchy or the police union or even an attempt to horse-trade? The reaction by the Queensland police stands in stark contrast to the overt opposition displayed by the police in New York and Philadelphia and the more subtle bartering approach adopted by the police in the United Kingdom, Canada and other Australian states to the introduction of much less powerful bodies with more limited functions.

Before the Fitzgerald Inquiry, the power of the Queensland police had been centralised. To a degree it was held by the commissioner of police who had direct access to the premier and, it can be argued, was protected by his patronage. The police union, particularly members from the Criminal Intelligence Branch, also had considerable influence and power within the department. Indeed, the police union was so influential that it has been alleged by a veteran senior police officer that pre-Fitzgerald, it could influence the direction of a person's career.

However, by the time Lewis was stood down as police commissioner, the police department's power had all but dissipated. Control of, and influence over, police issues had shifted to the Inquiry. The department continued to operate and handle the day-to-day policing functions but all important managerial and administrative decisions were made by the Inquiry. Fitzgerald was consulted at all times and directed how things should operate (interview with Queensland Commissioner of Police Mr Jim O'Sullivan). In effect, he had become "the de facto commissioner of police" (interview with former president of Queensland Police Union of Employees, Senior Sergeant John O'Gorman). He also became the de facto police minister as the government had virtually ceased making any policy decisions in relation to police until after Fitzgerald had brought down his blueprint for reform and, as mentioned earlier, it and the alternative government had already committed themselves to fully implementing the policies recommended by Fitzgerald.

Attitude of police union

The Fitzgerald Inquiry also had the effect of reducing the power of the police union. Then Senior Sergeant (now Inspector) John O'Gorman became president of the union a few days before Fitzgerald brought down his report, but because the previous president Colin Chant had suffered ill health for some time, O'Gorman had been involved in most discussions with the Inquiry. When asked why the union had not even tried to bargain with the government over the functions and powers of the CJC, O'Gorman explained that "the union didn't really have anything to horse-trade. In terms of the public perception we had a stable full of criminals" (interview with former president of Queensland Police Union of Employees, Senior Sergeant John O'Gorman).

Even though O'Gorman emphatically believes that was not the case, he acknowledged that it was the position the Queensland police force had to get back from. The union, he said, "had to live with the reality that police were seen to have sunk into the mud, we had to get ourselves washed off and get back to our job". To do this "the union had to swallow the bitter pill that we had criminals masquerading as police officers and that kicked a lot of us around" (interview with former president of Queensland Police Union of Employees, Senior Sergeant John O'Gorman). These realities weakened any bargaining position the union may have had.

But O'Gorman maintains that the position adopted by the union was not so much a negative one of having to go along with the reforms because there was no alternative, rather, it was a positive pro-Fitzgerald approach motivated by the desire to win back public support for the police service. As he explained, the union recognised that:

> The Fitzgerald Inquiry was a watershed, not only in police history but in Queensland history. Therefore, it had to stand back and have a good hard look at all that Fitzgerald had uncovered and recommended. We had to throw it into neutral, let it come to a stop and start again because what we had before hadn't worked. A complaints system controlled by the police would not have the faith of the public and would have been resisted by various pressure groups . . . and the Police Complaints Tribunal among all the rest hadn't worked. (interview with former president of Queensland Police Union of Employees, Senior Sergeant John O'Gorman)

The will was there to support something that would work.

Fitzgerald's recommendations concerning the CJC were examined by the union, and even though there were reservations about certain aspects of the model, the decision was made to support it. O'Gorman also added that:

> [He] didn't want to go down in history as the president of a union that had the opportunity to help clean up the police, and put things in place that would help to keep it clean, and then abandon it all for the sake of some coppers saying – oh wasn't he a tough bugger – what a hero. (interview with former president of Queensland Police Union of Employees, Senior Sergeant John O'Gorman).

O'Gorman firmly believes that the union gained more respect from rank and file police and from the community they serve by supporting the Fitzgerald reform process than it would have by simply making a lot of negative noises. Throughout O'Gorman's presidency the union continued to strongly support the reform process and one of its central planks, the Criminal Justice Commission. However, it should be noted that even though O'Gorman supported the concept of a CJC, that support was not universal throughout the QPS. Rumours about the dire consequences for Queensland police and the policing function from the establishment of an external, independent civilian oversight body were commonplace. But with the union on-side it proved impossible for disgruntled police officers to mobilise a movement against the CJC. O'Gorman and the union executive's stand adds weight to the argument that unions are important players in any reform process. Their input is not always negative.

Conclusion

The Fitzgerald Inquiry stands as an almost unique reminder to the community of what can be achieved when governments are not indirectly operating a commission of inquiry's control levers through limited terms of reference, inadequate resources and an unrealistic time-frame. In this instance, an inquiry which was established to look at possible police misconduct and associated matters ended up covering the way in which units of public administration did business in Queensland and outlining a blueprint for reform of the police service and parts of the political system. A precedent has been set in terms of community expectations which suggests that it may not be as easy for governments to stonewall the introduction of similar inquiries into police misconduct, to indirectly control them or to ignore their recommendations to the degree they have in the past. If this proves to be the case police accountability could be improved.

The Fitzgerald legacy also demonstrates that when the power of the police hierarchy and police union is neutralised, and the union supports the need for reform, it is possible to introduce a civilian oversight model in which the structure, functions and lines of accountability are based on the perceived requirements for effective, ongoing accountability and reform, rather than on the art of compromise, which has influenced the legislative framework of many other oversight bodies.

Because of the status afforded the Fitzgerald Report, it was not immediately electorally viable for the government to grant the CJC the powers and functions outlined by Fitzgerald but to undermine them by not adequately resourcing the Commission. In this respect, the Fitzgerald Inquiry also demonstrates what is possible when electoral imperatives transcend police-government relations. When this happens, government intent is skewed toward political survival and in 1989 in Queensland that survival was tied to effective police and public sector accountability, as detailed by Fitzgerald.

The adoption of a policy based on some notion of a rational plan rather than on concessions to the powerful police lobby group could see the introduction of new models for oversighting the complaints against police; models similar to the CJC, which has the capacity to be proactive and reactive, and which also has responsibility for working with police to review and implement reforms on a continuous basis. It is not being suggested that other jurisdictions slavishly adhere to the CJC blueprint. However, because it concentrates on dealing with the cause as well as symptoms of police misconduct, the Criminal Justice Commission model offers a unique opportunity to improve police behaviour and police accountability in the long term – governments willing. As the following chapter demonstrates it has much to recommend it to policy makers interested in effective police accountability.

8

THE CRIMINAL JUSTICE COMMISSION

Introduction

The models used to oversight complaints against police are gradually changing. These days many can monitor, supervise and reinvestigate police investigations and, in some jurisdictions, can conduct their own investigation from the outset. Even though progression along Petterson's theoretical spectrum has not been uniformly linear, the trend has been from left to right: that is away from police-controlled systems and toward greater civilian involvement in the process.

Queensland's Criminal Justice Commission sits to the extreme right-hand side of the spectrum in terms of its reactive powers and has many of the characteristics of the Civilian External Investigatory/Adjudicative and Civilian Review models discussed in Chapter Four. On a theoretical spectrum defining proactive powers, the CJC may well prove to be the most innovative oversight body yet established and when its reactive and proactive powers and functions are combined, it can be argued that there never has been a similar accountability institution. Unlike many of the models discussed to date, the CJC is not a variation on a theme. It was a bold attempt by the Fitzgerald Inquiry (1989) to put structures and processes into place which would guard, as much as possible, against history simply repeating itself once the Commission of Inquiry and all that it revealed became yesterday's news. The CJC has many exceptional features and, external relations permitting, could well prove to be the parent model for a new generation of oversight body.

This chapter begins by outlining how the challenges facing Fitzgerald and his team led to the CJC model. It then discusses the current structure, functions, jurisdiction and accountability mechanisms which form its framework. The chapter is mainly descriptive as there is no detailed account of this unique approach to civilian oversight in the literature.

The challenge

After summarising and synthesising all of the information which had come to hand throughout his two year inquiry, Fitzgerald and his team set about creating an exceptional and particular organisation; one which could fulfil a multiplicity of important roles and functions on behalf of the people of Queensland; a body in which "the external overview and critical assessment of the Police Force" would be an important but not an "isolated factor" (Fitzgerald 1989, 308).

The challenge was to design a workable model which could effectively address a myriad of issues in a cohesive and integrated manner. The model had to draw together strands which had previously been unravelled or disconnected, while at the same time ensuring, as much as possible, that the new agency was immune from what the Inquiry had shown were the often negative and sometimes fatal effects of party politics.

The need to give an external, independent body responsibility for investigating, monitoring and reviewing complaints against police has been widely canvassed in previous chapters of this book. Thus, it is sufficient to say that the dismal failure of the police-controlled system for dealing with complaints against police led to the inevitable conclusion that any system which resided with the police service was doomed to fail. Referring to Queensland's Internal Investigation Section, the Fitzgerald Report noted that its approach was "a good indicator of the inability of police, without external independent supervision to act objectively and effectively when investigating each other" (1989, 289). It was decided, therefore, that the CJC should have an official misconduct division which, among other things, would deal with complaints against police in the traditional reactive manner.

Beyond police misconduct and corruption

The Inquiry revealed that official misconduct was not limited to the police. The cooperation of other public officials in key positions throughout various units of public administration is important to the success of the corrupt. Evidence was uncovered of other forms of public sector corruption and misconduct and the central role it played in facilitating major and organised crime (Fitzgerald 1989, 299). As a result, the CJC's Official Misconduct Division was not confined to handling complaints against the police. Similar to many Ombudsman models, it was also given responsibility for investigating official misconduct by other public servants. As there are often links between organised crime and official misconduct, the OMD was also charged with investigating major and organised crime.[1] Because the Fitzgerald Inquiry exposed the dubious and corrupt conduct of some politicians and the difficulty they had in delineating their private interests from their public duties, the OMD was also given the power to address allegations of official misconduct involving members of the Legislative Assembly, the Parliamentary Service and the Executive Council. As will be suggested in Chapter Nine, the ability to oversight the conduct of politicians has certainly prevented the fulfilment of Fitzgerald's idea of creating an accountability institution that would escape the negative effects of party politics.

The Inquiry team was aware that punishment alone had not and never could have a significant, long-term effect on the elimination of misconduct and corruption. Consequently, it was decided that the OMD should also have a corruption prevention function.[2] Along with its reactive, investigative role, the division was charged with undertaking a proactive educative or liaison function which offered advice and assistance on how to improve management systems and detect official misconduct in police and other public sector departments and agencies (Fitzgerald 1989, 314).

Who should control intelligence

Leaving aside matters of police misconduct and inefficiency, the Inquiry also found that Queensland's police information system was not and could not provide an effective intelligence service (Fitzgerald 1989, 317). When reviewing who should take control of the intelligence function, consideration was given to making it completely external to the police. However, concerns were expressed about the practical wisdom of such a move. It was felt that the idea would be so abhorrent to police that they would retaliate by refusing to contribute any information. If this were to happen, the effectiveness of any database would be greatly diminished. The compromise was that the CJC would control the pinnacle of

---

1 In May 1998 the Criminal Justice Commission's jurisdiction to investigate organised and major crime was removed. A new institution, the Queensland Crime Commission is now responsible for investigating such matters (See *Crimes Commission Act 1997*).

2 As noted earlier, the corruption prevention function was made the responsibility of a corruption prevention division in 1992. In 1998 this division was merged with the Research Division to form the Research and Prevention Division.

intelligence information and oversight the police intelligence function[3] (interview with senior member of Fitzgerald Inquiry).

What to do with witness protection

Witness protection was moved from the Police Service to the CJC for the very logical reason that it did not make sense to allow it to remain under the control of the police when some witnesses were giving evidence against them. It was considered "quite foolish" to expect the police department to perform this function, not because those involved in witness protection were considered corrupt, but because of the conflict of interest that would inevitably arise from such an arrangement (interview with senior member of Fitzgerald Inquiry).

The need for independent, publicly available research

Throughout the course of the Inquiry there was overwhelming, compelling and depressing evidence of research into criminal justice and related issues being deliberately buried in police headquarters and other Queensland Government departments. To ensure that this could not happen in the future, the Fitzgerald team decided that research relating to the criminal justice system had to be a function of the independent Criminal Justice Commission. Queensland needed a "fearless" research unit, one that "did not have to worry about party political agendas". The lessons of history had made it abundantly clear that only through an independent body would "politically sensitive issues be aired in public" (interview with senior member of Fitzgerald Inquiry).

Importantly, the CJC's research function is,

> [N]ot only independent in determining its agenda but also in selecting methods of research, preparation of reports and papers and publishing recommendations. Regardless of whether or not the recommendations accord with government policy, the process by which the reports are tabled in the Parliament guarantees that the public of Queensland is afforded access to results of the research. (Criminal Justice Commission 1991a, *Annual Report*, 62).

Mindful that the police reform process could easily flounder at the implementation stage of the policy process, the Fitzgerald team also gave

3 The *Crimes Commission Act 1997* removed the CJC's responsibility for gathering intelligence in relation to organised and major crime and its responsibility for monitoring the intelligence function of the QPS (Parliamentary Criminal Justice Committee 1998, 120-27).

the independent Research and Co-ordination Division[4] responsibility for continually reviewing the effectiveness of the police department's programs and methods.

Another consideration in determining the CJC model was the need to have an independent organisation look after the sensitive data that the Inquiry had uncovered throughout its two-year life.

The putting together of the Criminal Justice Commission model was not a rushed attempt at dealing with institutional corruption and incompetence by cobbling together bits and pieces of other models. It was a well considered approach to cleaning up a decaying police and wider public sector system and, more importantly perhaps, of introducing structures and processes to prevent the decay returning. It was recognised that a return to past arrangements (as happened after the previous four inquiries mentioned in Chapter Seven) would eventually rot the institutional framework of Queensland society and virtually guarantee that it became, in effect, a police state.

The remainder of this chapter is devoted to describing the CJC and how this powerful and unique organisation is held accountable for its actions. This serves to contrast the way in which the CJC differs from the more traditional models addressed by many writers, including Goldsmith, Kerstetter and West.

The chair and part-time commissioners

The Commission consists of a full-time chairperson and four part-time commissioners. The chair must be a person who has served, or is qualified for appointment as a judge of the Supreme Court of Queensland, the Supreme Court of any other state or territory of the Commonwealth, or the High Court or Federal Court of Australia (*Criminal Justice Act 1989*).

In terms of the four part-time commissioners, one has to be a practising legal practitioner who has demonstrated an interest and ability in civil liberty issues; of the remaining three, all must have demonstrated an interest and ability in community affairs and one must have proven senior managerial experience in a large organisation (*Criminal Justice Act 1989*). The background of the four part-time commissioners reflects Fitzgerald's attempt to subject a bureaucracy driven by legal considerations to non-legal input at the highest decision-making level, and to ensure that such a potentially powerful organisation is constantly aware of the civil libertarian implications of its decision.

---

4 Now the Research and Prevention Division.

The chairperson or a part-time commissioner cannot be appointed without the support of a majority of members of the Parliamentary Committee which monitors and reviews the CJC, the Parliamentary Criminal Justice Committee (PCJC), and that majority must not consist wholly of members of the political party or parties which form the government (*Criminal Justice Act 1989*, sections 11(3), (4); 12(4)). The minister responsible for the administrative and financial resources of the CJC (initially the Premier, then Attorney-General and now the Premier) is also obliged to consult with the chairperson when appointing part-time commissioners (*Criminal Justice Act 1989* section 12(3)). This serves to limit the government's input into the appointment of the Commission and is consistent with Fitzgerald's attempt to try to make the administration of criminal justice an apolitical function. Subject to certain qualifications, Commission members' tenure is for not less than two years but not more than five.

In addition to assisting with the general running of the organisation, part-time members also concentrate on particular functions of the CJC. This allows them to gain a level of expertise in certain key areas and helps to fulfil Fitzgerald's criteria that they should bring practical expertise to their role.

Staff of the CJC

As at 30 June 1998 the CJC has an approved establishment of 262 employees of which some 92 are seconded police officer (Criminal Justice Commission 1998, 80).[5] Its actual staff rates are broken up as follows: Official Misconduct Division 141; Corporate Services 40; Witness Protection 28; Intelligence 23; Research 18; Executive including Office of General Counsel 6; and Corruption Prevention 6 (Criminal Justice Commission 1998, 80).

The Commission staff are either employed for a finite period on contract or seconded from other public sector organisations for a fixed term.

Organisational units within the CJC

The Commission has the power to establish or disband organisational units and has done so from time to time. It currently has five divisions:

5 Police seconded to the CJC are bound by the secrecy provisions of the *Criminal Justice Act*. During the time of their secondment, they are not obliged to obey, provide information or to account to any other police officer save police seconded to the Commission.

Official Misconduct, Intelligence, Witness Protection, Research and Prevention and Corporate Services. With the exception of the Research and Prevention Division and the position of General Counsel which for a time was the Division of General Counsel, the organisational structure remain much the same as that recommended by Fitzgerald.

A brief description of the principal functions of those divisions and other key units in the CJC is outlined below.

The Official Misconduct Division

The Official Misconduct Division accounts for a little over half of the Commission's employees. It investigates alleged or suspected misconduct and official misconduct by police, alleged or suspected official misconduct by people holding office in other units of public administration and up until May 1998 investigated major and organised crime. The Division is not exclusively complaints driven, it can and does investigate matters on its own initiative. It also has a preventive role in that it offers advice or assistance by way of liaison or education to law enforcement bodies, units of public administration, companies, auditors and other people or institutions concerned with detecting and preventing official misconduct (*Criminal Justice Act 1989*).

OMD currently has two investigative complaints teams and four multidisciplinary teams.[6] If a matter is particularly complex or if it is envisaged that it will be a prolonged investigation the case is referred to a multidisciplinary team. Multidisciplinary teams (MDTs) are also used to support the Commission's public inquiries. They consist of lawyers, financial analysts, seconded police and intelligence analysts.

The *Criminal Justice Act* makes provision for the establishment of a Complaints Section within the OMD and for all matters relating to misconduct by police officers and official misconduct by officers in units of public administration to be forwarded to the Section for assessment. The Section consists of a chief officer, an assessment unit, two investigative complaints teams, a review unit, a senior financial analyst and support staff (Criminal Justice Commission 1995a, 110). The Commission assesses all complaints, including those that are anonymous. Depending

6 Before recent changes it also had a team which was part of the Joint Organised Crime Task Force (JOCTF) with the Queensland Police Service. The JOCTF, was established in December 1992, and was jointly managed by the CJC and the QPS. It comprised an equal number of CJC and QPS investigators and included intelligence analysts, financial analysts and legal staff (Criminal Justice Commission 1995a, 111). It was disbanded in 1998.

on how they are classified, the CJC conducts its own investigation from the outset and, in the case of police, also monitors, supervises or reviews investigations conducted by officers of the Queensland Police Service.

The Complaints Section's review function in terms of police is largely confined to matters relating to major incidents such as police shootings, high speed pursuits, serious injury or attempted suicides in police custody.

Its monitoring or supervising function is used when a complaint, assessed as possibly constituting criminal or official misconduct, is referred to the QPS for a preliminary investigation. This is mainly done when, for geographical and resource reasons, the CJC is unable to immediately attend. In such instances the CJC retains responsibility for the investigation and police have to follow strict and detailed CJC guidelines. They are advised who is to be interviewed and what aspects their report is to cover. Upon receipt of the police report, the complaint is subject to the normal assessment process and the officer(s), the subject of the complaint, is usually interviewed by CJC personnel.

As mentioned earlier, OMD also carries out proactive investigations. These often result from long-term analysis of intelligence and other information, or after material is received which suggests on-going misconduct or corruption.

Intelligence Division

The Intelligence Division's functions include the provision of specialist criminal intelligence data for official misconduct investigations and any other criminal activity which is beyond the scope of normal police investigations. It does this by creating and maintaining a database of intelligence information on criminal activities and on those who engage in it (Criminal Justice Commission 1995a, 9). The Division's data base is also used to provide support to investigations conducted by the OMD and other law enforcement agencies, to monitor trends in corruption, official misconduct and misconduct and to prepare strategic assessments. As well as collecting information from reactive investigations, the division has developed a proactive data collection strategy which allows it to adopt a more strategic approach to serious police corruption issues (Criminal Justice Commission 1998, 70). In discharging its functions, Intelligence is obliged to ensure the security and confidentiality of its database and records.

Stringent restrictions apply to access and entitlement to access information. Data is reviewed in administrative files every two years and criminal intelligence files every five years. There is an instruction that data should be "purged" if it is no longer relevant, no longer useful, out of date, inaccurate or incorrect. The dissemination of all material from intelligence to external agencies is audited quarterly by a principal analyst of the data management section and twice a year by the Director of Intelligence. The Intelligence Division is externally audited by the Parliamentary Criminal Justice Committee and the Parliamentary Criminal Justice Commissioner. The *Crimes Commission Act 1997* makes the Parliamentary Criminal Justice Commissioner responsible for reviewing annually the Commission's intelligence data. The purpose of the review is to: consider the appropriateness of the data held by the Commission; whether it unnecessarily duplicates data held by the Crimes Commission and/or the Queensland Police Service: and the level of cooperation which exists between the three agencies (Parliamentary Criminal Justice Committee 1998, 122).

Witness Protection Division

The Witness Protection Division which is staffed by police officers seconded to the CJC provides a witness protection service to people assisting the CJC or other law enforcement agencies with their investigations. In doing so it provides a 24-hour lifeline for witnesses, offers on-call protection and close personal protection and, if necessary, relocates and provides new identities (Criminal Justice Commission 1995a, 9). These services are offered on a long- or short-term basis depending on particular needs. Since it was established in 1989, the division has provided protection to 694 people (CJC 1998, 74).

The chairperson of the CJC has ultimate responsibility for the Division but the day-to-day management has been delegated to the Director of Operations, who is also an assistant commissioner of police seconded to the CJC. The Division operates with three teams which share responsibility for the protection of various witnesses. The Division is also obliged to maintain a register on persons who have assumed new identities. The only persons permitted to access the register are the chairperson and executive director of the CJC and the director of the Witness Protection Division.

Research and Prevention Division

Much of the work of the Research and Prevention Division has been addressed in Chapter Four. In summary, the Research and Prevention Division conducts research and makes recommendations about matters which have, or could have, an impact on the administration of criminal justice in Queensland. It is also obliged to monitor, review and oversight, on a continuing basis, the effectiveness of QPS programs, particularly those relating to the CJC's recommendations or policy instructions on community policing, crime prevention and matters affecting the selection, recruitment, training and career progression of members of the police service. Another function of the Division is to prepare reports and suggest directions and/or remedial action to the commissioner of police on matters arising from its research. When undertaking these functions, the Division takes into account the activities, findings and recommendations of agencies outside Queensland which are also concerned with the administration of criminal justice (*Criminal Justice Act 1989*).

The Division's corruption prevention function includes an educative role in that it offers and gives advice and assistance to the police and other units of public administration in relation to the detection and prevention of official misconduct. The Research and Prevention Division is also engaged in promoting proactive strategies to Queensland's police and the wider public sector. This is done, in part by advising principal officers and boards of management on how best to meet their obligation to report alleged official misconduct. The Division also advises management on ways to reduce exposure to official misconduct through risk management assessments.

Corporate Services Division

Corporate Services supports the work of the CJC through the development and implementation of human resource and administrative policies and procedures; by making recommendations to assist the CJC meet its organisational, staffing and budgetary needs and by establishing procedures to meet external and internal accountability obligations (Criminal Justice Commission 1998, 7).

Other key units

Other key units within the CJC are the Office of General Counsel, the Office of the Commission and Commissioner for Police Service Reviews.

Office of General Counsel

The Office of General Counsel provides advice and representation to the Commission, the Chairperson and all Divisions. The Office consists of the General Counsel, the Official Solicitor and a support officer.

Office of the Commission

The Office of the Commission provides secretarial support to the Criminal Justice Commission and coordinates accountability processes and corporate governance procedures. It is answerable to the Executive Director who heads the Corporate Services Division but it is not a part of that Division (Criminal Justice Commission 1998, 7).

The Media and Communication manager forms part of the Office of the Commission. The manager is responsible for acting as the primary point of contact for media inquiries and for facilitating media conferences and interviews with CJC staff. He/she provides media releases on CJC activities and publications and initiates stories about the Commission's activities through metropolitan, regional and national media outlets. The manager also responds to a multitude of requests for information across Australia. By having its own Media and Communications manager, the CJC is able to accurately inform the community about the work of the Commission. This helps to raise the public's awareness about the role of the Commission and how it functions.

Commissioner for Police Service Reviews

The CJC's part-time commissioners and former part-time commissioners act as Commissioners for Police Service Reviews. The review commissioners hear applications from aggrieved police personnel in relation to QPS decisions about promotions, transfers, stand downs, suspensions, dismissals (other than for misconduct) and disciplinary sanctions (other than for findings of misconduct or official misconduct). Review commissioners can only make recommendations, but if the commissioner of police does not act on a recommendation, he or she must briefly summarise the reasons why, and forward the explanation to the parties involved, including the review commissioner.

In accordance with the non-adversarial, informal nature of these proceedings (legal counsel is not permitted), the process is based on written submissions being exchanged before a hearing. The purpose of the hearing is to clarify and highlight matters of disquiet in terms of the selection process and/or in the case of promotions, the relative merits of the parties (Criminal Justice Commission 1998, 20).

CJC powers

The Criminal Justice Commission is a standing commission of inquiry. Its investigative powers are certainly wider than those bestowed on police. However, most are no greater than other bodies engaged in the oversighting of the complaints against police and other public servants. For example, the following CJC powers are common to the vast majority of police oversight bodies in Australia. They include:

- the ability to require a person to furnish a statement of information in relation to an investigation;
- the power to compel the production of records and things appertaining to an investigation;
- the ability to summons a person to attend and to give evidence;
- the power to conduct a hearing and to compel witnesses to give evidence on oath and to produce documents;
- the power to compel a person attending before the commission to furnish a statement of information, to give evidence and to reproduce records and things, notwithstanding that compliance could incriminate a person or would mean that the person was breaching a statutory duty or obligation to maintain confidentiality. The information supplied cannot be used against the person in a civil, criminal or disciplinary proceeding and cannot render a person liable for breach of the statute or obligation or to disciplinary action (Criminal Justice Commission 1991a, 9).

Unlike the National Crime Authority, the Australian Federal Police, the New South Wales Crime Commission, New South Wales Police Service, the New South Wales ICAC, the New South Wales Police Integrity Commission the Victorian Police and the South Australian Police, the CJC does not have telecommunication interception powers. In a 1995 issues paper (Criminal Justice Commission 1995f), the Commission argued that it, and the QPS, should be granted these powers. The CJC claimed that on the available evidence, telephone tapping powers would enhance its ability to combat major and organised crime, that telecommunication interception was less intrusive and more cost-effective than other forms of electronic surveillance already allowed for under Queensland law, and that it was inappropriate and impractical for the CJC and the QPS to be solely reliant on the cooperation of Commonwealth law enforcement agencies to access these types of powers (Criminal Justice Commission 1995f, 39). The Borbidge Government did introduce the Telecommunications (Interception) Queensland Bill into the parliament in March 1998. However, before the Bill was passed an election was called and the National-Liberal Party Coalition lost power. At the time of writing the Beattie Government, which has been in office for 12 months, has not acted to grant the Commission these powers .

The CJC does have some exceptional powers. When conducting an investigation it can apply to a judge of the Supreme Court for authority, to take possession of instruments of title and financial documents and to take possession of a passport or other travel documents. The CJC also has the power to copy and inspect bank records and records from financial institutions, insurance companies and stock and share brokers. A person holding an appointment in a unit of public administration, and any person associated with that person, can be required to furnish an affidavit relating to their assets (Criminal Justice Commission 1995c). Even though these powers are exceptional in terms of many police oversight bodies, the Police Integrity Commission in New South Wales, which deals with matters of serious police misconduct, has similar and potentially more oppressive powers.

CJC and politicians

As mentioned earlier, the Criminal Justice Commission's power with regard to elected officials extends to members of the state's Legislative Assembly, the Parliamentary Service, the Executive Council and local government members and officials (*Criminal Justice Act* 1989 section 3A(1)). The CJC's power to investigate allegations of official misconduct (dishonest or improper conduct which could constitute a criminal offence) by politicians has caused it more difficulties than any other power. It is an unusual mandate for a body which deals with complaints against police but it is not unique to the CJC. The Independent Commission Against Corruption in New South Wales investigates allegations of corrupt behaviour by "public officials" which includes MPs, ministers of the Crown, judges, all holders of public office, and employees of government departments and authorities as well as local government members and employees (Sturgess 1989, 6). Before the creation of the Police Integrity Commission in July 1996, ICAC also investigated alleged and suspected serious police misconduct.

Accountability of CJC

The cornerstone to the Criminal Justice Commission's ability to fulfil its role and functions is its independence. Accountability is the counter-balance. The Criminal Justice Commission is held accountable through a variety of formal mechanisms, the most significant being to a standing parliamentary committee.

Parliamentary Committee

The CJC was made accountable to a standing parliamentary committee, the Parliamentary Criminal Justice Committee, whose membership reflects the balance of power in the parliament. Even when the Legislative Assembly is dissolved a committee member's term of office continues until new members are appointed by the Legislative Assembly or a member resigns (Parliamentary Criminal Justice Committee 1998, 3). Committee members are eligible for re-appointment and the Chairperson is drawn from government members on the committee.

The parliamentary committee is charged with monitoring and reviewing the functions of the CJC in general and the OMD in particular. It is obliged to report to the legislative assembly: on any matter relating to the way in which the CJC discharges its functions and exercises its powers; on matters arising out of the CJC's annual report and other CJC reports; and on any matter referred to the committee by the legislative assembly. The committee is also obliged to conduct a three-yearly review on the activities of the CJC, and to report to the legislative assembly on any changes it believes should be made to the *Criminal Justice Act* and the powers and functions of the Commission (*Criminal Justice Act 1989* section 118(1)(f)). The committee also participates in the appointment or removal of the chairperson or part-time commissioners.

When undertaking its three-yearly review of the CJC, the PCJC calls for public submissions. In the vast majority of cases these submissions are released to the public and made available to the media for public comment and discussion. Following the release of the submissions, the Committee also holds public hearings at which selected people are invited to give oral evidence. A written report is tabled in the legislative assembly, but there is no obligation for it to be debated by the parliament.

It is rare for the three yearly review reports to be debated in parliament. This is despite the best efforts of the first PCJC which recommended that standing orders be changed so that parliament was obliged to debate the reports' findings and that the government be obliged to respond to reports within three months of their being tabled in the House (Parliamentary Criminal Justice Committee 1991e, 45-48). Neither recommendation has been acted on and many CJC reports lie on library shelves, seemingly of more interest to academics than politicians.

The committee meets regularly with the chairperson, part-time commissioners and directors of CJC divisions, usually every two months. Before these regular meetings the parliamentary committee receives a confidential report which, in effect, updates committee members on the activities of the Commission. The committee can request further information on any matter raised in the monthly written reports or inquire into any other matter brought to its attention. The CJC is obliged to answer any questions asked of it by the parliamentary committee unless the information concerns a highly sensitive current operation (Criminal Justice Commission 1998, 9).

Fitzgerald deliberately made an all party parliamentary committee responsible for monitoring and reviewing the CJC. This was done in what now seems to have been a naive attempt to make the administration of criminal justice 'an apolitical' function (Fitzgerald 1989, 309). With the exception of the first Parliamentary Criminal Justice Committee chaired by Labor's Peter Beattie, the parliamentary committees have not acted in the bipartisan manner envisaged by Fitzgerald. A partisan approach has been adopted on sensitive and controversial issues including the establishment of a government initiated inquiry into the CJC commonly referred to as the Connolly-Ryan Inquiry (see Chapter Nine), which co-opted the role of the parliamentary committee. At the time the committee was chaired by National Party member Vince Lester. He and his colleagues did nothing to try and prevent the committee's functions from take over by the National-Liberal Party executive. Because they did not have the numbers there was little the minority Labor Party members could do but express their dismay over the situation (*Weekend Australian* 21-22 Sept 1996, 5).

The political reality, which the Fitzgerald team did not and perhaps could not provide for, was party politics and the way in which executive power would be exercised to try and over-ride designated parliamentary functions.

Parliamentary Criminal Justice Commissioner

In 1997 a new accountability mechanism, the office of Parliamentary Criminal Justice Commissioner was established. It has wide-ranging powers which allows it to audit and review the records and activities of the CJC including the register in relation to listening device applications. The Parliamentary Criminal Justice Committee can refer complaints made against officers of the Criminal Justice Commission to the Parliamentary Commissioner for investigation (Criminal Justice Commission 1998, 9).

Public Interest Monitor (PIM)

The position of Public Interest Monitor was created by the Borbidge Government in 1998. Its responsibilities include monitoring applications by the CJC for listening devices, surveillance warrants and covert search warrants (Criminal Justice Commission 1998, 9).

In its 1998 Annual Report the CJC expressed disquiet about the role of PIM in respect of the CJC. It pointed out that the Public Interest Monitor has full access to confidential CJC information. It may appear in the Supreme Court on any application the CJC makes for a listening device, ask questions and make submissions on the appropriateness of the application.

The CJC also noted its concern about the process used to appoint the Public Interest Monitor and Deputy Public Interest Monitor. Both positions are government appointments. As the CJC points out, one of its applications to the Supreme Court could relate to official misconduct by parliamentarians, political staffers or senior public servants. As a result, it is vital that any person appointed to the position have, and be seen to have, bipartisan support.

Another less than ideal aspect of the Borbidge Government's appointment of the Public Interest Monitor is that, as a practising barrister, he has acted for police who are the subject of investigation by the CJC. As the Commission explains, "The barrister appointed as PIM has frequently acted for police officers under investigation by the CJC and continues to act in some cases for such officers, despite the clear potential for a conflict of interest" (Criminal Justice Commission 1998, 91-92).

Judicial Review Act

The Criminal Justice Commission supported the introduction of the *Judicial Review Act 1991* and is subject to the Act "except in relation to providing reasons for decisions it makes in discharging its investigative, intelligence and witness protection functions". The Commission sought this exemption to prevent the legislation being used to "prejudice Commission operations" (Criminal Justice Commission 1992, 10).

Freedom of information

Queensland's *Freedom of Information Act 1992* allows members of the community statutory rights to access documents of the Commission, including policy documents. The CJC supported Freedom of Information (FOI) legislation and did not seek a blanket exemption from it. However, it did forewarn that it would apply for exemptions "to protect the integrity and confidentiality of the discharge of its functions and responsibilities and its sources of information. In particular it [would] ensure that the legislation [was] not used as a window into the Commission's investigative, intelligence and witness protection functions" (Criminal Justice Commission 1992, 101).

Sections of the *Freedom of Information Act* allow a person or organisation to claim an exemption from the release of certain information. For example, the CJC has done this in relation to the gathering of intelligence and the conduct of the witness protection program. However, as was pointed out in the Commission's 1995 *Annual Report*, "a mere claim does not guarantee success as it may be rejected by the external review process" (Criminal Justice Commission 1995a, 94).

Review by Supreme Court

If any person feels that an investigation by the OMD is being conducted unfairly or that the complaint or information which is the basis of the investigation (or proposed investigation) does not warrant such action, he/she may seek injunctive relief from a Supreme Court judge. However, an order from the Supreme Court cannot prevent or inhibit the investigation in question if further facts emerge which may indicate that the order is unjustified. Under these circumstances, the CJC can apply to a Supreme Court judge for revocation of the order. The judge can revoke or vary the terms of the order as he or she thinks fit (Criminal Justice Commission 1990a, 13).

The CJC's power to use a listening device is restricted by the statutory requirement that a Supreme Court judge must scrutinise all applications (Criminal Justice Commission 1992, 10). Even though it is not obliged to do so, the Commission also supplies a report to the Court on how the listening device is to be used.

Any application for the issue of a warrant to enter, search and seize by the CJC must also be made to a Supreme Court judge. Other functions which require the CJC to seek the approval of a Supreme Court judge were outlined in the section headed "CJC powers".

Accountability to complainants

The *Criminal Justice Act* ensures accountability to complainants by requiring the director of the Official Misconduct Division to advise them if no action has been taken on a complaint and the reasons for that decision. If action has been taken, the complainant must be advised as to the nature of the action, why it was considered appropriate and the result of the action. Wherever practicable, complainants are debriefed by a complaints officer. This is usually done by telephone but if this is not possible a letter is sent inviting them to contact the CJC if they require further information.

Public investigative hearings

The *Criminal Justice Act* places a *prima facie* obligation on the CJC to hold open investigative hearings. However, it does have the discretion to conduct a closed hearing if it believes that the subject matter or nature of the evidence is such that public disclosure would be unfair to an individual, or would not be in the public interest. In a few instances the CJC has been criticised for the way in which it exercised this discretion, particularly in relation to its inquiry into what is commonly referred to as the Cape Melville incident.[7]

Public documents/public seminars

The Commission is accountable to the public through the release of its research papers, issues papers and reports. These reports are widely distributed to public libraries, or can be purchased through the CJC or the government printing office for a nominal sum. Other smaller, more user-friendly reports are distributed to relevant agencies and individuals free of

---

7 For further details refer to *A Report of an Investigation into the Cape Melville Incident*, CJC 1994.

charge. The CJC also conducts public seminars as part of its independent research function.

Complaints against members of the CJC

People who are dissatisfied with the investigations or activities of the CJC can complain to the Parliamentary Criminal Justice Committee. By agreement with the Committee, the Criminal Justice Commission is obliged to refer any complaint against its own officers to the Director of Public Prosecutions (DPP). Complaints are investigated by a senior crown prosecutor nominated by the DPP and a senior police officer nominated by the commissioner of the Queensland Police Service. These investigators report to the DPP who advises the CJC and the Attorney-General of the outcome and makes recommendations based on the findings.

Internal accountability

The chairperson, part-time commissioners, staff and consultants are obliged to submit statutory declarations of personal particulars and of private interests and associations and to sign confidentiality agreements. Summaries of pecuniary interests and personal and political associations have to be updated annually for the chair and part-time commissioners. The newly established Office of the Commission plays a coordinating role in internal accountability processes and corporate governance.

Conclusion

Examining the Commission's structure, functions and powers it is possible to juxtapose its reactive features against Goldsmith's External, Investigatory/Adjudicative category, Kerstetter's Civilian Review model and most of the other reactive features identified in Chapter Four as being fundamental to a civilian oversight body's citizen watchdog role and come to the conclusion that the Commission has most of the reactive powers needed for an oversight body to effectively respond to complaints against police conduct and related issues. It is also possible to look at its range of proactive features which are primarily undertaken by its Research and Prevention Division (see Chapter Five) and argue that in this respect the CJC is leading the way in terms of civilian oversight models.

The catalyst for this new form of civilian oversight was the institutional corruption uncovered by the Fitzgerald Inquiry. It was so significant that adapting models from other jurisdictions or tinkering with existing structures and processes in an incremental fashion were not viable options. If the Queensland reform process was to have a positive, long-lasting effect, ground-breaking policies were required. In theory at least the CJC is a near ideal police accountability institution. Whether it can be in practice may have more to do with its relationship with government than with the police service.

The CJC has been operational for some nine years. During that time it has overcome many of its teething problems some of which were self inflicted. However it has reached the stage where, in terms of its police oversight role, it is now in a position to concentrate on making the links, the "loops", between its reactive and proactive functions and, therefore, to operate in an holistic manner. But as will be shown in the following chapter, its ability to fulfil its potential in this regard has often been impeded by the nature of its relationship with governments, particularly with the Borbidge National-Liberal coalition government

9

THE CJC AND THE POLITICAL SYSTEM

Introduction

Unhelpful tensions between oversight bodies and governments can exist when the oversight body's jurisdiction is limited to police and other public servants (the Ombudsman) and when it is confined solely to police (Police Complaints Authorities). Strained relations arise from time to time regardless of the scope of the oversight body's jurisdiction and can often be traced to structural factors. Also any independent, civilian oversight agency can have its attention distracted from its police oversight role if resources, physical and monetary, are continually being diverted and consumed by the effects of its relationship with governments. The nature of the relationship can also impact negatively on the outcome of negotiations when the oversight body is trying to influence government policy in terms of powers, resources and support. The CJC and other oversight bodies share these problems to varying degrees. But, because the CJC has the power to investigate suspected or alleged official misconduct by politicians, it often finds itself embroiled in issues which have more to do with party politics than police and public sector probity.

Even though the unusual scope of the Commission's coverage serves to magnify oversight body-government tensions, it is not the sole cause of them. This chapter continues the case study of the CJC. In doing so, it shows how structural tensions, its independent status and personality clashes have added to the problems which arise from the commission's major difficulty: its political oversight role.

Structural tensions

Independent external civilian oversight bodies are usually established to investigate, monitor and/or review complaints against police and other public servants. Under these circumstances, friction with government is inevitable. It occurs, in part, because the government and not the oversight body is ultimately accountable for the actions of public servants. This helps to explain the degree of structural tension which exists and why, when an investigation by an oversight body exposes serious misconduct or corruption by public servants, governments, as Pearce (1992, 1993) explains, often try to shoot the messenger rather than heed the message.

Structural tensions are compounded by the somewhat unique constitutional position many independent accountability institutions occupy. They are often described as the "fifth wheel on the constitutional coach". In the British, Canadian and Australian contexts, this "fifth wheel" tends to interfere with the traditional Westminster system of responsible government, where ministers are theoretically accountable to parliament for the actions of their department. But when an independent oversight body reports to the parliament and not to a minister, it bypasses the authority and influence of the executive. As a result these type of accountability agencies are viewed by governments, at best, as political irritants and at worst as obstructionist institutions with a secret agenda designed to shift power from the government to the oversight body.

Queensland's Goss Labor Government had been in power for just four months when the CJC became operational in April 1990. Tensions between oversight body and government were immediate. They surfaced initially in terms of the Commission's proactive independent research function which the government viewed as a political irritant.

Proactive research function

As discussed in Chapter Four, one of the most innovative and (potentially) effective aspects of the CJC model, in terms of changing police behaviour and keeping the community and the parliament informed about police and other criminal justice issues, is its capacity to undertake independent research and to publicly report its findings. However, it has also been a source of great friction with government, particularly in the Commission's formative years. The right to determine policy is fundamental to government and, while it may seek advice from several quarters, who it consults, and whether or not it makes the advice it receives public, is at the government's discretion. The CJC's research function interferes with that disclosure option, thereby lessening the government's ability to control the debate in terms of criminal justice issues.

Part of the prescribed agenda set for the CJC by the Fitzgerald Report was a general review of the criminal law in relation to prostitution, SP bookmaking, illegal gambling and illicit drugs. Because of the high probability that the debate on such politically sensitive issues would be hijacked by party political considerations, Fitzgerald deliberately recommended that research into these matters be undertaken by the independent CJC. This way the Queensland community would have access to impartial, professional research to help it come to an informed decision after open, public debate.

Even though the Commission's research reports are only one avenue of policy advice to government and parliament, some of its early findings proved to be politically unacceptable as they did not coincide with the Goss Labor Government's stated agenda. The CJC's task of conducting research and reporting via the parliament, meant that an important control lever on public information had slipped from the executive's grasp. This was an experience they did not like.

It seems as though the Research Division was operating as intended and at this early stage of the reform process the extent of public sector and political corruption exposed by the Fitzgerald Inquiry was still crystal clear in the minds of many in the community. As a result, the Goss Government's combative tactics, which included pre-emptive strikes on CJC findings by the Premier, were not well received. Even though the CJC was still in favour with the public,[1] it was on its way to being well and truly out of favour with the government.

Functional tensions

Power to investigate politicians' behaviour

The shaky relationship between the Goss Government and CJC, which arose from structural tensions, took a decided turn for the worse with the release of the *Report on an Investigation into Possible Misuse of Parliamentary Travel Entitlements by Members of the 1986-1989 Queensland Legislative Assembly* in December 1991 (Criminal Justice Commission 1991c). This investigation brought the CJC's multiple coverage into play,

1 Once the Commission completed its politically sensitive Fitzgerald agenda, tensions between the CJC and governments over its research function dissipated.

in particular its capacity to investigate the conduct of politicians. The investigation into parliamentary members' travel entitlements was brought about by the Commission invoking its own motion powers. While inaugural CJC Chairman Sir Max Bingham pointed out that the Commission was bound under the *Criminal Justice Act* to investigate allegations that parliamentary travel entitlements were being abused, many MPs disagreed and accused the CJC of exceeding its authority. Sir Max said that "the message coming from all sides [of politics] was to pack it in", with some callers intimating that the inquiry was putting the future prospects of the Commission at risk (Walker 1995, 173).

The independent CJC refused to bow to political pressure and the inquiry continued, taking some 12 months to complete. Part of the delay resulted from the refusal by former and present members of parliament to voluntarily answer questions. This meant that in the majority of cases the Commission had to use its powers under the Act to obtain the necessary information. Its decision to do so placed a further strain on relations between oversight body and government.

When the report was released it found, inter alia, that there was:

> Cogent evidence suggesting that the Parliamentary Travel Entitlements Scheme was abused by a significant number of the Members of the 1986-1989 Queensland Legislative Assembly. The evidence raises a strong suspicion that those Members used daily travelling allowances, in combination with other entitlements, to fund private excursions, on some occasions alone, but generally with their spouses, and often with family members (Criminal Justice Commission 1991c; iii).

However, the available evidence would not substantiate dishonest conduct to the high level of proof needed in criminal matters, proof beyond reasonable doubt and, on the advice of one of Queensland's leading QCs, the Criminal Justice Commission's report did not name names. The Commission chose instead to use case studies.

The report had negative consequences for the Labor, Liberal and National Parties and for the relationship between the CJC and politicians on all sides of the political divide. The media quickly put names to some case studies and before long the CJC "travel rorts" report, as it became known, had claimed some high profile political scalps.

Criticism of the CJC report by parliamentarians was across party lines and set the tone for future relationships between many politicians and the Commission. As might be expected, some of the harshest criticisms came from those most affected by the report's findings. They included comments such as "the CJC had dished out kangaroo-court style justice in an unprofessional, subjective, sloppy, judgmental and pathetic report" and that it "had too much power" (*Courier-Mail* 12 Dec 1991, 2).

Such disparaging comments from those responsible for setting accountability standards in the community can have a negative effect on the institution being criticised. However, given the findings of the CJC investigation, public sentiment remained with the Commission and not with those doing the criticising. As a result, government action was kept in check by the weight of public opinion.

While all this was going on, the focus of attention by the community, the CJC, the government and the PCJC shifted from the police reform process (which was still in its infancy) to the ethical standard of Queensland's politicians but, more particularly, to the battle which ensued between the government, the opposition parties and the CJC over the Commission's role in bringing those standards to the attention of the public.

Personality factors

Structural and functional tensions with the government and wider political system were not the only problems this embryonic accountability institution was experiencing. Personality factors exacerbated already tense relations between the CJC and the first Goss Government. From the outset Premier Goss and Sir Max Bingham had a difficult relationship. The cause was a mutual lack of trust, which at times spilled into the public arena. Unhelpful comments were made by both about each other. However, because the Fitzgerald reform agenda was still being supported by many in the media and by the community, the government had to find a way to live with the CJC. But it was also important for the CJC's credibility and survival that the chair of the Commission find a way to work with the government. It seems that compromises were reached as, toward the end of Sir Max's term as chair, public comments by both sides became less strident.

When Robin O'Regan became the second chair of the CJC, tensions between the premier and head of the Commission eased. However, personality issues were a factor in the relationship which developed between the second Parliamentary Criminal Justice Committee chaired by Labor's Ken Davies and the CJC when it was chaired by O'Regan.

The matter which brought their tense relationship into the public arena was the CJC's rejection of a PCJC directive that the Commission conduct an internal investigation into a breach of security within its own organisation. O'Regan took the view that it was not appropriate for the CJC to investigate itself. He arranged instead for an inspector of police, supervised by the Director of Public Prosecutions, to conduct an inquiry.

When the Commission rejected the PCJC's "strong advice" that it conduct its own inquiry, the PCJC admitted that it did not have the power to order the CJC to do so. Davies claimed this left his Committee with no option but to carry out its own public inquiry into the matter (Parliamentary Criminal Justice Committee 1994c, 1, 2).

The way in which the PCJC conducted its inquiry provides a useful illustration of structural tensions between the CJC and PCJC and the degree to which they can get out of control when power games, influenced by personality factors, take precedence over the responsibility to rationally and objectively monitor and review.

From the opening minutes of the inquiry, the Committee's animosity toward present and former staff of the CJC was evident. Indeed, it could be said that the Committee's behaviour, particularly in the first two days of public hearings was an abuse of its considerable powers and did nothing toward achieving Fitzgerald's goal of restoring citizens' faith in their democratic institutions.

The inquiry had no terms of reference. This was verified by chairperson Ken Davies on the first day of the inquiry (Parliamentary Criminal Justice Committee 1994c, 8). The lack of any terms of reference account for some of the Committee's irrelevant questions which did not appear to be connected to the reason it gave for establishing the inquiry.

Legal representation was denied to two former members of the CJC. This was despite the fact that all people appearing before the inquiry were required to give evidence under oath or affirmation. Witnesses were treated as though in a court of law but not given the protection of the law. A former research director of the Parliamentary Criminal Justice Committee issued a press statement describing the hearing as a "travesty of justice".

Much of the blame for the nature of the relationship rests with the parliamentary committee. In the struggle to try to exercise power over the CJC, the Davies Parliamentary Committee lost sight of the fact that its role was to monitor and review the CJC, not control it. It appeared to mistake bullying for effectiveness and operated on the basis of conflict, ignoring the benefits that could flow from a professional, arm's-length but constructive relationship between an oversight body and the political institution to which it reports.

Part-time commissioner and respected criminologist Professor Ross Homel whose term coincided with part of the Davies PCJC's term, describes the first 12 months of his appointment as akin to being in "a constant artillery barrage. You never knew when the next shell was going to fall. With one political crisis after another and a parliamentary committee that was unhelpful, it was totally all-consuming. There was no time to focus or reflect on critical issues" (interview with Professor Ross Homel).

The desire to exert political power rather than monitor and review the Commission's principal functions also had the effect of diverting the focus and hence the valuable resources (time, money and people) of both organisations away from their central tasks.

Too often the Davies PCJC became distracted from its primary function. Instead of probing and questioning the CJC on its police oversight role, both reactive and proactive, it spent an inordinate amount of time locked in power battles with the Commission. In responding to the demands of the Davies PCJC, the CJC also spent a disproportionate amount of resources having to prepare for PCJC inquiries. In many instances resources could have been better spent on short and long term police accountability issues.

Unhelpful personal relations can hinder the effectiveness of any organisation which oversights complaints against police, regardless of the scope of its jurisdiction. In the case of the CJC personality clashes between a Premier and chair of the CJC and between a PCJC and the Commission served to heighten already tense relationships between oversight body and government. They were made even worse by the way in which the CJC was used as a political football by people on both sides of the political divide.

Political football

Politicians use the CJC to lodge complaints about members of other political parties and then announce to the media that the person is under investigation by the Commission. They do this in the hope that it will get them positive publicity and will impact negatively on their opponents. Their complaint usually has more to do with party political advantage than with concerns about increased integrity and probity among units of public administration The CJC is also aware of the difficult situation in which it finds itself in relation to politically sensitive and volatile investigations. It acknowledges that matters referred to it by politicians often consume more resources than is desirable.

The genesis of the politically controversial Cape Melville Inquiry (Criminal Justice Commission 1994d) was a letter to the Commission from the National Party Shadow Minister for Environment and Heritage Doug Slack. Attached to Slack's letter was an anonymous letter which, among other things, alleged serious misconduct by a senior public servant, and that pressure had been applied not to charge a person because he was the brother of the Premier's former private secretary. Slack's letter expressed the view that the allegations outlined in the anonymous letter were most serious and warranted a full investigation by the CJC (Criminal Justice Commission 1994d, 1-2).

After a 10-months investigation, the CJC found that "All of the allegations of impropriety contained in the letter have been found to be untrue" (Criminal Justice Commission 1994d, 2). It also added that it was suspicious of the motives of the anonymous complainant given that he or she chose to bring the matter to the attention of a member of the opposition as opposed to reporting it to the police, the Ombudsman or the Minister for the Environment and Heritage. The CJC further pointed out that by making the complaint to a politician in the first instance, the anonymous complainant could reasonably expect that it would be used for party political advantage (Criminal Justice Commission 1994d, 3).

When, after a lengthy and detailed investigation, the Commission recommended that no charges be laid against members of the Premier's staff, the then leader of the opposition Rob Borbidge declared publicly that the report a "whitewash". Because of the politically charged nature of the issue, the Cape Melville Inquiry placed the CJC in a no-win position. Which ever answer was "right" according to the investigation, it was inevitably going to be labelled "wrong" by the opposing sides of politics, particularly when they had lodged the complaint.

In the lead-up to the important Mundingburra by-election in February 1996 (of which more later), the then Shadow Attorney-General Denver Beanland lodged a complaint with the CJC alleging that the Labor Party had offered inducements to a sitting member so he would not run as a candidate in the election. After lodging the complaint, Beanland followed up by writing two letters to the CJC within a space of 14 days. These letters demanded a speedy investigation "in recognition of the clear public interest to resolve the matter promptly" (*Courier-Mail* 2 Sept 1996, 1). Beanland's demands were played out through the media. In an effort to comply with them, the CJC devoted considerable resources to the investigation (*Courier-Mail* 7 Sept 1996). The investigation was finalised within the time-frame demanded by Beanland. When the Commission found the allegations were unfounded Beanland accused it of a "whitewash" and tried to cast doubt on the quality of the investigation by describing it as "quite incredibly quick" (*Courier-Mail* 7 Sept 1996).

Even though many of the criticisms levelled at the CJC by politicians do not stand up to rational examination, they can have a negative impact on the community's perception of the external, independent oversight body. Unless the public clearly distinguishes between the Commission's various functions, which is unlikely, the continual undermining of the CJC for party political purposes can have a detrimental effect on its credibility as a police oversight agency. The Police Complaints Tribunal case study clearly demonstrates the consequences for police accountability when an oversight body is discredited in the eyes of the community and honest police. This seems to have been ignored by those doing the criticising for party political advantage.

The above examples of governments and alternative governments trying to undermine the Commission for partisan political reasons pales into insignificance when compared with the Borbidge National-Liberal Party coalition government's attempt to emasculate the Criminal Justice Commission.

Attempts to destroy the Criminal Justice Commission

Some extraordinary happenings in Queensland during 1996-97 saw the Borbidge National-Liberal Party Coalition Government launch an unprecedented attack on the Criminal Justice Commission which threatened its ability to deliver effective police accountability. The events surrounding this government's assault on the CJC are complex. They cover:

- the police union's campaign in the Mundingburra by-election;
- a memorandum of understanding (MOU) between the then leader of the National-Liberal Party opposition Rob Borbidge, then Shadow Minister for Police Russell Cooper and president of the Queensland Police Union Gary Wilkinson;
- the government-appointed Bingham review of the Queensland Police Service;
- the CJC-appointed Carruthers Inquiry established to examine the memorandum of understanding;

- the government-appointed Connolly-Ryan Inquiry established to review the Criminal Justice Commission, which included an examination of the Carruthers Inquiry (an inquiry into an inquiry); and
- the CJC's budget.

While each of these event will be dealt with separately, they are to a lesser or greater degree intertwined. They demonstrate:

(a) how the police union and politicians united to try and weaken considerably the CJC's ability to be an effective police accountability institution;

(b) how, when the scheme became the subject of an inquiry by the CJC, the government launched an on-going and vicious attack on the oversight body which, it can be argued, was designed to emasculate it;

(c) the unrelenting way in which the Borbidge Government attacked the CJC;

(d) how government-oversight body relations can influence government intent; and

(e) how that intent can hinder effective police accountability.

Memorandum of understanding

In February 1996 a crucial one seat by-election was held in the Queensland seat of Mundingburra. At stake was the ability to form government in Queensland. Throughout the lead-up to the election, the police union campaigned consistently and vigorously against the incumbent Goss Labor Government which held the seat by only 16 votes. While the union's campaign did not specifically support any political party, it was openly anti-Labor. The seat was won by the Liberal Party and, with the support of Queensland's only independent member of parliament, delivered government to the National-Liberal Party Coalition.

Three weeks after the election Queensland's *Courier-Mail* newspaper broke the story that the president of the police union Gary Wilkinson had negotiated a deal with incoming Premier Rob Borbidge, and incoming Police Minister Russell Cooper when they were in opposition which, among other things, would greatly curtail the powers of the CJC, significantly weaken several post-Fitzgerald disciplinary measures and reverse many other crucial Fitzgerald-inspired police reforms.[2] It also delivered unprecedented power to the police union, particularly in relation to senior Queensland Police Service appointments (*Courier-Mail* 27 Feb 1996, 1; *Courier-Mail* 28 Feb 1996, 18).

The *Courier-Mail*'s story forced the recently sworn-in Police Minister Russell Cooper to admit that the MOU had been drawn up and signed some three weeks before the by-election but that its contents had not been made known to the voters of Mundingburra before they had cast their votes. Some of the more disturbing elements of the memorandum in relation to complaints against police which were "agreed"[3] to by Borbidge and Cooper include the following:

> DISCIPLINE
>
> A. The CJC shall be responsible for serious criminal matters only.
>
> B. Simple offences, misconduct and discipline matters shall be dealt with by the QPS.
>
> D. Double jeopardy shall no longer apply. Once an officer has been dealt with in any jurisdiction, no further action shall be taken against him over the same matter.
>
> Response: Items A, B, . . . D . . . are agreed.

Item 27 also impacts directly on the role and functions of the CJC. It states that:

> (27) The Government shall take advice from the QPUE [Queensland Police Union Executive] when selecting the next Commissioner of Police and shall not select an individual for his position that the Union has genuine reasons for opposing.
>
> Response: Agreed.

The CJC's powers in respect of complaints against police have already been outlined (see Chapter Eight). Suffice is to say that if the memorandum of understanding had not been exposed by the media it would almost certainly have become government policy. When implemented, the

---

2 The change in the Presidency of the police union appears to have signalled a change in attitude by the union toward the Criminal Justice Commission.

3 At the Connolly-Ryan Inquiry the meaning of the word "agreed" in the Memorandum of Understanding was analysed. Borbidge, Cooper and some members of the union offered their interpretations of the word. They included that "agreed" did not mean "agreed", rather it "indicates only an agreement to have the matter reviewed"; "that agreed meant agreed, but also that it was consistent with coalition policy"; that "agreed meant agreed to be reviewed" and that agreed "indicates only an agreement to have the matter reviewed" (Transcripts from Connolly-Ryan Inquiry).

items listed above under "DISCIPLINE" would have turned the CJC into a token police accountability body.

If item 27 had been implemented, a Fitzgerald inspired safeguard designed to prevent the politicisation of the office of commissioner would have been removed. Presently the government is obliged to consult with the chair of the Commission before appointing or dismissing a commissioner of police. Presuming that the Coalition Government did not intend to abolish the CJC or remove the chairperson's right to be consulted about the position of police commissioner, it can be assumed that by including this item in the memorandum, the union would have been able to veto persons from a short list of potential commissioners, before the CJC had seen the names of those candidates.

The Mundingburra by-election presented Gary Wilkinson, the police union president, elected after O'Gorman stood down in March 1995, and his executive with the window of opportunity they were looking for to reassert union power and severely weaken the CJC's role in the complaints against police process. However, it can be argued that Wilkinson may not have bothered to include the CJC's police oversight role in the controversial memorandum of understanding if he did not feel confident that his demands would be "agreed" to by influential members of a National-Liberal Party Coalition Government. It can also be argued that continued criticism by prominent National and Liberal members toward the CJC in general, and its investigative capabilities in particular, could have encouraged the president of the union to feel assured that his demands would be "agreed" to.

The furore which followed the exposure of the MOU left Police Minister Cooper little choice but to forward it to the CJC so it could be examined with "proper diligence".[4] Because one of the "agreed" items in the memorandum was the curtailment of the CJC's powers in relation to police misconduct, the chair of the CJC, on independent legal advice, engaged a retired Supreme Court judge from another Australian state, His Honour Kenneth Carruthers QC, to conduct an inquiry.

However, before the revelations about the MOU, Police Minister Cooper announced the establishment of a committee to review the QPS which he later claimed at the Carruthers Inquiry was linked to the Memorandum of Understanding. Before discussing the ramifications of

4 Police Minister Cooper wrote to the chair of the CJC Frank Clair saying, inter alia, that "attached is a copy of that memorandum of understanding and I would be grateful if you could review it and advise if, in your considered view, there is anything improper in it" (*Courier Mail* 29 Feb 1996, 17).

the CJC-appointed Carruthers Inquiry and the subsequent government-appointed Connolly-Ryan Inquiry, the government-appointed committee established to review the QPS will be addressed.

Bingham Inquiry

One of the first things incoming Police Minister Cooper did after his party's coalition partners won the Mundingburra by-election was announce that he would establish a committee to review the Queensland Police Service (*Courier-Mail* 22 Feb 1996, 2). At that time the person tipped to head the inquiry was a former assistant commissioner of police who had been critical of the Criminal Justice Commission and who had a less than friendly relationship with a strong supporter of the Fitzgerald reform program, Commissioner of Police Jim O'Sullivan. As revealed later at the Carruthers Inquiry, this was the same person from whom Cooper had sought advice in January 1996 in relation to the police union's "wish-list of policy demands that later became the core of the controversial memorandum of understanding between the coalition and the union" (*Australian* 14 June 1996, 6). However, when the furore over the existence of the alleged secret memorandum broke, it seems that the government quickly changed its mind and the inaugural chair of the CJC Sir Max Bingham accepted the appointment as chair of the Queensland Police Service Review.

The Bingham review committee's charter "to conduct a broad ranging review of the Queensland Police Service with a view to identifying areas in which its efficiency, effectiveness and accountability can be improved in order to ensure the best service delivery" (a) clearly cut across many of the major functions of the CJC and (b) by definition necessitated a partial review of the CJC – a function which as per the Fitzgerald blueprint for reform was deliberately made the responsibility of the all party Parliamentary Criminal Justice Committee.

The then chair of the CJC Frank Clair argued publicly that reviewing the QPS was a function of the CJC but, accepting the inevitable, went on to say that "if the CJC is not to conduct the review, it should at least have a representative in the process" (*Courier-Mail* 28 Feb 1996, 7). Clair had to fight vigorously for CJC representation and, after several letters were exchanged, the government agreed to the directors of the CJC's Official Misconduct Division and Research and Co-ordination Division being members. To do otherwise so soon after the revelations of the contents of the MOU could have reflected badly on the government.

The Bingham committee's *Report on the Review of the Queensland Police Service* (1996, 42) was generally well received but a couple of matters proved to be controversial The first dealt with the appropriateness of the police minister meeting with the police union without the police commissioner being present.[5] This issue, which is linked to the Memorandum of Understanding, also relates to matters that were then being considered by the Carruthers Inquiry. It was also the subject of critical comment in the Fitzgerald Report which recommended that "any contact between the unions and government ministers, including the Premier, should only occur with the police commissioner and his minister being present" (Fitzgerald 1989, 280).

The second controversy surrounded dissension between CJC committee members and Sir Max Bingham over the interpretation of a recommendation. The difference of opinion is not so much the issue here as the attack on the CJC which followed the disagreement.

---

5 The Bingham committee came to the conclusion that such a restriction appeared to be "impracticable and undesirable". In defence of its position, the committee's report argued that, "all parties will benefit from the development of a frank, open, constructive and reasonable set of relations. Meetings between the unions and minister on one hand and the unions and the Commissioner on the other, need not necessarily involve the other party, so long as due care is taken as has been indicated" (Queensland 1996, 42)

The *Courier-Mail* felt that the report took "a very optimistic view of the contribution the unions can make in relation to policy and administration, while largely ignoring the dangers demonstrated by recent experiences between Borbidge, Cooper and Wilkinson" (*Courier-Mail* 20 Aug 1996, 14).

Commenting on his committee's approach to the issue, Sir Max explained "the committee felt that it was unduly constraining the union to pin it down to the sort of terms that Fitzgerald thought were appropriate at the time . . . there has been a lot of water under the bridge since then" (*Australian* 20 Aug 1996, 4). He further argued that "it's time to get rid of the almost paranoid attitude that people had about the police union in the past and to settle down to a sensible working relationship" (*Courier-Mail* 21 Aug 1996, 13).

Scott Emerson, commenting on Bingham's perspective expressed surprise that "[S]ir Max Bingham, the inaugural chair of the Fitzgerald-recommended anti-corruption body, the Criminal Justice Commission, had 'consigned' Fitzgerald's view to history . . . by labelling it paranoid" (*Australian* 20 Aug 1996, 4). The most strident criticism of this aspect of the report came from the Australian Council for Civil Liberties which saw the review committee's position in relation to police unions as an "invitation back to the pre-Fitzgerald days". Its president, Terry O'Gorman, making the link between the matter under review by the Carruthers Inquiry and the Bingham committee's position, asked the pertinent question, "What the hell is the Carruthers Inquiry all about . . . other than a graphic example of what happens when that very important Fitzgerald recommendation has been ignored?" (*Australian* 20 Aug 1996, 4).

Sir Max Bingham used the media to publicly criticise the Commission, claiming that it was tying to "undermine the work of the rest of the committee". He suggested that there had been a less than harmonious relationship between the CJC and the Police Service Review from the beginning,

He further pointed out that:

> If you read our report carefully, you will see a number of areas in which the performance of the CJC in respect of its monitoring role has been less than adequate. There's been inefficiencies there [in the police service] that have been apparent to the CJC for at least a couple of years, and they haven't remedied them (*Sunday Mail* 1 Sept 1996, 4).

These comments by Sir Max appear to support the argument that the government-appointed Bingham review was also taking over a major role of the PCJC: to monitor and review the CJC.

The establishment of the Bingham review committee could be perceived by the public as a vote of no confidence by the government in the CJC's police oversight role (reactive and proactive). If it was not for Clair's successful efforts to have the CJC represented on the committee, public opinion may have been further damaged.

There is also the question of whether there is a conflict of interest when the former chair of the independent CJC is subsequently engaged by the government to review a principal function of the CJC. The review committee looked at the operations of the QPS since the establishment of the CJC. This would, by necessity, involve a review of the CJC's police oversight and review role and would have to include Sir Max's term as chair of the Commission from 1989 to 1992. Consequently, there is, in effect, an element of Caesar judging Caesar for part of the period under review.

Despite assurances to the contrary, it can be argued that the government was trying to undermine the CJC by distancing it from one of its primary functions, its police oversight and review role. This argument gains more credibility because assurances about the CJC's involvement in the implementation of the review committee's recommendations were not met. Apparently, when the Bingham review committee was first mooted, Commissioner O'Sullivan was assured by Police Minister Cooper that "the CJC will have final veto of any recommendations that may come out of that review" (*Courier-Mail* 29 Feb 1996, 17) and a story in the *Sunday Mail* on 1 September 1996 reported Sir Max as saying that "the CJC would be invited to participate on the committee that would impliment [sic] the Bingham report". Despite these assurances, the Commission was not part of the implementation committee. The CJC was temporarily sidelined and the QPS found itself with two bodies, one of which was critical of the other, involved in the recommendation and implementation of reforms to the Service. This is not a helpful scenario for effective accountability.

Carruthers Inquiry and Connolly-Ryan Inquiry

The Carruthers Inquiry terms of reference required it to examine the events surrounding the creation and execution of the previously mentioned memorandum of understanding. Given the serious nature of the issues being examined and the positions held by some people called to give evidence before it, it was inevitable that the Carruthers Inquiry and the CJC would be subjected to criticism by the government. But it is doubtful that anyone could have anticipated the direction the attack would eventually take, or its ferocity.

The longer the Carruthers Inquiry sat, the greater the animosity by the National-Liberal Party Government toward the CJC. In July 1996, Carruthers indicated that the evidence before him suggested that Police Minister Cooper had tried to harness the police union's "political muscle" in the crucially important Mundingburra by-election and that Cooper and Wilkinson had deliberately tried to keep the MOU secret. In August, Carruthers explained that it was the secrecy element that concerned him (*Courier-Mail* 16 Aug 1996, 2).

After the public hearings ended Carruthers began work on his report which was expected to be completed toward the end of November 1996.

There was more at risk for the government than a finding of criminal conduct against a government minister, the ability to govern could have been at stake. Any threat to that position had to be averted, with whatever means were available and at any cost, even if that cost meant undermining totally the body established, inter alia, to deal with complaints against police and oversight of the ongoing Fitzgerald inspired police reform process. The nearer Carruthers got to handing down his report, the more the CJC had to defend itself from attack by Premier Borbidge, Police Minister Cooper and other members of the National-Liberal Party Coalition Government.

In September 1996 National Party backbencher Allan Grice made serious allegations in parliament about the head of the CJC's Official Misconduct Division Mark Le Grand. Apparently, Grice's allegations were what prompted state cabinet to bring forward a promised inquiry into the CJC. National Party leader and Premier Rob Borbidge justified cabinet's decision on the pretext that there were "too many unresolved issues for the sake of the CJC, its accountability and its future"[6] (*Courier-Mail* 17 Sept 1996, 1). These unresolved issues were related in part to Grice's very recent allegations.

CJC Chairman Frank Clair condemned the proposed inquiry as "executive interference", adding that "he expected the 'programme of degradation' against the Commission would intensify in the lead-up to Carruthers' report" (*Courier-Mail* 16, 17, 18 Sept 1996, 1). He saw the government's attacks on the CJC as a bid to undermine the Commission and an attempt to save Police Minister Cooper from the political fallout of the Carruthers Inquiry (*Courier-Mail* 16 Sept 1996, 1).

When the government-initiated inquiry's into the CJC was brought forward, the decision about who should head it also became an issue. The *Courier-Mail* newspaper, which supported the idea of an inquiry, made it clear that:

> It should not be a former Queensland Supreme Court judge, such as Peter Connolly QC, who only a few months ago provided Police Minister, Russell Cooper, with an opinion to be used in his defence in a CJC hearing being conducted by Kenneth Carruthers QC. Whatever the validity of Mr Connolly's advice in that matter (and Mr Carruthers may well reject some of his propositions) it would be inappropriate for him to investigate a body which in effect puts his "client on trial" (*Courier-Mail* 19 Sept 1996, 16).

The wisdom of this line of argument was confirmed by Justice Thomas when he closed down the Connolly-Ryan Inquiry on the grounds of "ostensible bias" (see pages 170-173). However, ignoring this opinion and those of many others in the community, one of the two retired Queensland judges appointed to conduct the inquiry into the CJC was Peter Connolly QC.[7] The other was Kevin Ryan QC. They were given royal commission powers and "a virtually unlimited brief".

It was now becoming apparent that the Borbidge Government was determined to take control of the CJC's future so that it and not the parliament could determine its role, functions, powers and fate. But what

---

6 Initially the attorney-general said that it would be more appropriate if the inquiry into the CJC were to commence after the Carruthers Inquiry had handed down its findings (*Courier-Mail* 3 Sept 1996, 4). Beanland submitted to cabinet that "the methodology for a judicial inquiry into the performance and accountability of the CJC be implemented in late 1996 or early 1997" (*Courier-Mail* 2 Sept 1996, 2).

7 In response to continued concern about Connolly's appointment, the State Government passed a regulation which enabled Connolly to absent himself from his inquiry's investigations into the Carruthers Inquiry (*Courier-Mail* 5 Dec 1996, 5).

the government had not accounted for was Carruthers' reaction to the Connolly-Ryan Inquiry's terms of reference.

Carruthers QC resigned before bringing down his report saying that the government setting up of the Connolly-Ryan Commission, with powers wide enough to embrace his continuing inquiry, constituted a potential threat to his independence.[8]

He documented the salient points of the legal opinion he sought before taking the decision to resign. They were that:

> a. Although it is part of my duty to recommend whether or not criminal charges should be brought against Mr Borbidge and Mr Cooper (amongst others), both of those persons are members of the government which established the Connolly-Ryan Commission.
>
> b. In other words, two of the persons into whose conduct, and possible misconduct, I am currently inquiring have participated in setting up a Commission of Inquiry into my Inquiry into them.
>
> c. The position is rendered more extreme by the fact that one of the two commissioners so appointed has been counsel who advised Mr Cooper in relation to certain of the conduct I am obliged to investigate (Carruthers QC, His Honour Kenneth 1996, Resignation Speech, 29 Oct).

Grave concerns for the future of the CJC followed Carruthers' resignation. The *Australian*, Australia's national daily newspaper, editorialised that "Despite the Government's protestations, that inquiry [the Connolly-Ryan Inquiry] – timed as it was to coincide with Mr Carruthers' deliberations – was a transparent attempt to erode his (Mr Carruthers) status and the credibility of the CJC" (31 Oct 1996, 12).

The government's reaction to Carruthers' resignation was to further attack the CJC. Borbidge, in a ministerial statement to the Queensland parliament, claimed that, "If ever the people of this state needed a justification for a careful assessment of the CJC, its appointees, its

---

8 Carruthers explained that:

Because the Connolly-Ryan Commission regarded it as a distinct possibility that they would wish to inquire into the conduct of my inquiry, they wished me to preserve, evidently for examination by them, every scrap of paper, every thought recorded in writing, and every argument or proposition communicated by me or to me in writing. As was made clear by Mr Hanger . . . it was intended by him that his staff should be able now to inspect and copy such documents.

My immediate view, which I continue to hold after deep reflection, and after taking legal advice, was that this was an actual interference with my independence because it was an assertion of control over my inquiry, moment by moment, while that inquiry was still underway. Not only was the Commission seeking to exert control over me directly, but it was also asserting control over staff seconded to me by the CJC. (Carruthers QC, His Honour Kenneth 1996, Resignation Speech, 29 Oct.)

policies, its actions, its expenditure and its effectiveness, this travesty of public duty by Mr Carruthers is it" (*Courier-Mail* 31 Oct 1996, 4).

The day after Carruthers' resignation,[9] Connolly and Ryan convened their government-appointed inquiry into the CJC and confirmed that they intended to investigate the conduct of the Carruthers Inquiry. On the same day, Mr Connolly made disparaging remarks about Mr Carruthers on a radio program, the inappropriateness of which was confirmed in the Supreme Court of Queensland (see pages 170-173).

Two days after Carruthers' resignation, the CJC briefed two barristers to review the evidence collected by the Carruthers' Inquiry. Their report found that there was no evidence to support criminal charges of electoral bribery against the Premier, the police minister, or against members of the police union executive, as the memorandum of understanding had not resulted in any tangible benefits (as defined under the *Electoral Act 1992*) to the parties of the MOU. Based on the barristers' findings, the CJC issued a report in December 1996 clearing all those involved in the memorandum of understanding of electoral bribery in relation to the MOU.

Even with the politically charged climate of the time, what followed this CJC report can be best described as a savage, unprecedented assault on the CJC by Premier Borbidge and Police Minister Cooper – an attack which may have done the CJC permanent damage. Cooper likened the Carruthers Inquiry to a European Cold War "show trial", claiming that it "struck at the heart of the democratic process" (*Sunday Mail* 22 Dec 1996, 6). He questioned the political allegiance of staff of the CJC saying that "Without naming names, they are card carrying members of the ALP Labor lawyers" (*Sunday Mail* 22 Dec 1996, 6).[10]

Choosing to ignore the fact that the CJC had acted on independent legal advice in appointing a retired judge from interstate, Cooper continued his barrage of criticism claiming that the Carruthers Inquiry "was loaded and they couldn't find any self-respecting judge in Queensland retired or otherwise to do the job so they shopped around until

---

9 Carruthers resigned on 29 October 1996.

10 Cooper's statement seemed hypocritical given that the inaugural chair of the CJC, Sir Max Bingham QC, had a distinguished 17-year career in Liberal Party politics in the Australian state of Tasmania. He was Attorney-General, Deputy Premier, Minister for Police and Minister for Education in Liberal Party Governments and the leader of the opposition. He was appointed to the position of CJC chairperson by the National Party Government of which Cooper was Premier. Sir Max's professionalism when chair of the CJC transcended party politics. There was absolutely no reason for Cooper to imply anything different in relation to other officers of the CJC.

they found one in New South Wales and brought him up here [to Queensland] to do their wicked will" (*Sunday Mail* 22 Dec 1996, 6).

Borbidge reacted to the CJC report by dumping "a torrent of criticism" on the Commission. He questioned whether its chair Frank Clair should continue in his position and claimed that the CJC's actions made "the KGB in its hey day look like a kindergarten picnic" (*Courier-Mail* 21 Dec 1996, 1; *Australian* 23 Dec 1996, 5).

It should be remembered that these extraordinary attacks on the Criminal Justice Commission resulted from its clearing Borbidge and Cooper of any criminal conduct on an issue that was referred to it in the first place by Police Minister Cooper. It begs the question of what might have happened to the CJC if the legal opinion had gone the other way.

Commentators were now describing the relationship between the CJC and the government as "poisonous". However, what followed at the Connolly-Ryan Inquiry not only inflamed the already "poisonous" relationship between the Borbidge Government and the CJC, it almost brought the Commission "to its knees".

Connolly-Ryan Inquiry

Some extraordinary happenings surrounded the setting-up and running of the *Commission of Inquiry Pursuant to Orders in Council dated 7 October 1996*, sometimes referred to as the *Inquiry into the Effectiveness of the CJC* but more commonly as the Connolly-Ryan Inquiry.[11] The

11 The Terms of Reference for the Commission of Inquiry are:

1. To examine and make recommendations in relation to the future role, structure, powers and operations of the Criminal Justice Commission established under the *Criminal Justice Act 1989*;
2. Without limiting in any manner the generality of paragraph 1:–
   (a) To examine and review whether the functions and responsibilities of the Criminal Justice Commission set out in the *Criminal Justice Act 1989* remain appropriate and provide a proper legislative framework for the future operations of the Criminal Justice Commission having regard to:–
      (i) the original purpose for which the Criminal Justice Commission was established;
      (ii) the extent to which such original purpose has been fulfilled;
      (iii) whether there are any functions currently vested in the Criminal Justice Commission which should now be performed by another agency or entity; and
      (iv) the appropriateness of the operational priorities previously determined by the Criminal Justice Commission and the relevance of these priorities to the proper objectives of the Criminal Justice Commission;

appointment of Peter Connolly to chair the inquiry into the CJC and his inappropriate public comments about Carruthers (a subject of his inquiry) have already been mentioned. However, controversy surrounding Connolly does not stop there. While escorting a part-time commissioner of the CJC to a private hearing of his inquiry, Connolly QC, the supposedly impartial chair, remarked that "now that our side of politics is back in power we can do a proper critique of the Fitzgerald experiment" (Criminal Justice Commission 1998, 97).

The manner in which the Connolly-Ryan Inquiry was being conducted was causing concern to many in the community. In June 1997 some 8 months after the inquiry was established, Mr Carruthers and the

---

(*cont*)

(b) To examine and review Divisions 4, 5, 6 and 7 of Part 2 of the *Criminal Justice Act 1989*;

(c) To examine and review the confidentiality provisions of the *Criminal Justice Act 1989*;

(d) To examine and review whether the Parliamentary Criminal Justice Committee established under Part 4 of the *Criminal Justice Act 1989*, is the most appropriate model for monitoring and reviewing the operations of the Criminal Justice Commission, or whether there are other or additional accountability measures that should be put in place;

(e) To examine and review when a periodic review or audit of the operations of the Criminal Justice Commission should be undertaken;

(f) To identify what legislative or other action should be taken by the Government of the State of Queensland in relation to the future role, structure, powers and operations of the Criminal Justice Commission;

(g) To examine and review the past operations of the Criminal Justice Commission with a view to making recommendations concerning the performance, efficiency, effectiveness and accountability of the Criminal Justice Commission and its various organisational elements;

(h) To examine and review the policies that have been adopted by the Criminal Justice Commission in relation to:–

(i) the manner and form of any proceedings which have been instituted on behalf of the Criminal Justice Commission under the *Criminal Justice Act 1989*;

(ii) the criteria for the selection and engagement of persons to undertake duties for and on behalf of the Criminal Justice Commission, being persons who are not staff of the Criminal Justice Commission in terms of Section 64 of the *Criminal Justice Act 1989*; and

(iii) the allocation of resources and funds between the various Divisions of the Criminal Justice Commission in the discharge of the statutory functions of the Criminal Justice Commission;

(i) To examine all the events, facts and circumstances involved and surrounding, or relevant to, the allegations which are contained in the Hansard Reports of Proceedings for the Legislative Assembly of Queensland of 13 September 1996 at pages 2915-2918.

(Terms of Reference for the Connolly-Ryan Inquiry 1997)

CJC commenced action in the Supreme Court of Queensland to prevent it proceeding further on the grounds of apprehended bias. The CJC relied on the following matters, which are outlined in their 1997-98 Annual Report, as being indicative of that bias. They were:

- adverse comments made by both Connolly and Ryan during their Inquiry to and about CJC witnesses;
- the refusal of the Commissioners (Connolly and Ryan) to accept an application by the CJC to call certain witnesses relevant to issues before the Inquiry;
- the continued expressions of disapproval by Mr Connolly in relation to the CJC's claim of legal professional privilege in respect of some material, even though the claim had been upheld by the Queensland Supreme Court;
- adverse comments by Mr Connolly in relation to the conduct of the CJC's Counsel and solicitors;
- the favourable treatment afforded to witnesses whose evidence was adverse to the CJC, in contrast to the adverse treatment afforded to witnesses whose evidence was seen to be favourable to the CJC; and
- the absence of intervention by the Commissioners when derogatory and inappropriate questions were put to CJC witnesses by Counsel. For example, when one Counsel referred to the CJC as "Gestapo Headquarters at Toowong" (Criminal Justice Commission 1998, 98).

On 5 August 1997 His Honour Justice Thomas of the Queensland Supreme Court brought down his judgment in relation to the apprehended bias claim. He highlighted several incidents throughout the Connolly-Ryan Inquiry which he indicated could be of concern to "a fair-minded and informed member of the public". They included:

- Mr Connolly's acceptance of the commission to investigate the conduct of the CJC in circumstances where his former client, Mr Cooper was sorely aggrieved by the conduct of the Criminal Justice Commission;
- Mr Connolly's disparaging remarks about Mr Carruthers;
- Mr Connolly's expression of political alignment while his inquiry into the CJC was current;

- Mr Connolly's conduct of hearings in a manner which was apparently more supportive of witnesses adverse to the CJC than those who are favourable to it; and
- Mr Connolly's uneven conduct in terms of the issue of alleged impropriety by the Director of the CJC's Official Misconduct Division which included a refusal to receive evidence that would support the Director's defence (Criminal Justice Commission 1998, 98).

Justice Thomas found, inter alia, that there was "overwhelming evidence of ostensible bias against Mr Connolly with respect to matters that his Commission had to consider". He ordered that "there be a declaration that the Commissioners [Connolly and Ryan] are disqualified from further proceeding with the subject Inquiry and an injunction should be granted restraining them forthwith from so proceeding". The Connolly-Ryan Inquiry was shut down.

As well as continually bombarding the Commission with criticism and establishing a committee to undertake one of the CJC's principal functions (the Bingham committee), the Borbidge Government also established the Connolly-Ryan Inquiry which:

- allegedly threatened the independence of an existing CJC inquiry, the Carruthers Inquiry which, inter alia, was examining the conduct of the premier and police minister; and
- usurped the role of the all party Parliamentary Criminal Justice Committee.

During their time in office the Borbidge National-Liberal Party Coalition Government also cut the CJC's budget by nearly 7 percent. This translated into a $2.7 million reduction in operating funds (Courier-Mail 13 September 1996, 1).

Even though the unrelenting and savage attacks on the Commission by the Borbidge coalition government can be sourced to the CJC's political oversight role, they had negative consequences for the Commission's police accountability function.

A CJC report to parliament *The Impact of the Connolly/Ryan Inquiry on the Criminal Justice Commission* outlines in some detail the impact the Inquiry had on the Commission.

Impact of the Connolly-Ryan Inquiry

When established, it was announced that the Connolly-Ryan Inquiry would last for three months. It had been running for 10 months when it was prematurely closed down by the Supreme Court of Queensland. During that time 126 days of hearings required the attendance of CJC staff.

The inquiry made 277 specific requests to the Criminal Justice Commission for information, some of which consumed a considerable amount of time. For example, one Summons to Produce required the Commission to supply the names and addresses of all past and present employees of the CJC and any consultants they had engaged since the establishment of CJC in 1989. This request covered a 7 year time span. It took 116 hours of staff time to comply with the direction. Another Summons to Produce required the CJC to produce all material relating to the Carruthers Inquiry. Fifty-five boxes of material had to be examined for legal professional privilege and photocopies made of all documents which had to be produced. This took 401 hours of staff time.

The CJC estimated that from the first Summon to Produce on 29 October 1996 until the closure of the Connolly-Ryan Inquiry in August 1997, a total of 17,234 hours were devoted to the Inquiry. This translates into 2377 working days or 12.64 persons working full-time for the 10 month period. These figures do not include the time spent on Inquiry matters by the Commission's chairperson, his executive assistant or the part-time commissioners.

The CJC report also highlights how each of the divisions were effected. For the purpose of this book only those divisions which play a significant role in the Commission's police oversight function will be mentioned.

The Official Misconduct Division's Complaints database revealed that there was an increase in the finalisation times for older matters and an increase in the number of incomplete complaints. The diversion of resources to the Connolly-Ryan Inquiry also meant that there were less resources to investigate complex matters. This led to a reduction in the number of completed official misconduct investigations being referred to Misconduct Tribunals.

The Manager of the Complaints Section's Initial Assessment Unit had to devote 31 working days attending to Inquiry matters. Consequently he was often unavailable to discuss complaints matters with the Chief Officer, Complaints. This led to a delay in finalising complaints.

For a five week period commencing mid-June 1997 the Deputy Chief Officer of the CJC's Review Unit's time was virtually devoted to responding to Connolly-Ryan Inquiry submissions. As a result, files were not reviewed. This contributed to substantial time delays in the review of QPS investigations. As the overwhelming majority of complaints referred to the CJC are about police, it can be safely assumed that the CJC's reactive police oversight role was adversely effected.

Research staff had the primary responsibility for the preparation, coordination, presentation and editing of the Commission's major submission to the Inquiry as well as the Chairperson's statement. The Division's legal staff were heavily involved with matters arising out of the Inquiry, with one officer's time being devoted almost exclusively to such matters. Because the Office of General Counsel's time was devoted exclusively to the Connolly-Ryan Inquiry, legal staff in the Research Division had to undertake the work normally carried out by General Counsel. The net result of this for the then Research and Coordination Division in terms of its police related responsibilities were:

- the delayed completion of several projects, including a major report on the implementation and impact of Fitzgerald Inquiry recommendations for the reform of the police complaints and disciplinary process;
- a delay in the commencement of work on a report (requested by the Parliamentary Criminal Justice Committee) about the transfer of prosecution functions from the police to the Director of Public Prosecutions; and
- a reduction in the resources available to monitor significant developments in the QPS and the follow-up of prior recommendations in these areas.

The Inquiry also took approximately three days a week of the Chairperson's time and more than half the time of his Executive Assistant. Part-time commissioners were involved directly in activities surrounding the Inquiry and had to attend certain hearings.

The Connolly-Ryan Inquiry also caused a major drain on the financial resources of the Commission. The direct financial costs have been estimated at $1,696,839.00. This money was spent on legal representation, external consultants and stationery and photocopying charges. These expenses occurred at a time when resources were already severely strained because of the previously mentioned budget cuts. There were no provisions in the CJC's budget for these additional costs but repeated requests to Attorney-General Denver Beanland by the Commission for its budget to be supplemented were denied.

A matter not taken up in the CJC's report to parliament, which could also have an adverse effect on the Criminal Justice Commission as an effective police oversight body, concerns a direction by the Connolly-Ryan Inquiry, that the CJC hand over to the inquiry the records of 700,000 phone calls made over the past three years. This demand could make some police and members of the public nervous about contacting the independent CJC in the future. It may also reduce the flow of information the Commission receives from informers and other intelligence sources and have implications for its witness protection program. These areas are directly and indirectly linked to the Commission's police oversight and review function.

Other spin-off effects

This chapter has already suggested that the Queensland Police Union, under the presidency of Gary Wilkinson, used political means to try to dismantle CJC powers, and that it may have been encouraged to do so by the attitude and actions of National and Liberal Party politicians towards the CJC. Neither of these issues will be re-canvassed here. However, the actions of the National-Liberal Party Government, in particular, could negatively impact on the Commission's police oversight role in other ways.

The behaviour of politicians toward the Commission could provide police management and the police union with ammunition if and/or when they try to reassert their power in the complaints against police process. Police can source adverse comments about the CJC back to governments and alternative governments. For example, the police department and/or the union could argue that the Commission's investigations are "quite incredibly quick", a "whitewash", a "witch hunt" or that the CJC conducts "KGB"-style investigations and therefore should not be involved in the complaints against police process.

It is not being argued that governments and opposition parties should not criticise the CJC. What is being questioned is the motive and intent that drives the criticism and its long-term effect on the Commission's credibility. It needs to be remembered that if honest police and the public lose confidence in the integrity of the police oversight agency they will not use it. Queensland's history clearly demonstrates that when that happens police corruption flourishes more easily.

Its difficult relationship with government creates particular problems for the Commission; problems which raise the question of whether, because the Fitzgerald Inquiry found corruption in the political system as well as the police force, the CJC ended up being asked to do an impossible job: oversighting police and other public servants' conduct, while at the same time investigating the suspected and alleged official misconduct of its masters. The scope of its jurisdiction means that the possibility continually exists for the Commission's effectiveness as a police oversight body to be undermined by the consequences of its political oversight function. However, it does not automatically follow that tensions between the CJC and governments would disappear if it no longer oversighted the conduct of politicians, only that they would not occur at the heightened level they often do.

The simple answer to reducing the level of tension between governments, alternative governments and the Criminal Justice Commission would be to remove the Commission's political oversight role. But if that were to happen, future memorandums of understanding between politicians and police unions may not be subject to the same level of independent, public scrutiny.

It is worth reiterating that the improper relationship between police and government was found, by the Fitzgerald Inquiry, to be a significant factor in the breakdown of police accountability in Queensland. It allowed police misconduct and corruption to flourish.

As much as there are negative consequences for the CJC from its political oversight role, not all of the spin-off effects for police accountability are negative – for the Queensland community at least.

Conclusion

A body which oversights complaints against police is always vulnerable to attack by the powerful police pressure group. Such attacks can bring about the demise of the oversight body as experienced, for example, in Philadelphia and Victoria, Australia. If the oversight body's coverage includes other public sector departments and agencies, it can find itself fighting on two fronts. But when its functions extend to conducting publicly available, independent research into politically sensitive criminal justice issues, which may conflict with government policy, and investigating the conduct of its masters, it can find itself encircled by powerful, hostile opponents. Under these circumstances the best chance the oversight body has of being properly resourced, receiving adequate powers or in extreme circumstances of surviving, is public opinion. But when government intent is focused on undermining any support the public has for the oversight body, it can find itself in a vulnerable and precarious position.

Many other police oversight bodies would appreciate having the reactive powers and range of proactive functions the CJC does. However, because its multiple coverage extends to politicians, the CJC often finds itself charged with an unenviable task. It has to regulate those who, in turn, are responsible for the Commission's budget, role, functions and powers. Any evaluation of the Criminal Justice Commission's effectiveness would need to take these factors into account.

CONCLUSION

For too long police in liberal democratic societies controlled and operated the system whereby dishonest and unscrupulous police were held accountable for their actions. The "code of silence", the "them against us" syndrome and, in some instances, the politicisation of the policing function meant that, in practice, police were rarely brought to account for their dishonest and abusive behaviour.

Even though scandals periodically exposed how police were abusing the trust and powers conditionally granted them by society, and violating rather than protecting people's civil rights, governments failed to remove their virtual monopoly over the complaints against police process. Government failure to adequately protect one of the basic tenets of liberal democratic societies, the rights of the individual, can be explained in part by the power of the police and the symbiotic relationship which exists between police and government. But despite the privileged position of police, the bottom line for all governments is staying in power. As citizens started to organise into opposing pressure groups and lobby for more open and effective police accountability procedures, governments, sensing the mood of the electorate, responded to their demands. Some 40 years ago, policies which allowed civilians to participate in the police complaints process gradually began to be introduced, but progress has been patchy and confined.

Police objected strongly to their loss of control and even though they frequently did not win the battle against civilian involvement, they have used their considerable power to influence the scope of civilian participation and the stage at which they are permitted to become involved in the complaints process. Consequently, in too many jurisdictions, civilian oversight bodies are confined to asking police questions about a police investigation into the misconduct of other police some time after the investigative process is complete.

Being denied the most basic of oversight powers, the ability to investigate from the initial stage of the complaints process, means that too many external, civilian oversight bodies are trying to keep police accountable for their behaviour while blindfolded. Those with first-hand knowledge of what is required to effectively oversight police conduct, the heads of civilian oversight agencies, point out how this arrangement only creates a false sense of security for the public. Citizens believe that governments have established external, civilian bodies which can protect their rights by making police accountable for the use of their considerable power, when, in reality they cannot.

Even when governments grant civilian oversight agencies the core reactive powers they need to effectively discharge their responsibilities they usually fail to adequately resource them. As a result, they are unable to operationalise what powers they do have. Inadequate reactive powers and resources places civilian oversight bodies in a subordinate position to those they are oversighting and compromises their effectiveness as accountability institutions. Under these circumstances, it is not logical or wise to evaluate the effectiveness of the civilian oversight process on the basis of what can be defined as bad policy.

The unsatisfactory situation many "reactive only" bodies find themselves in does not appear to concern some governments. They understand that as long as they are seen to have responded to citizens' demands for greater police accountability, they can claim to have listened to the will of the people. They also understand that once the scandal which led to an increased interest in police accountability passes, the media and citizens lose interest in the more mundane aspects of civilian oversight.

Establishing bodies which are handicapped by insufficient powers can help ease the tense relationship which often develops between police and governments at the policy formulation stage of the complaints against police policy process. Police, acting as a pressure group, use this phase to exert their considerable power. As the oversight body is not yet an entity, it is unable to counter police demands about when and how civilians should be involved.

Police argue that in a liberal democratic society they are entitled to be involved in pressure group politics. However, in relation to complaints against police, governments have to decide if police should be instrumental in setting police accountability principles. In other words, should what constitutes acceptable police behaviour and appropriate sanctions for misbehaviour be set according to standards which are acceptable to police departments, unions and the police culture, or according to community norms.

Institutional tensions in the civilian oversight process are not confined to police and government. They naturally occur between oversight bodies and police. They also arise between oversight bodies and government.

Because the overwhelming majority of police oversight bodies can only react to complaints, they are perceived as the bearer of bad news. Governments sometimes respond to such news by attacking the messenger rather than heeding the message. But oversight bodies do not have to be simply reactive bodies which use a Band-Aid approach to treat symptoms. They can, governments willing, treat the cause of police misconduct and help to prevent it occurring and recurring. Indeed, as argued in this book, prevention is an essential part of civilian oversight process. By integrating reactive and proactive policies an holistic approach to police misconduct and associated issues becomes possible. Until this happens, civilian oversight can not be a truly effective method of police accountability.

An holistic approach also help ease tensions in the relationship between police and oversight body and oversight body and government. The message conveyed by an institution which adopts an integrated approach can often be positive, and a positive message is more palatable for politicians and police to digest. It is also a more appealing one for them to pass on to the community.

The reactive-proactive Criminal Justice Commission model outlined in this book goes part of the way to countering the institutional tensions which arise from police-government and police-oversight body relations. For example, its integrated, holistic approach to police misconduct and associated issues helps to ease tensions in police-oversight body relations. The reduction of party political interference in police reform processes and police-related research also takes partial account of some problems which can arise in police-government relations and puts a layer between police and government, which may be beneficial in preventing the politicisation of the policing function.

The CJC model is a leap forward in the complaints against police process. By dealing with the cause and prevention of police misconduct, it offers a new approach to old problems – a "one-stop shop" strategy to police misconduct, corruption and associated issues. This stands in stark contrast to the somewhat fragmented approach found in Goldsmith's and Kerstetter's models. Even though Bayley and Perez go one step further and advocate a reactive, proactive approach, they do not go far enough, nor do they account for the impact external relations can have on the civilian oversight process.

The CJC model came into being when relationships between the police and government were under severe strain and the power of the police department and police union had been temporarily negated. Because of these unusual circumstances, Fitzgerald was able to have his recommendations for a near ideal police oversight body implemented "lock, stock and barrel". However, unlike most bodies which oversight police, his model widens the jurisdiction of the CJC to include politicians.

It has already been acknowledged that because of its unusual jurisdiction, the Criminal Justice Commission case study offers a more severe example of oversight body-government relations. However, coupled with the case study on the Police Complaints Tribunal, it highlights the fact that external relations need to be included when analysing and evaluating the effectiveness of the civilian oversight process.

BIBLIOGRAPHY

Alderson, John 1984, *Law and Disorder*, Hamish Hamilton, London.

Alderson, John 1992, "The police", in *Criminal Justice Under Stress*, eds E Stockdale and S Calase, Blackstone Press, London.

Alderson, John 1993, Police: The social contract theory and its practical implications, paper presented at national conference, *Keeping the Peace: Police Accountability and Oversight*, Royal Institute of Public Administration Australia and NSW Office of the Ombudsman, Sydney, 20-21 May.

Alpert, Geoffrey and Dunham, Roger 1988, *Policing Urban America*, Waveland Press, Illinois.

Annual Report of Her Majesty's Chief Inspector of Constabulary for 1995/96, HMSO, London.

Ascoli, D 1979, *The Queen's Peace*, Hamish Hamilton, London.

Australian Law Reform Commission 1975, *Report no 1: Complaints Against Police*, AGPS, Canberra.

Australian Law Reform Commission 1978, *Report no 9: Complaints Against Police, Supplementary Report*, AGPS, Canberra.

Australian Law Reform Commission 1996, *Complaints Against the AFP and NCA*, Draft Recommendation Paper, July, ALRC, Sydney.

Avery, J 1981, *Police: Force or Service*, Butterworths, Sydney.

Bachrach, P and Baratz, MS 1962, "Two faces of power", *American Political Science Review*, vol 56, pp 947-52.

Bachrach, P and Baratz, MS 1963, "Decisions and nondecisions: An analytical framework", *American Political Science Review*, vol 57, pp 633-42.

Barton, Peter G 1970, "Civilian review boards and the handling of complaints against the police", *University of Toronto Law Journal*, vol 20, pp 448-69.

Baxter, John and Koffman, Laurence (eds) 1985, *Policing and the Rule of Law in Police: The Constitution and the Community*, Professional Books Limited, London.

Bayley, David H 1983, "Accountability and control of police: Lessons for Britain", in *The Future of Policing*, ed T Bennett, Institute of Criminology, Cambridge.

Bayley, David H 1985a, "Control of the police", in *Patterns of Policing: A Comparative International Analysis*, Rutgers University Press, New Brunswick, NJ.

Bayley, David H 1985b, "Police in political life", in *Patterns of Policing: A Comparative International Analysis*, Rutgers University Press, New Brunswick, NJ.

Bayley, David H 1991, "Preface", in *Complaints Against the Police: The Trend to External Review*, Clarendon, Oxford.

Bayley, David H 1992a, "Comparative organization of the police in English-speaking countries", in *Modern Policing*, eds M Tonry and N Morris, The University of Chicago Press, Chicago.

Bayley, David H 1992b, *Police Brutality and Civilian Oversight*, Occasional paper of the International Association of Civilian Oversight of Law Enforcement, 2nd issue, IACOLE, Ohio.

Bell, John 1986, "PACE and complaints against the police", *Policing*, vol 2, no 4, pp 283-93.

Beral, Howard and Sisk, Marcus 1964, "The administration of complaints by civilians against the police", *Harvard Law Review*, vol 77, pp 499-518.

Bingham, M 1992, "Criminal Justice Commission: Performance Report", in *Keeping them Honest: Democratic Reform in Queensland*, eds A Hede, S Prasser and M Neylan, University of Queensland Press, St Lucia.

Bingham, M 1993, "The Criminal Justice Commission: Agenda and program", in *Public Sector Reform Under the First Goss Government: A Documentary Sourcebook*, ed G Davis, Royal Institute of Public Administration Australia and Centre for Australian Public Sector Management, Griffith University, Brisbane.

Bingham, M 1994, "The politicisation of crime", in *Unpeeling Tradition: Contemporary Policing*, eds K Bryett and C Lewis, Macmillan, Melbourne.

Bittner, Egon 1990, *Aspects of Police Work*, Northeastern University Press, Boston.

Blecker, Robert 1989, "Policing the police", in *Police and Policing: Contemporary Issues*, ed DJ Kenney, Praeger, New York.

Boateng, Paul 1985, "Crisis in accountability", in *Police: The Constitution and the Community*, eds J Baxter and L Koffman, Professional Books Limited, London.

Bowden, T 1978, *Beyond the Limits of the Law: A Comparative Study of the Police in Crisis Politics*, Penguin Books, London.

Brereton, David and Ede, Andrew 1996, The police code of silence in Queensland: Assessing the impact of the Fitzgerald reforms, paper presented to the 11th Annual Conference of Australian and New Zealand Society of Criminology, Wellington, Jan, rev draft 16 Feb, pp 1-23.

Brogden, Mike, Jefferson, Tony and Walklate, Sandra 1988, *Introducing Policework*, Unwin Hyman, London.

Brown, David 1985a, "Civilian review of complaints against the police: A survey of United States literature" in *Policing Today*, eds K Heal, R Tarling and J Burrows, HMSO, London.

Brown, David 1985b, *Civilian Review of Complaints against the Police: A Survey of United States Literature*, Research and Planning Unit paper no 19, HMSO, London.

Brown, David 1987, *The Police Complaints Procedure: A Survey of Complainants" Views*, Home Office Research Study no 93, HMSO, London.

Brown, Lee P 1975, "Police review boards: An historical and critical analysis", in *Critical Issues in Criminal Justice*, ed DO Schultz, Charles C Thomas, Illinois.

Brown, Lee P 1991, "The Civilian Review Board: Setting a goal for future obsolescence", *The Police Chief*, July, p 6.

Bryett, Keith and Lewis, Colleen (eds) 1994, *Unpeeling Tradition: Contemporary Policing*, Macmillan, Melbourne.

Carruthers QC, His Honour Kenneth 1996, Resignation Speech, 29 Oct.

Change Implementation Team 1995, "Team-based approach to future operations", *Platypus Magazine*, no 47, pp 14-21.

Chevigny, Paul 1995 *Edge of the Knife: Police Violence in the Americas*, The New Press, New York.

City of New York 1994, Commission to investigate allegations of police corruption and the anti-corruption procedures of the police department, Commission Report (The Mollen Commission Report), New York.

Clifford, W 1981, Policing a democracy, Keynote Address at Eleventh National Conference, Australian Crime Prevention Councils, Canberra, 31 Aug.

Clifford, W 1982, *Policing a Democracy*, Australian Institute of Criminology, Canberra.

Coaldrake, P 1989a, "Changing the system", *Legal Service Bulletin*, vol 14, no 4, Aug, pp 159-60.

Coaldrake, P 1989b, *Working the System: Government in Queensland*, University of Queensland Press, St Lucia, Qld.

Coaldrake, P 1991, "The campaign", in *Political Crossroads: The 1989 Queensland Election*, eds R Whip and C Hughes, University of Queensland Press, St Lucia, Qld.

Coaldrake, P and Wanna, J 1988, Not like the good old days: The political impact of the Fitzgerald Inquiry into police corruption in Queensland, paper presented at the Australasian Political Studies Association Conference, University of New England, Armidale, NSW, Aug.

Cohen, B 1985, "Police complaints procedure: Why and for whom?", in *Police: The Constitution and the Community*, ed J Baxter and L Koffman, Professional Books Ltd, London.

Commission of Inquiry into Possible Illegal Activities and Associated Police Misconduct (The Fitzgerald Inquiry) 1987-89, Brisbane.

Commission of Inquiry into the Future Role, Structure, Powers and Operation of the Criminal Justice Commission (The Connolly-Ryan Inquiry) 1997, Brisbane.

Commission to Investigate Allegations of Police Corruption and the Anti-corruption Procedures of the Police Department (The Mollen Commission) 1994, New York.

Commonwealth and Defence Force Ombudsman *Annual Reports 1989-90; 1990-91; 1992*, AGPS, Canberra.

Commonwealth Ombudsman, *Annual Report 1994-98*, AGPS, Canberra.

Communist Party of Australia 1977, *Law in Disorder: Politics, the Police and Civil Liberties in Queensland*, State Committee, Communist Party of Australia, Fortitude Valley, Qld.

Compton, RL 1995, "Self-managing work teams: Evolution, revolution or commonsense?", *Management*, Sept, pp 5-8.

Corns, Chris 1992a, "Inter-agency relations: Some hidden obstacles to combating organised crime", *The Australian and New Zealand Journal of Criminology*, vol 25, no 2, July, pp 169-85.

Corns, Chris 1992b, "Lawyers and police: An uneasy marriage in the NCA's fight against organised crime", *The Australian and New Zealand Journal of Criminology*, vol 25, no 3, Dec, pp 231-54.

Corns, Chris 1994, "Reply to rejoinder to my article "Lawyers and police: An uneasy marriage in the NCA's fight against organised crime"", *The Australian and New Zealand Journal of Criminology*, vol 27, no 2, Sept, pp 172-73.

Cribb, M 1991, "The National Party", in *Political Crossroads: The 1989 Queensland Election*, eds R Whip and C Hughes, University of Queensland Press, St Lucia, Qld.

Criminal Justice Act 1989 (Qld).

Criminal Justice Commission 1990a, *Annual Report*, CJC, Brisbane.

Criminal Justice Commission 1990b, *Reforms in Laws Relating to Homosexuality: An Information Paper*, CJC, Brisbane.

Criminal Justice Commission 1990c, *Report on Gaming Machine Concerns and Regulations*, CJC, Brisbane.

Criminal Justice Commission 1991a, *Annual Report*, CJC, Brisbane.

Criminal Justice Commission 1991b, *Regulating Morality? An Inquiry into Prostitution in Queensland*, September, CJC, Brisbane.

Criminal Justice Commission 1991c, *Report on an Investigation into Possible Misuse of Parliamentary Travel Entitlements by Members of the 1986-1989 Queensland Legislative Assembly*, CJC, Brisbane.

Criminal Justice Commission 1991d, *Review of Prostitution-related Laws in Queensland: An Information and Issue Paper*, March, CJC, Brisbane.

Criminal Justice Commission 1991e, *Submission on Monitoring of the Functions of the Criminal Justice Commission*, CJC, Brisbane.

Criminal Justice Commission 1992, *Annual Report*, CJC, Brisbane.

Criminal Justice Commission 1993a, *Annual Report*, CJC, Brisbane.

Criminal Justice Commission 1993b, *Attitudes towards Queensland Police Service: Second Survey*, CJC, Brisbane.

Criminal Justice Commission 1993c, *Cannabis and the Law in Queensland: A Discussion Paper*, Government Printer, Brisbane.

Criminal Justice Commission 1993d, *Report on a Review of Police Powers in Queensland: Volume I: An Overview*, CJC, Brisbane.

Criminal Justice Commission 1994a, *Annual Report*, CJC, Brisbane.

Criminal Justice Commission 1994b, *A Report of an Investigation into the Arrest and Death of Daniel Alfred Yock*, CJC, Brisbane.

Criminal Justice Commission 1994c, *A Report on an Investigation into the Cape Melville Incident*, CJC, Brisbane.

Criminal Justice Commission 1994d, *Implementation of Reform within the Queensland Police Service: The Response of the Queensland Police Service to the Fitzgerald Inquiry Recommendations*, CJC, Brisbane.

Criminal Justice Commission 1994e, *Informal Complaint Resolution in the Queensland Police Service: An Evaluation*, CJC, Brisbane.

Criminal Justice Commission 1994f, *Report by the Criminal Justice Commission on its Public Hearings Conducted by the Honourable RH Matthews QC into the Improper Disposal of Liquid Waste in South-East Queensland, Volume I: Report Regarding Evidence Received on Mining Issues*, July, CJC, Brisbane.

Criminal Justice Commission 1994g, *Report on an Investigation Conducted by the Honourable RH Matthews QC into the Improper Disposal of Liquid Waste in South-East Queensland, Volume II: Transportation and Disposal*, October, CJC, Brisbane.

Criminal Justice Commission 1994h, *Submission to the Parliamentary Criminal Justice Committee on its Review of the Criminal Justice Commission's Activities*, July, CJC, Brisbane.

Criminal Justice Commission 1995a, *Annual Report*, CJC, Brisbane.

Criminal Justice Commission 1995b, *Ethical Conduct and Discipline in the Queensland Police Service: The Views of Recruits, First Year Constables and Experienced Officers*, CJC, Brisbane.

Criminal Justice Commission 1995c, *External Oversight of Complaints Against Police in Australia: A Cross-jurisdictional Analysis*, CJC, Brisbane.

Criminal Justice Commission 1995d, Media Release, 3 March.

Criminal Justice Commission 1995e, *Report on an Inquiry Conducted by the Honourable DG Stewart into Allegations of Official Misconduct at the Basil Stafford Centre*, March, CJC, Brisbane.

Criminal Justice Commission 1995f, *Telecommunications Interception and Criminal Investigation in Queensland: A Report*, CJC, Brisbane.

Criminal Justice Commission 1996a, *Annual Report*, CJC, Brisbane.

Criminal Justice Commission 1996b, *Informal Complaint Resolution in the Queensland Police Service: Follow-up Evaluation*, CJC, Brisbane.

Criminal Justice Commission 1996c, *Submission to the Queensland Police Service Review Committee*, July, CJC, Brisbane.

Criminal Justice Commission 1997, *Annual Report*, CJC Brisbane.

Criminal Justice Commission 1998, *Annual Report*, CJC Brisbane.

Critchley, TA 1967, *A History of Police in England and Wales, 900-1966*, Constable, London.

Curran, James T 1972, "Toward an ethical police service", in *Police and Law Enforcement: An AMS Anthology*, eds JT Curran, A Fowler and RH Ward, AMS Press Inc, New York.

Dahl, R 1956, "The concept of power", *Behavioural Science*, vol 1, pp 201-15.

Dahl, R 1957, "The concept of power", *Behavioural Science*, vol 2, pp 201-5.

Dahl, R 1958, "A critique of the ruling elite model", *American Political Science Review*, vol 52, no 2, pp 463-69.

Dahl, R 1961, *Who Governs?*, Yale University Press, New Haven.

Dahl, R 1978, "Pluralism revisited", *Comparative Politics*, vol 10, pp 191-203.

Dahl, R 1982, *Dilemmas of Pluralist Democracy: Autonomy vs Control*, Yale University Press, New Haven.

Daley, Robert 1978, *Prince of the City: The True Story of a Cop Who Knew Too Much*, Houghton, Mifflin, Boston.

Davis, Glyn 1995, *A Government of Routines: Executive Coordination in an Australian State*, Macmillan, Melbourne.

Davis, G and Wanna, J 1988, "The Fitzgerald Commission: The politics of inquiries", *Canberra Bulletin of Public Administration*, no 55, June, pp 78-83.

Davis, G, Wanna, J Warhurst, J and Weller, P 1988, *Public Policy in Australia*, Allen and Unwin, Sydney.

Davis, G, Wanna, J Warhurst, J and Weller, P 1993, *Public Policy in Australia*, 2nd edn, Allen and Unwin, Sydney.

Day, Patricia and Klein, Rudolf 1987, *Accountabilities: Five Public Services*, Tavistock, London.

Dickie, P 1989, *The Road to Fitzgerald and Beyond*, University of Queensland Press, St Lucia, Qld.

Dixon, David 1995a, "Change in policing, changing police", *The Australian and New Zealand Journal of Criminology*, Special Supplementary Issue, pp 62-66.

Dixon, David 1995b, "Crime, criminology and public policy", *The Australian and New Zealand Journal of Criminology*, Special Supplementary Issue, pp 1-5.

Dugan, John R and Breda, Daniel R 1991, "Complaints about police officers: A comparison among types and agencies", *Journal of Criminal Justice*, vol 19, no 2, pp 165-71.

Dunham, Roger G and Alpert, Geoffrey P 1993, *Critical Issues in Policing: Contemporary Readings*, 2nd edn, Waveland Press, Illinois.

Elliott, JF and States, Mitchell H 1980, "The concept of power and the police", *Journal of Police Science and Administration*, vol 8, no 1, pp 87-93.

Emy, Hugh V and Hughes, Owen E 1988, *Australian Politics: Realities in Conflict*, Macmillan, Melbourne.

Ericson, Richard V 1981, "Rules for police deviance", in *Organisational Police Deviance: Its Structure and Control*, ed CD Shearing, Butterworths, Toronto.

Etter, Barbara and Palmer, Mick (eds) 1995, *Police Leadership in Australasia*, The Federation Press, Sydney.

Fenna, Alan 1998, *Introduction to Australian Public Policy*, Longman, Sydney.

Findlay, Mark 1988a, "Institutional responses to corruption: Some critical reflections on the ICAC", *Criminal Law Journal*, vol 12, pp 271-85.

Findlay, Mark 1988b, "Lessons in fighting corruption", *Legal Services Bulletin*, vol 13, no 4, Aug, pp 141-45.

Findlay, Mark and Zvekic, Ugljesca 1993, *Alternative Policing Styles: Cross-Cultural Perspectives*, United Nations Interregional Crime and Justice Research Institute, Kluwer Law and Taxation Publishers, Deventer-Boston.

Finnane, Mark 1987a, "Police complaints Queensland style", *Legal Services Bulletin*, vol 12, no 2, pp 75-76.

Finnane, Mark 1987b, "The Fitzgerald Commission: Uncovering the Lewis years", *Legal Services Bulletin*, Oct, pp 210-14.

Finnane, Mark 1988, "The Fitzgerald Commission: Law, politics and state corruption in Queensland", *Australian Journal of Public Administration*, vol XLVII, no 4, Dec, pp 332-42.

Finnane, Mark 1994, *Police and Government: Histories of Policing in Australia*, Oxford University Press, Melbourne.

Fogel, David 1987, "The investigation and disciplining of police misconduct: A comparative view – London, Paris, Chicago", *Police Studies*, vol 10, no 1, Spring, pp 1-15.

Fosdick, Raymond 1920, *American Police Systems*, The Century Co, New York.

Freckelton, Ian 1988a, "Sensation and symbiosis", in *Police in Our Society*, eds I Freckelton and H Selby, Butterworths, Sydney.

Freckelton, Ian 1988b, "The Police Complaints Authority: Shooting the messenger", *Legal Services Bulletin*, vol 13, no 2, April, pp 58-60.

Freckelton, Ian 1991, "Shooting the messenger: The trial and execution of the Victorian Police Complaints Authority", in *Complaints Against the Police: The Trend to External Review*, ed A Goldsmith, Clarendon Press, Oxford.

Freckelton, Ian and Selby, Hugh 1987, "Police accountability: How serious the commitment?", *Legal Services Bulletin*, vol 12, no 2, April, pp 66-70.

Freckelton, Ian and Selby, Hugh 1989, "Piercing the blue veil: An assessment of external review of police", in *Australian Policing: Contemporary Issues*, eds D Chappell and P Wilson, Butterworths, Sydney.

Friedrich, Carl J 1940, "The nature of administrative responsibility", in *Public Policy*, ed CJ Friedrich, Harvard University Press, Cambridge, MA.

Fyfe, James 1985, *Reviewing Citizens" Complaints against Police in Police Management Today: Issues and Case Studies*, International City Management Association, Washington, DC.

Geller, William A (ed) 1985, *Police Leadership in America: Crisis and Opportunity*, American Bar Foundation/Praeger, New York.

Gellhorn, Walter 1966, "Police review boards: Hoax or hope?", *Columbia University Forum*, Summer, pp 5-10.

Glare, K 1985, "Complaints against police", *Police Life*, May, pp 78-79.

Gleeson, AM 1993, Police accountability and oversight: An overview, paper presented at national conference, *Keeping the Peace: Police Accountability and Oversight*, Royal Institute of Public Administration Australia and NSW Office of the Ombudsman, Sydney, 20-21 May.

Goldring, John and Blazey, Patricia 1993, Constitutional and legal mechanisms of police accountability in Australia, paper presented at national conference, *Keeping the Peace: Police Accountability and Oversight*, Royal Institute of Public Administration Australia and NSW Office of the Ombudsman, Sydney, 20-21 May.

Goldsmith, Andrew J 1988, "New directions in police complaints procedures: Some conceptual and comparative departures", *Police Studies*, vol 11, no 1, Spring, pp 60-71.

Goldsmith, Andrew J 1990, External review and self-regulation in police complaints procedures: A "community policing" perspective, paper presented at conference, *The Police and the Community*, Australian Institute of Criminology, Canberra, 23-25 Oct.

Goldsmith, Andrew J (ed) 1991a, *Complaints Against the Police: The Trend to External Review*, Clarendon Press, Oxford.

Goldsmith, Andrew J 1991b, "External review and self-regulation: Police accountability and the dialectic of complaints procedures", in *Complaints Against the Police: The Trend to External Review*, ed A Goldsmith, Clarendon Press, Oxford.

Goldsmith, Andrew J 1993, "And that's the way it is": Institutional legitimacy and the limits of forensic realism for police complaints system, paper presented at national conference, *Keeping the Peace: Police Accountability and Oversight*, Royal Institute of Public Administration Australia and NSW Office of the Ombudsman, Sydney, 20-21 May.

Goldsmith, Andrew J and Farson, Stuart 1987, "Complaints against the police in Canada: A new approach", *The Criminal Law Review*, September, pp 615-23.

Goldstein, Herman 1977, "The corruption problem", in *Policing a Free Society*, ed H Goldstein, Ballinger Publishing Co, Cambridge, MA.

Goldstein, Ralph 1985a, "Complaints and the Ombudsman", *Australian Federal Police Journal*, vol 6, no 13, Oct, pp 15-16.

Goldstein, Ralph 1985b, "Complaints and the Ombudsman", *Australian Federal Police Journal*, vol 6, no 14, Nov, pp 26-27.

Goldstein, Ralph 1986, “Complaints and the Ombudsman”, *Australian Federal Police Journal*, vol 7, no 2, Feb, pp 21-22.

Goode, Matthew 1973, “Administrative systems for the resolution of complaints against the police: A proposed reform”, *Adelaide Law Review*, vol 5, no 1, Dec, pp 55-78.

Goode, Matthew 1987, “Controlling police misconduct, complaints against the police and the process of law reform: As it happens – an academic war story”, in *Government Illegality*, ed P Grabosky assisted by I le Lievre, Australian Institute of Criminology Proceedings no 17, Australian Institute of Criminology, Canberra.

Goode, Matthew 1991, “Complaints against the police in Australia: Where we are now, and what we might learn about the process of law reform, with some comments about the process of legal change”, in *Complaints Against the Police: The Trend to External Review*, ed A Goldsmith, Clarendon Press, Oxford.

Goodsell, Charles T (ed) 1981, *The Public Encounter: Where State and Citizen Meet*, Indiana University Press, Bloomington.

Grant, Alan 1976, “Complaints against the police: The North American experience”, *Criminal Law Review*, June, pp 338-43.

Griffith, Curt T and Verdun-Jones, Simon N 1989, *Canadian Criminal Justice*, Butterworths, Toronto.

Griswold, David B 1994, “Complaints against the police: Predicting dispositions”, *Journal of Criminal Justice*, vol 22, no 3, pp 215-21.

Guyot, Dorothy 1991, *Policing as Though People Matter*, Temple University Press, Philadelphia.

Hague, Rod and Harrop, Martin 1982, *Comparative Government: An Introduction*, Macmillan, London.

Hain, Peter 1979, “Introduction”, in *Policing the Police, Volume 1, The Complaints System: Police Powers and Terrorism Legislation*, eds P Hain, D Humphry and B Rose-Smith, John Calder, London.

Hain, Peter, Humphry, Derek and Rose-Smith, Brian (eds) 1979, *Policing the Police, Volume 1, The Complaints System: Police Powers and Terrorism Legislation*, John Calder, London.

Ham, C and Hill, M 1984, *The Policy Process in the Modern Capitalist State*, Wheatsheaf, Sussex.

Ham, C and Hill, M 1993, *The Policy Process in the Modern Capitalist State*, 2nd edn, Harvester Wheatsheaf, London.

Hann, Robert, McGinnis, James, Stenning, Philip and Farson, Stewart 1985, “Municipal police governance and accountability in Canada: An empirical study”, *Canadian Police College Journal*, vol 9, no 1, pp 1-85.

Harrison, John and Cragg, Stephen 1991a, “Police complaints”, in *Police Misconduct: Legal Remedies*, 2nd edn, Legal Action Group, London, pp 26-55.

Harrison, John and Cragg, Stephen 1991b, "What can be done", in *Police Misconduct: Legal Remedies*, 2nd edn, Legal Action Group, London, pp 1-10.

Hawice, RJ 1984, "Do police have industrial muscle?", *Police Union Review*, Oct, pp 44-47.

Hawker, B 1981, "Police, politics, protest and the press: Queensland 1967-81", *Alternative Criminology Journal*, vol 4, July, pp 57-91.

Heclo, H 1972, "Review article: Policy analysis", *British Journal of Political Science*, vol 2, January.

Heclo, H 1978, "Issue networks of the executive establishment", in *The New American Political System*, ed A King, AGI, Washington.

Heneley, Terry 1988, "Civilian review boards: A means to police accountability", *The Police Chief*, vol LV, no 9, Sept, pp 45-47.

Hewitt, Patricia 1982, *A Fair Cop: Reforming the Police Complaints Authority*, National Council for Civil Liberties, London.

Hoffman, Paul and Crew, John 1991, *On the Line*, American Civil Liberties Union, San Francisco.

Hogarth, John 1982, "Police accountability", in *The Maintenance of Order in Society*, ed R Donclan, Proceedings of symposium, Centre of Criminology, University of Toronto, Canadian Police College, Ottawa.

Hogg, Russell and Hawker, Bruce 1983a, "The politics of police independence, pt. I", *Legal Services Bulletin*, vol 8, no 4, Aug, pp 169-75.

Hogg, Russell and Hawker, Bruce 1983b, "The politics of police independence, pt. II", *Legal Services Bulletin*, vol 8, no 5, Oct, pp 221-24.

Home Office 1993, *Police Reform: A Police Service for the Twenty-First Century. The Government's Proposals for the Police Service in England and Wales*, HMSO, London.

Home Office F2 Division 1993, *Review of Police Discipline Procedures*, Consultation paper, HMSO, London.

Hudson, James R 1971, "Police review boards and police accountability", *Law and Contemporary Problems*, vol 36, pp 515-38.

Humphry, Derek 1979, "The complaints system", in *Policing the Police, Volume 1, The Complaints System: Police Powers and Terrorism Legislation*, eds P Hain, D Humphry and B Rose-Smith, John Calder, London.

Hunt, David 1993, Police authority, police responsiveness and the rights of the individual: What is the right balance? paper presented at national conference, *Keeping the Peace: Police Accountability and Oversight*, Royal Institute of Public Administration Australia and NSW Office of the Ombudsman, Sydney, 20-21 May.

Hurley, Seán D 1995, *Community Policing and Civilian Oversight of Police: Some Preliminary Thoughts*, Occasional paper of the International Association for Civilian Oversight of Law Enforcement, IACOLE, Ohio.

Inquiry into Allegation of Police Misconduct in Relation to SP Bookmaking at Southport (The O'Connell Inquiry) 1977, Brisbane.

International Association for Civilian Oversight of Law Enforcement (IACOLE) 1985, *Proceedings on First International Conference on Civilian Oversight of Law Enforcement*, IACOLE, Toronto, Canada.

Jaensch, D 1991, *Parliament, Parties and People: Australian Politics Today*, Longman Cheshire, Melbourne.

James, Steve and Warren, Ian 1995, "Culture and ethics: The case of police rule-breaking", *Res Publica*, vol 4, no 3, pp 1-4.

Jefferson, T and Grimshaw, R 1984, *Controlling the Constable*, Frederi Muller, London.

Keim, Stephen 1987, "Police: Police complaints system in Queensland – possible improvements", *Legal Services Bulletin*, vol 12, no 6, Dec, pp 275-77.

Kelling, George L and Moore, Mark H 1988, "The evolving strategy of policing", *Perspectives on Policing*, series no 4, US Department of Justice, National Institute of Justice, Nov.

Kelly, William and Kelly, Nora 1976, *Policing in Canada*, Macmillan, Toronto.

Kerstetter, Wayne A 1985, "Who disciplines the police? Who should?", in *Police Leadership in America: Crisis and Opportunity*, ed WA Geller, Praeger, New York.

Kingsley, R, Lea, J and Young, J 1986, *Losing the Fight Against Crime*, Basil Blackwell, Oxford.

Kirby, Michael D 1976, "New light on complaints against police", in *Proceedings of the Institute of Criminology, Sydney University Faculty of Law, no 29, Seminar on Complaints against Police*, Government Printer, Sydney, pp 11-32.

Kirby, Michael D 1992, "Mediation: Current controversies and future directions", *Australian Dispute Resolution Journal*, Aug, pp 139-48.

Knight, RC 1982, "Police and politics: Political control", *The Australian Police Journal*, vol 36, no 2, April, pp 75-81.

Koffman, Laurence 1985, "Safeguarding the rights of citizens", in *Police: The Constitution and the Community*, eds J Baxter and L Koffman, Professional Books Limited, London.

La Marsh Research Program on Violence 1983, *Police Misconduct in Metropolitan Toronto: A Study of Formal Complaints*, York University, Canada.

Lambert, John L 1986, *Police Powers and Accountability*, Croom Helm, Kent.

Landa, David E 1993, Serving the customer, paper presented at national conference, *Keeping the Peace: Police Accountability and Oversight*, Royal Institute of Public Administration Australia and NSW Office of the Ombudsman, Sydney, 20-21 May.

Landa, David E 1994, The Ombudsman surviving and thriving into the 2000's: The challenge, paper presented at the 25th Biennial Conference, International Bar Association, Melbourne, 13 Oct.

Landa, David and Lewis, Colleen 1996, "Making the police accountable for their conduct", in *Australian Policing: Contemporary Issues*, 2nd edn, Butterworths, Sydney.

Landau, Tammy 1994, *Public Complaints Against the Police: A View from Control*, ed CD Shearing, Butterworths, Toronto.

Lenihan, Denis 1994, "Lawyers, police and the National Crime Authority: A rejoinder to Dr Corns", *The Australian and New Zealand Journal of Criminology*, vol 27, no 2, Sept, pp 160-71.

Lessnoff, Michael 1986, *Social Contract: Issues in Political Theory*, Macmillan, London.

Leuci, Robert 1989, "A process of erosion: A personal account", in *Police and Policing: Contemporary Issues*, ed DJ Kenney, Praeger, New York.

Levenson, Howard and Fairweather, Fiona 1992a, "Police: Criminal Evidence Act 1984", in *Police Powers: A Practitioner's Guide*, Legal Action Group, London.

Levenson, Howard and Fairweather, Fiona 1992b, "Police complaints procedures", in *Police Powers: A Practitioner's Guide*, Legal Action Group, London.

Levenson, Howard and Fairweather, Fiona 1992c, "Remedies", in *Police Powers: A Practitioner's Guide*, Legal Action Group, London.

Lewis, Clare E 1991, "Police complaints in metropolitan Toronto: Perspectives of the Public Complaints Commissioner", in *Complaints Against the Police: The Trend to External Review*, ed A Goldsmith, Clarendon Press, Oxford.

Lewis, Clare E, Linden, Sidney B, and Keene, Judith 1986, "Public complaints against police in metropolitan Toronto: The history and operation of the Office of the Public Complaints Commissioner", *Criminal Law Quarterly*, vol 29, pp 115-44.

Lewis, Colleen 1988, Police accountability Queensland style, unpublished Honours thesis, Griffith University, Brisbane.

Lewis, Colleen 1992, "Police accountability: Unintended consequences of the reform process", in *Keeping Them Honest: Democratic Reform in Queensland*, eds A Hede, S Prasser and M Neylan, University of Queensland Press, St Lucia, Qld.

Lewis, Colleen 1994, "Independent external civilian review of police conduct", in *Unpeeling Tradition: Contemporary Policing*, eds K Bryett and C Lewis, Macmillan, Brisbane.

Lewis, Norman and Birkinshaw, Patrick 1993, *When Citizens Complain: Reforming Justice and Administration*, Open University Press, Buckingham and Philadelphia.

Lewis, Terence Murray 1988, Submission to the Fitzgerald Inquiry, 11 Oct.

Lindblom, Charles E 1959, "The science of muddling through", *Public Administration Review*, vol 19, pp 79-88.

Lindblom, Charles E 1977, *Politics and Markets: The World's Political-Economic Systems*, Basic Books, Inc, New York.

Lindblom, Charles E 1979, "Still muddling, not yet through", *Public Administration Review*, vol 39, pp 517-26.

Loveday, Barry 1987, "Developments in police complaints procedure: Britain and North America", *Occasional Paper New Series no 22*, Department of Government and Economics, City of Birmingham Polytechnic, Dec.

Loveday, Barry 1993, "The local accountability of the police in England and Wales: Future prospects", in *Accountable Policing: Effectiveness, Empowerment and Equity*, eds R Reiner and S Spencer, Institute for Public Policy Research, London.

Lukes, Steven 1974, *Power: A Radical View*, Macmillan, London.

Lustgarten, Laurence 1986, "Chief constables: police authorities", in *The Governance of Police*, Sweet-Maxwell, London.

Lynch, Peter 1988, "Complaints against the police in Victoria: The need for reform", *The Law Institute Journal*, vol 62, no 5, May, pp 395-97.

McCormack, Robert J 1989-90, "Confronting police corruption: Organizational initiatives for internal control", *Criminal Justice*, Annual Edition 89/90, pp 90-94.

McDougall, Allan K 1988a, *Policing: The Evolution of a Mandate*, Canadian Police College, Ottawa.

McDougall, Allan K 1988b, *The Police Mandate: An Historical Perspective*, The Canadian Police College, Ottawa.

MacFarlane, Steve 1996, *Union News 5*, Queensland Police Union of Employees, Cairns, Queensland.

McLeay, EM 1990, "Defining policing policies and the political agenda", *Political Studies*, vol XXXVIII, no 4, Dec, pp 620-37.

McMahon, Maeve 1988, "Police accountability: The situation of complaints in Toronto", *Contemporary Crises*, vol 12, no 4, pp 301-27.

McMahon, Maeve and Ericson, Richard 1984, *Policing Reform: A Study of the Reform Process and Police Institution in Toronto*, Research Report, Centre of Criminology, University of Toronto, Canada.

Maguire, M 1991, "Complaints against the police: The British experience", in *Complaints Against the Police: The Trend to External Review*, ed A Goldsmith, Clarendon Press, Oxford.

Maguire, M and Corbett, C 1989, "Patterns and profiles of complaints against police", in *Coming to Terms with Policing: Perspectives on Policy*, eds R Morgan and DJ Smith, Routledge, New York.

Maguire, M and Corbett, C 1991, *A Study of the Police Complaints System*, HMSO, London.

Marenin, Otwin 1985, "Police performance and state rule: Control and autonomy in the exercise of coercion", *Comparative Politics*, vol 18, no 1, Oct, pp 101-22.

Marin, Rene J 1993, Police management and accountability, Key Address at national conference, *Keeping the Peace: Police Accountability and Oversight*, Royal Institute of Public Administration Australia and NSW Office of the Ombudsman, Sydney, 20-21 May.

Marshall, Geoffrey 1965, *Police and Government*, Methuen, London.

Marshall, Geoffrey 1978, "Police accountability revisited", in *Policy and Politics*, eds D Butler and A Halsey, Macmillan, London.

Marshall, Geoffrey 1985, "The police: Independence and accountability", in *The Changing Constitution*, eds J Jowell and D Oliver, Oxford University Press, Oxford.

Masterman, G 1985, Keynote address, paper presented to the *First International Conference on Civilian Oversight of Law Enforcement*, International Association for Civilian Oversight of Law Enforcement, Toronto, Canada, pp 35-52.

Masterman, G 1987, The first three years of the new complaints system, Special Report to Parliament, Sydney.

Masterman, G 1988, "External review: The New South Wales experience", in *Police in Our Society*, eds I Freckelton and H Selby, Butterworths, Sydney.

Meyer, John C 1977, Complaints of police corruption, Monograph, no 9, Criminal Justice Centre, New York.

Miliband, R 1977, *Marxism and Politics*, Oxford University Press, Oxford.

Milte, Kerry and Weber, Thomas A 1977, *Police in Australia: Development, Functions and Procedures*, Butterworths, Melbourne.

Moore, David and Wettenhall, Roger 1994, *Keeping the Peace: Police Accountability and Oversight*, University of Canberra and The Royal Institute of Public Administration, Canberra.

More, Harry W 1989, "Review of police conduct", in *Critical Issues in Law Enforcement*, 4th edn, ed HW More, Anderson Publishing Co, Cincinnati, OH.

More, Harry W 1992, *Special Topics in Policing*, Anderson Publishing Co, Ohio.

Morgan, Rod 1989, "Policing by consent: Legitimating the doctrine", in *Coming to Terms with Policing: Perspectives on Policy*, eds R Morgan and DJ Smith, Routledge, London.

Morton, James 1993, *Bent Coppers: A Survey of Police Corruption*, Little, Brown and Co, London.

Nader, Ralph 1972, "A code for professional integrity", in *Police Law Enforcement: An AMS Anthology*, eds JT Curran, A Fowler and RH Ward, AMS Press Inc, New York.

National Commission on Law Observance and Enforcement (the Wickersham Commission) 1931, Washington.

Nelson, Penelope 1986, "Beyond the blue curtain: The Ombudsman's role in investigating complaints against the police in New South Wales, *Australian Journal of Public Administration*, vol XLV, no 3, Sept, pp 230-38.

New South Wales Ombudsman 1990a, *Annual Report*, State Government Printing Service, Sydney.

New South Wales Ombudsman 1990b, *Special Report to Parliament pursuant to Section 31 of the Ombudsman Act: The independence and accountability of the Ombudsman*, Report to the Hon NF Greiner, Premier of New South Wales, NSW Ombudsman, Sydney.

New South Wales Ombudsman 1991a, *Annual Report*, State Government Printing Service, Sydney.

New South Wales Ombudsman 1991b, *Special Report to Parliament Pursuant to Section 31 of the Ombudsman Act: The Effective Functioning of the Office of the Ombudsman*, NSW Ombudsman, Sydney.

New South Wales Ombudsman 1992, *Annual Report*, State Government Printing Service, Sydney.

New South Wales Ombudsman 1993, *Annual Report*, State Government Printing Service, Sydney.

New South Wales Ombudsman 1994, *Annual Report*, State Government Printing Service, Sydney.

New South Wales Ombudsman 1995, *Annual Report*, State Government Printing Service, Sydney.

New South Wales Police Academy 1992, Seminar on Police and Government, Executive Development Program, Seminar 1.

Oliver, I 1987, *Police, Government and Accountability*, Macmillan, London.

Over, JE 1982, "Independent element: Yes or no", *The Police Journal*, vol LV, no 3, pp 238-43.

Page, RW 1976, "Commentary", in *Proceedings of the Institute of Criminology, Sydney University Faculty of Law, no 29, Seminar on Complaints against Police*, Government Printer, Sydney, pp 87-90.

Page, Robert W and Swanton, Bruce 1983, "Complaints against police in New South Wales: Administrative and political dimensions", *Australian Journal of Public Administration*, vol XLII, no 4, Dec, pp 503-28.

Palmer, Alasdair 1994, "Noble cause corruption", *The Police Journal*, March, pp 30-32.

Palmer, MJ 1993, The trend to external review, paper presented at national conference, *Keeping the Peace: Police Accountability and Oversight*, Royal Institute of Public Administration Australia and NSW Office of the Ombudsman, Sydney, 20-21 May.

Parliamentary Criminal Justice Committee 1991a, Report on prostitution, Report no 12, 12 November, Legislative Assembly of Queensland.

Parliamentary Criminal Justice Committee 1991b, Review of the Committee's operations and the operations of the Criminal Justice Commission, Part A: Submissions, vol 1, Public submissions, Report no 9, 16 July.

Parliamentary Criminal Justice Committee 1991c, Review of the Committee's operations and the operations of the Criminal Justice Commission, Part A: Submissions, vol 2, CJC Submissions and Minutes of Evidence taken on 6 and 13 June 1991, Report no 9, 16 July.

Parliamentary Criminal Justice Committee 1991d, Review of the Committee's operations and the operations of the Criminal Justice Commission, Part A: Submissions, vol 2B, CJC Submissions and Minutes of Evidence taken on 6 and 13 June 1991, Report no 9, 16 July.

Parliamentary Criminal Justice Committee 1991e, Review of the operations of the Parliamentary Criminal Justice Committee and the Criminal Justice Commission, Part B: Analysis and recommendations, Report no 13, December, Legislative Assembly of Queensland.

Parliamentary Criminal Justice Committee 1992a, Report on the public hearing held on 25 June 1992 into allegations made by Mr Richard Chesterman QC (past member of the Misconduct Tribunals), on 23 June 1992 in the *Courier-Mail* and the *Australian* newspapers, Report no 16, 13 July, Legislative Assembly of Queensland.

Parliamentary Criminal Justice Committee 1992b, Review of the operations of the Parliamentary Criminal Justice Committee and the Criminal Justice Commission, Part C: A report pursuant to section 4.8(1)(f) of the *Criminal Justice Act 1989*, Report no 18, August, Legislative Assembly of Queensland.

Parliamentary Criminal Justice Committee 1992c, The Committee's recommendations on changes to the method of appointment and conditions of service of members of the Misconduct Tribunals, Report no 17, 28 July, Legislative Assembly of Queensland.

Parliamentary Criminal Justice Committee 1993a, A review of the past twelve months operation of the Parliamentary Criminal Justice Committee of the 47th Parliament, Report no 22, 10 December, Legislative Assembly of Queensland.

Parliamentary Criminal Justice Committee 1993b, Transcript of Proceedings: Police Powers Review of Volumes I-III, Legislative Assembly of Queensland, 16 December, Brisbane.

Parliamentary Criminal Justice Committee 1993c, Transcript of Proceedings: Police Powers Review of Volumes I-III, Legislative Assembly of Queensland, 17 December, Brisbane.

Parliamentary Criminal Justice Committee 1994a, Report on the inquiry into the CJC's failure to account for two copies of the November 1993 Monthly Report to the PCJC and related matters, Report no 25, 5 August, Legislative Assembly of Queensland.

Parliamentary Criminal Justice Committee 1994b, Submissions to Parliamentary Criminal Justice Committee: The Three-yearly Review of the Criminal Justice Commission, Volume One and Two, August, PCJC, Brisbane.

Parliamentary Criminal Justice Committee 1994c, Transcripts of Proceedings: Inquiry into the CJC's Failure to Account for Two Copies of the November Monthly Report to the PCJC, 19-21 April, Brisbane.

Parliamentary Criminal Justice Committee 1995, A report of a review of the activities of the Criminal Justice Commission pursuant to s 118(1)(f) of the *Criminal Justice Act 1989*, Report no 26, 6 Feb, Legislative Assembly of Queensland.

Parliamentary Criminal Justice Committee 1998, A Report of a review of the activities of the Criminal Justice Commission pursuant to s 118(1)(f) of the *Criminal Justice Act 1989*, Report no 45, June, Legislative Assembly of Queensland.

Patience, Allan (ed) 1985, *The Bjelke-Petersen Premiership 1968-1983*, Longman Cheshire, Melbourne.

Pearce, Dennis 1992, "Impact of external review on government administration: The Commonwealth experience", *Australian Journal of Public Administration*, March, vol 51, no 1, pp 10-16.

Pearce, Dennis 1993, "The Ombudsman: Review and preview the importance of being different", *The Ombudsman*, vol 11, pp 13-36.

Perez, Douglas W 1994, *Common Sense about Police Review*, Temple University Press, Philadelphia.

Petterson, Werner E 1991, "Police accountability and civilian oversight of policing: An American perspective", in *Complaints Against the Police: The Trend to External Review*, ed A Goldsmith, Clarendon Press, Oxford.

Philips, Sir Cyril 1984, "Change and reform in the system of dealing with complaints against the police", *Policing*, vol 2, no 1.

Pike, Michael S 1985, "Independence and accountability", in *The Principles of Policing*, Macmillan, London.

Plehwe, Rudolph and Wettenhall, Roger 1993, Policing in Australia: An historical perspective, paper presented at national conference, *Keeping the Peace: Police Accountability and Oversight*, Royal Institute of Public Administration Australia and NSW Office of the Ombudsman, Sydney, 20-21 May.

Police Complaints and Discipline Procedures 1983, HMSO, London.

Police Complaints Authority 1988, *Triennial Review 1985-1988*, HMSO, London.

Police Complaints Authority 1990, *Report to the Home Secretary on Procedures for the Supervision of Investigation of Complaints against the Police*, HMSO, London.

Police Complaints Authority 1991, *Triennial Review 1988-91*, HMSO, London.

Police Complaints Authority 1994a, *Annual Report for the Year Ended 30 June 1994*, HMSO, London.

Police Complaints Authority 1994b, *Triennial Review 1991-94*, HMSO, London.

Police Complaints Authority 1995, *Police Complaints Authority: The First Ten Years*, HMSO, London.

Police Complaints Tribunal *Annual Report* 1982, 1983, 1984, 1985, Government Printer, Brisbane.

Police Complaints Tribunal 1986a, *Annual Report*, Government Printer, Brisbane.

Police Complaints Tribunal 1986b, *Report on Complaints by Barry Mannix*, Government Printer, Brisbane.

Police Complaints Tribunal *Annual Report* 1987, 1988, 1989, 1990, Government Printer, Brisbane.

Polsby, Nelson W 1963, *Community Power: Political Theory*, Yale University Press, New Haven.

Pomeroy, Wesley A Carroll 1985, "The source of police legitimacy and a model for police misconduct review: A response to Wayne Kerstetter", in *Police Leadership in America: Crisis and Opportunity*, ed WA Geller, Praeger, New York.

Prasser, Scott 1994, "Royal Commissions and public inquiries: Scope and uses", in *Royal Commissions and the Making of Public Policy*, ed P Weller, Macmillan, Melbourne.

Prasser, S, Wear, R and Nethercote, J (eds) 1990, *Corruption and Reform: The Fitzgerald Vision*, University of Queensland Press, St Lucia, Qld.

Procter, Craig 1985, "The police", in *The Bjelke-Petersen Premiership 1968-1983: Issues in Public Policy*, ed A Patience, Longman Cheshire, Melbourne.

Public Sector Management Commission 1993, *Review of the Queensland Police Service*, Government Printer, Brisbane.

Punch, Maurice 1983, "Officers and men: Occupational culture, inter-rank antagonism, and the investigation of corruption", in *Control in the Police Organisation*, ed M Punch, MIT Press, Cambridge, MA.

Queensland Council for Civil Liberties 1994, *Submission to the Parliamentary Criminal Justice Committee. Re: Three-yearly Review of Operation of the Criminal Justice Commission*, July, Brisbane.

Queensland Police Department *Annual Report* 1980, 1983, 1984, 1985, 1986, 1987, 1988, 1989, 1990, 1991, 1992, 1993, 1994, 1995, 1996, 1997, 1998, Government Printer, Brisbane.

Queensland Police Service 1996, *Submission to the Queensland Police Service Review*, May, QPS, Brisbane.

Queensland Police Service Review 1996, *Report on the Review of the Queensland Police Service*, Kingswood Press, Brisbane.

Queensland Police Union of Employees 1994, *Submission in Relation to the Three-yearly Review of the Operation of the Criminal Justice Commission*, June, Brisbane.

Ransley, Janet 1992, "Reform of parliamentary processes: An assessment", in *Keeping Them Honest: Democratic Reform in Queensland*, eds A Hede, S Prasser and M Neylan, University of Queensland Press, St Lucia, Qld.

Ransley, Janet 1994, "The powers of Royal Commissions and controls over them", in *Royal Commissions and the Making of Public Policy*, ed P Weller, Macmillan, Melbourne.

Reiner, Robert 1978, *The Blue-coated Worker: A Sociological Study of Police Unionism*, Cambridge University Press, Cambridge.

Reiner, Robert 1983, "The politicisation of the police in Britain", in *Control in the Police Organisation*, ed M Punch, The MIT Press, London.

Reiner, Robert 1985, *Politics of the Police*, Wheatsheaf, Sussex.

Reiner, Robert 1989, "Where the buck stops: Chief constables" views on police accountability", in *Coming to Terms with Policing: Perspectives on Policy*, eds R Morgan and DJ Smith, Routledge, New York.

Reiner, Robert 1991a, "A much lower pedestal", *Policing*, vol 7, no 3, Autumn, pp 225-38.

Reiner, Robert 1991b, "Chief constables in England and Wales: A social portrait of a criminal justice elite", in *Beyond Law and Order*, eds R Reiner and M Cross, Macmillan, London.

Reiner, Robert 1992, "Policing a postmodern society", *The Modern Law Review*, vol 55, no 6, Nov, pp 761-81.

Reiner, Robert 1993, "Police accountability: Principles, patterns and practices", in *Accountable Policing: Effectiveness, Empowerment and Equity*, eds R Reiner and S Spencer, Institute for Public Policy Research, London.

Reiner, Robert and Spencer, Sarah (eds) 1993, *Accountable Policing: Effectiveness, Empowerment and Equity*, Institute for Public Policy Research, London.

Reiss, Albert J 1992, "Police organisation", in *The Twentieth Century, in Modern Policing*, eds M Tonry and N Morris, University of Chicago Press, Chicago.

Reith, Charles 1952, *The Blind Eye of History: A Study of the Origins of the Present Police Era*, Faber and Faber, London. Reprinted in 1975 by Montclair, NJ Patterson Smith.

Report of a Commission of Inquiry Pursuant to Orders in Council (The Fitzgerald Report) 1989, Government Printer, Brisbane.

Report of a Commission to Investigate Allegations of Police Corruption and the City's Anti-Corruption Procedures (The Knapp Report) 1972, The City of New York, New York.

Report of a Working Party appointed by the Home Secretary CMND 8193: The Establishment of an Independent Element in the Investigation of Complaints against Police, HMSO, London, pp 1-11.

Report of the Board of Inquiry into Allegations Against Members of the Victorian Police Force (The Beach Report) 1978, Government Printer, Melbourne.

Report of the Board of Inquiry into Allegations of Corruption in the Police Force in Connection with Illegal Abortion Practices in the State of Victoria (The Kaye Report) 1971, Government Printer, Melbourne.

Report of the Commission to Inquire into New South Wales Police Administration (The Lusher Report) 1981, Government Printer, Sydney.

Report of the Commission to Investigate Allegations of Police Corruption and the Anti-Corruption Procedure of the Police Department (The Mollen Report) 1994, The City of New York, New York.

Report of the Committee Appointed to Examine and Advise in Relation to the Recommendations made in Chapter 8 of Volume 1 of the Report of the Board of Inquiry Appointed for the Purpose of Inquiring into and Reporting upon Certain Allegations against Members of the Victoria Police Force: Part II – Investigation of Complaints against Police, 1979-80, Government Printer, Melbourne.

Report of the Committee of Inquiry into the Enforcement of Criminal Law in Queensland (The Lucas Report) 1977, Government Printer, Brisbane.

Reuss-Ianni, Elizabeth and Ianni, Francis AJ 1983, "Street cops and management cops: The two cultures of policing", in *Control in the Police Organisation*, ed M Punch, MIT Press, Cambridge, MA.

Ritchie, Ella 1992, "Law and order", *Power and Policy in Liberal Democracies*, ed M Harrop, Cambridge University Press, Cambridge.

Robilliard, St John and McEwan, Jenny 1986, *Police Powers and the Individual*, Basil Blackwell, Oxford.

Robinson, Cyril D, Scaglion, Richard and Olivero, J Michael 1994, *Police in Contradiction: The Evolution of the Police Function in Society*, Greenwood Press, Westport, CT.

Rowett, GD 1986, "Investigating complaints against the police", *Victoria Police Association Journal*, vol 51, no 3, pp 25, 27, 29, 31, 35, 37, 39, 41, 43, 45, 47, 49, 51.

Royal Commission into Rumours of Police Misconduct in Relation to the National Hotel (The Gibbs Inquiry) 1964, Brisbane.

Royal Commission into the New South Wales Police Service 1996a, *Interim Report*, February, Sydney.

Royal Commission into the New South Wales Police Service 1996b, *Interim Report: Immediate Measures for the Reform of the Police Service of New South Wales*, November, Sydney.

Royal Commission on the Dismissal of Harold Hubert Salisbury 1978, Report, Government Printer, Adelaide.

Royal Commission on the September Moratorium Demonstration 1970, Report, Government Printer, Adelaide.

Ruchelman, Leonard 1974, *Police Politics: A Comparative Study of Three Cities*, Ballinger, Cambridge, MA.

Russell, Kenneth V 1978, "Complaints against the police", *The Police Journal*, vol LI, no 1, pp 34-44.

Sallman, Peter and Willis, John 1984, *Criminal Justice in Australia*, Oxford University Press, Melbourne.

Sanders, Andrew 1993, "Controlling the description of the individual officer", in *Accountable Policing: Effectiveness, Empowerment and Equity*, eds R Reiner and S Spencer, Institute for Public Policy Research, London.

Scarman, Lord 1986, *The Scarman Report: The Brixton Disorders 10-12 April 1981*, Penguin Books, Middlesex.

Scranton, Phil 1985, "The crisis in police accountability", in *The State of the Police*, Pluto Press, London.

Selby, Hugh 1985, "Investigating the police", *Public Interest Journal*, no 12, March, pp 10-12.

Selby, Hugh 1986, "Point of view", *Australian Federal Police Association Journal*, Jan, pp 11-12.

Selby, Hugh 1988, "Internal investigations: Too little, too late", in *Police in our Society*, eds I Freckelton and H Selby, Butterworths, Sydney.

Seneviratne, M 1994, *Ombudsmen in the Public Sector*, Open University Press, Buckingham.

Shearing, Clifford D 1992, "Changing police cultures: The bottom-up view", *Platypus*, July, pp 15-16.

Sherman, Lawrence W 1995, "The truly conceited: Ex Cathedra doctrine and the policing of crime", *The Australian and New Zealand Journal of Criminology*, Special Supplementary Issue, pp 45-51.

Skolnick, Jerome H 1966, *Justice Without Trial: Law Enforcement in Democratic Society*, 2nd edn, Macmillan, New York.

Skolnick, Jerome H 1993, Police accountability in the United States, paper presented at national conference, *Keeping the Peace: Police Accountability and Oversight*, Royal Institute of Public Administration Australia and NSW Office of the Ombudsman, Sydney, 20-21 May.

Skolnick, Jerome H and Fyfe, James J 1993, *Above the Law: Police and the Excessive Use of Force*, The Free Press, New York.

Slattery, JP 1976, "Complaints against police", in *Proceedings of the Institute of Criminology, Sydney University Faculty of Law, no 29, Seminar on Complaints against Police*, Government Printer, Sydney, pp 33-42.

Smith, RFI and Weller, P (eds) 1978, *Public Service Inquiries in Australia*, University of Queensland Press, St Lucia, Qld.

Smith, Roger 1992, "Is anybody listening?", *New Law Journal*, vol 142, no 6556, 12 June, p 816.

Solesbury, W 1976, "The environmental agenda: An illustration of how situations may become political issues and issues may demand responses from government: Or how they may not", *Public Administration*, vol 34, winter, pp 379-99.

South Australia 1983, *Report of the Committee on Complaints Against the Police: A Committee Established to Examine and Report to the Chief Secretary on the Establishment of an Independent Authority to Receive and Investigate Complaints from the Public about Police Activities*, Government Printer, Adelaide.

South Australia Police Complaints Authority 1995, *Annual Report 1992-1994*, State Government Printing Service, Adelaide.

Sparrow, M 1992, "Complaints against police and department management: Making the connection", *The Police Chief*, vol LIX, no 8, Aug, pp 65-73.

Spencer, Sarah 1985, "Campaigning for democratic control of the police", in *Called to Account: The Case for Police Accountability in England and Wales*, National Council for Civil Liberties, London.

Stenning, Philip C 1981a, *Legal Status of the Police*, Law Reform Commission of Canada, Ottawa.

Stenning, Philip C 1981b, *Police Commissions and Boards in Canada*, Research Report, The Centre of Criminology, University of Toronto.

Stenning, Philip C 1981c, "The role of police boards and commissions as institutions of municipal police governance", in *Organisation of Police Deviance: Its Structure and Control*, ed CD Shearing, Butterworths, Toronto.

Stoddard, Ellwyn R 1972, "The informal "code" of police deviancy: A group approach to "blue coat crime"", in *Police Law Enforcement: An AMS Anthology*, eds JT Curran, A Fowler and RH Ward, AMS Press Inc, New York.

Stubbs, Julie 1992, *Complaints Against Police in New South Wales*, New South Wales Bureau of Crime Statistics and Research, Sydney.

Sturgess, Gary 1989, "Independent Commission Against Corruption (ICAC)", *Criminology Australia*, June/July, pp 5-10.

Sturgess, Gary 1994, "Guarding the polity: The NSW Independent Commission Against Corruption", in *Royal Commissions and the Making of Public Policy*, ed P Weller, Macmillan, Melbourne.

Sturgess Inquiry into Sexual Offences Involving Children and Related Matters (The Sturgess Inquiry) 1985, Brisbane.

"Summary of recommendation" 1993, *New Law Journal*, vol 143, no 6608, 9 July, pp 993-96.

Sunahara, David F 1992, "Public inquiries into policing", *Canadian Police College Journal*, vol 16, no 2, pp 135-56.

Swanton, B 1979, *Police Institutions and Issues: American and Australian Perspectives*, Australian Institute of Criminology, Canberra.

Sykes, Gary W 1993, "The functional nature of police reform: The "myth" of controlling the police", in *Critical Issues in Policing: Contemporary Readings*, 2nd edn, eds G Dunham and GP Alpent, Waveland Press Inc, Illinois.

Sykes, Richard E 1977, "A regulatory theory of policing: A preliminary statement", in *Police and Society*, ed DH Bayley, Sage Publications, Beverly Hills and London.

Tasmania Ombudsman *Annual Report* 1990, 1991, 1992, 1993, 1994, 1995, 1996, 1997, 1998, State Government Printing Service, Hobart.

Taylor, Peter 1984, *Smoke Ring: The Politics of Tobacco*, The Bodley Head, London.

Terrill, Richard J 1980, "Complaints procedures against police: The movement for change in England, Canada and Australia", *Police Studies*, vol 3, pp 37-46.

Terrill, Richard J 1982, "Complaints procedures: Variations on the theme of civilian participation", *Journal of Police Science and Administration*, vol 10, no 4, pp 398-407.

Terrill, Richard J 1985, "Complaints procedures: Variations on the theme of civilian participation", in *Critical Issues in Law Enforcement*, 4th edn, ed HW More Jr, Anderson Publishing Co, Cincinnati, pp 122-41.

Terrill, Richard J 1990, "Alternative perceptions of independence in civilian oversight", *Journal of Police Science and Administration*, vol 17, no 2, June, pp 77-83.

Terrill, Richard J 1991, "Civilian oversight of the police complaints process in the United States: Concerns, developments, and more concerns", in *Complaints Against the Police: The Trend to External Review*, ed A Goldsmith, Clarendon Press, Oxford.

Tink, Andrew 1992, Watchdog or poodle? The Ombudsman and the police complaints system in New South Wales, paper presented at the 8th Annual Conference, The Australian and New Zealand Society of Criminology, Melbourne, Oct.

Toohey, Brian 1990, "Fitzgerald: A report without findings", *Criminology Australia*, Jan/Feb, pp 14-18.

Tregilgas-Davey, Marcus 1990a, "The police and accountability", *New Law Journal*, vol 140, no 6456, 18 May, pp 697-98.

Tregilgas-Davey, Marcus 1990b, "The police and accountability", *New Law Journal*, vol 140, no 6457, 25 May, pp 738-40.

Tully, John R 1987, "Internal investigations are a pain", *Law and Order*, March, pp 42-46.

Uglow, Steve 1988, *Policing Liberal Society*, Oxford University Press, Oxford.

Walker, Jamie 1995, *Goss: A Political Biography*, University of Queensland Press, St Lucia, Qld.

Walker, Samuel 1977, *Critical History of Police Reform: The Emergence of Professionalism*, Lexington Books, Lexington.

Walker, Samuel 1980, *Popular Justice: A History of American Criminal Justice*, Oxford University Press, New York and Oxford.

Walker, Samuel 1983, *The Police in America: An Introduction*, McGraw-Hill, New York.

Walker, Samuel 1992, *The Police in America: An Introduction*, 2nd edn, McGraw-Hill, New York.

Walker, Samuel and Bumphus, Vic W 1991, *Civilian Review of the Police: A National Survey of the 50 Largest Cities*, Department of Criminal Justice, University of Nebraska, Omaha.

Walker, Samuel and Bumphus, Vic W 1992, "The effectiveness of civilian review: Observations on recent trends and new issues regarding the civilian review of the police", *American Journal of Police*, vol XI, no 4, pp 1-26.

Walker, Samuel and Wright, B 1995, "Citizen review of the police, 1994: A national survey, fresh perspectives", *Police Executive Research Forum*, pp 1-15.

Wallace, Lyndon J 1992, "We're not perfect", *Policing*, vol 8, no 1, Spring, pp 73-77.

Wanna, J 1989, "A purchase on corruption", *Australian Left Review*, vol III, July/Aug, pp 26-31.

Wanna, J 1991, "Parliamentary commissions of review: The Criminal Justice Commission and the Electoral and Administrative Review Commission", in *Political Crossroads: The 1989 Queensland Election*, eds R Whip and C Hughes, University of Queensland Press, St Lucia, Qld.

Warhurst, John 1980, "Exercising control over statutory authorities: A study in government technique", in *Responsible Government of Australia*, eds P Weller and D Jaensch, Drummond Publishing, Melbourne.

Watt, Susan 1991, "The future of civilian oversight of policing", *Canadian Journal of Criminology*, vol 33, no 3-4, pp 347-62.

Weeks, John 1994, "Case of the emperor's new clothes", *Police: The Voice of the Service*, vol XXVI, no 12, Aug, pp 11-12.

Wegg-Prosser, Charles 1979, "Police conduct and discipline", in *The Police and the Law*, 2nd edn, Oyez Publishing, London.

Weller, Patrick 1979, "The study of public policy", in *Politics and Public Policy in Australia*, eds G Hawker, RFI Smith and P Weller, University of Queensland Press, St Lucia, Qld.

Weller, Patrick 1985, *First Among Equals: Prime Ministers in Westminster Systems*, Allen and Unwin, Sydney.

West, Paul 1988, "Investigation of complaints against the police: Summary report of a national survey", *American Journal of Police*, vol VII, no 2, pp 101-21.

West, Paul 1991, "Investigation and review of complaints against police officers: An overview of issues and philosophies", in *Police Deviance*, eds T Barker and D Carter, Anderson Publishing, Cincinnati, OH, pp 373-404.

Western Australia Parliamentary Commissioner for Administrative Investigations *Annual Report* 1990, 1991, 1992, 1993, 1994, 1995, 1996, 1997, 1998, State Government Printing Service, Perth.

Wettenhall, Roger 1977, "Government and the police", *Current Affairs Bulletin*, March, pp 12-23.

Whip, Rosemary 1991, "The candidates", in *Political Crossroads: The 1989 Queensland Election*, eds R Whip and C Hughes, University of Queensland Press, St Lucia.

Whip, Rosemary and Hughes, Colin A 1991, "Leader images", in *Political Crossroads: The 1989 Queensland Election*, eds R Whip and C Hughes, University of Queensland Press, St Lucia, Qld.

Whip, R, Western, J and Gow, D 1991, "Election issues", in *Political Crossroads: The 1989 Queensland Election*, eds R Whip and C Hughes, University of Queensland Press, St Lucia, Qld.

White, R and Richards, C 1992, "Police unions and police powers", *Current Issues in Criminal Justice*, vol 4, no 2, pp 157-74.

Whitton, E 1989, *The Hillbilly Dictator: Australia's Police State*, ABC, Sydney.

Wilson, OW and McLaren, Roy Clinton 1972, *Police Administration*, McGraw-Hill, New York.

Woodcock, John 1991, "Overturning police culture", *Policing*, vol 7, no 3, Autumn, pp 172-82.

Yin, Robert K 1981, "The case study crisis: Some answers", *Administrative Science Quarterly*, vol 26, no 1, pp 58-65.

Yin, Robert K 1994, *Case Study Research: Design and Methods*, Applied Social Research Methods Series, Sage Publications, Thousand Oaks, CA.

Young, Warren 1986, "Investigating police misconduct", in *Policing at the Crossroads*, eds N Cameron and W Young, Allen and Unwin, Wellington, New Zealand

Legislation

Australia Police Bill 1975 (Cth)

Complaints Against Police Bill 1985 (SA)

Complaints (Australian Federal Police) Act 1981 (Cth)

Criminal Justice Act 1989 (Qld)

Electoral Act 1992 (Qld)

Freedom of Information Act 1992 (Qld)

Judicial Review Act 1991 (Qld)

Ombudsman Act 1976 (Cth)

Parliamentary Committees Act 1995 (Qld)

Parliamentary Committees Bill 1995 (Qld)

Police (Complaints of Disciplinary Proceedings) Act 1985 (SA)

Police Act 1833 (NSW)

Police Complaints Tribunal Act 1982 (Qld)

Police Complaints Tribunal Act Amendment Bill 1987 (Qld)

Police Service Administration Act 1990 (Qld)

Parliamentary debates

Queensland

Queensland, Legislative Assembly 1982, *Debates*, 1 April.
Queensland, Legislative Assembly 1987, *Debates*, 14 Oct.
Queensland, Legislative Assembly 1990, *Debates*, 10 May.
Queensland, Legislative Assembly 1995, *Debates*, 30 April.

Western Australia

Western Australia, Legislative Assembly 1984, *Debates*, 14 Nov.

Newspaper articles

Australian 1988, 29 May.
Australian 1988, 21 June.
Australian 1990, 5 June.
Australian 1993, 12 March.
Australian 1993, 17 March.
Australian 1996, 20 August.
Australian 1996, 20 December.
Courier-Mail 1976, 5 October.
Courier-Mail 1987, 28 July.
Courier-Mail 1987, 21 August.
Courier-Mail 1987, 11 September.
Courier-Mail 1987, 18 September.
Courier-Mail 1987, 16 October.
Courier-Mail 1987, 21 October.
Courier-Mail 1987, 29 October.
Courier-Mail 1988, 26 January.
Courier-Mail 1988, 3 March.
Courier-Mail 1988, 25 June, Weekend 1.
Courier-Mail 1988, 2 September.
Courier-Mail 1988, 11 September.
Courier-Mail 1988, 12 October.
Courier-Mail 1988, 12 October.
Courier-Mail 1988, 12 October.
Courier-Mail 1988, 13 October.
Courier-Mail 1988, 21 October.
Courier-Mail 1989, 1 December.

Courier-Mail 1990, 6 June.
Courier-Mail 1991, 4 March.
Courier-Mail 1991, 3 August.
Courier-Mail 1992, 5 February.
Courier-Mail 1992, 4 March.
Courier-Mail 1992, 21 March.
Courier-Mail 1992, 10 April.
Courier-Mail 1993, 17 April.
Courier-Mail 1994, 4 May.
Courier-Mail 1994, 13 May.
Courier-Mail 1995, 8 March.
Courier-Mail 1995, 29 March.
Courier-Mail 1995, 26 April.
Courier-Mail 1996, 27 February.
Courier-Mail 1996, 28 February.
Courier-Mail 1996, 29 February.
Courier-Mail 1996, 16 August.
Courier-Mail 1996, 20 August.
Courier-Mail 1996, 21 August.
Courier-Mail 1996, 27 August.
Courier-Mail 1996, 2 September.
Courier-Mail 1996, 2 September.
Courier-Mail 1996, 3 September.
Courier-Mail 1996, 6 September.
Courier-Mail 1996, 7 September.
Courier-Mail 1996, 16 September.
Courier-Mail 1996, 17 September.
Courier-Mail 1996, 18 September.
Courier-Mail 1996, 19 September.
Courier-Mail 1996, 31 October.
Courier-Mail 1996, 5 December.
Courier-Mail 1996, 6 December.
Courier-Mail 1996, 21 December.
Sunday Mail 1991, 28 July.
Sunday Mail 1991, 22 December.
Sunday Mail 1992, 19 July.
Sunday Mail 1992, 29 August.
Sunday Mail 1992, 11 October.
Sunday Mail 1994, 20 March.
Sunday Mail 1994, 1 May.

Sunday Mail 1994, 27 August.
Sunday Mail 1996, 1 September.
Weekend Australian 1992, 28-29 November.
Weekend Australian 1993, 30-31 October.
Weekend Australian 1995, 1-2 April.
Weekend Australian 1996, 21-22 September.

Interviews

The status of persons interviewed reflects their position at the time of interview. Several people did not wish their comments to be attributed within the text of the book and a few did not wish to be identified at all. In these instances, generic position descriptions have been used.

Barnes, Mr Michael, Chief Complaints Officer, Official Misconduct Division, Criminal Justice Commission, March 1995, May 1996.

Beattie, Mr Peter, Chairperson, Parliamentary Criminal Justice Committee, December 1991.

Bevan, Mr David, Deputy Director, Official Misconduct Division, Criminal Justice Commission, July 1995.

Bingham, Sir Max, Chairperson, Criminal Justice Commission, December 1991.

Bingham, Sir Max, Former Chairperson, Criminal Justice Commission, May 1995.

Bleakley, Mr Robert, part-time Commissioner, Criminal Justice Commission, September 1995.

Boyce, Mr Peter, Police Complaints Authority, South Australia, December 1994.

Brereton, Dr David, Director, Research and Co-ordination Division, Criminal Justice Commission, May 1996.

Carter QC, His Hon Justice William, former Chairperson, Police Complaints Tribunal, Queensland, February 1996.

Clair, Mr Frank, Chairperson, Criminal Justice Commission, May 1996.

Couper, Ms Helen, Executive Legal Officer, Special Projects, Official Misconduct Division, Criminal Justice Commission, June 1995.

Davies, Mr Ken, Chairperson, Parliamentary Criminal Justice Committee, mid-1994.

Doonan, Chief Superintendent Patrick, Professional Standards Unit, Queensland Police Service, December 1995.

Ffrench, Mr Barry, part-time Commissioner, Criminal Justice Commission, February 1996.

Goss, Mr Wayne, former Premier of Queensland, March 1996.

Hailstone, Mr Robert, Director, Corruption Prevention Division, Criminal Justice Commission, August 1995.

Homel, Professor Ross, part-time Commissioner, Criminal Justice Commission, November 1995.

Irwin, Dr Janet, part-time Commissioner, Criminal Justice Commission, 1994.

Irwin, Mr Marshall, former General Counsel, Criminal Justice Commission, 1994.

James, Ms Susan, Manager, Information and Research Officer, Office of Police Complaints Commission, Ontario, Canada, October 1995.

Landa, Mr David, former Ombudsman for New South Wales, March 1995.

Le Grand, Mr Mark, Director, Official Misconduct Division, Criminal Justice Commission, November 1995.

McDonnell, Assistant Commissioner John, Director, Witness Protection Division, Criminal Justice Commission, June 1995.

Marjason, Mr Andrew, Principal Complaints Officer, Official Misconduct Division, Criminal Justice Commission, February 1995.

O'Gorman, Senior Sergeant John, President, Queensland Police Union of Employees, June 1995 and 1996.

O'Regan QC, Mr Robin, Chairperson, Criminal Justice Commission, April 1995.

O'Sullivan, Commissioner Jim, Commissioner of Police, Queensland Police Service, December 1995.

Packer, Mr Alan, Deputy Chief Officer, Complaints Section, Official Misconduct Division, Criminal Justice Commission, February 1995.

Peach, Sir Leonard, Chairperson, Police Complaints Authority, Britain, October 1995.

Robinson, Mr Ian, Deputy Chief Officer (Investigations), Official Misconduct Division, Criminal Justice Commission, May 1995.

Senior Adviser to Premier Michael Ahern and Premier Russell Cooper, 1994.

Senior Member of Fitzgerald Inquiry, April 1995.

Senior Police Officers seconded to Official Misconduct Division, Criminal Justice Commission, February-August 1995.

Shepherd, Mr David, Principal Legal Officer, Complaints Section, Official Misconduct Division, Criminal Justice Commission, June 1995.

Wyvill QC, Mr Lewis, Acting Chairperson, Criminal Justice Commission, June 1995.

Telephone interviews

Office of Northern Territory Ombudsman, March 1995.

Office of Tasmania Ombudsman, March 1995.

Office of the Commonwealth Ombudsman, March 1995.

Office of Victoria Deputy Ombudsman (Police Complaints), March 1995.

Office of Western Australia Parliamentary Commissioner for Administrative Investigations, March 1995

Index